C For Programmers

SECOND EDITION

C For Programmers

A Complete Tutorial Based on the ANSI Standard

SECOND EDITION

Leendert Ammeraal
Hogeschool Utrecht, The Netherlands

JOHN WILEY & SONS
Chichester · New York · Brisbane · Toronto · Singapore

Other Wiley Editorial Offices

John Wiley & Sons, Inc., 605 Third Avenue,
New York, NY 10158-0012, USA

Jacaranda Wiley Ltd, G.P.O. Box 859, Brisbane,
Queensland 4001, Australia

John Wiley & Sons (Canada) Ltd, 22 Worcester Road,
Rexdale, Ontario M9W 1L1, Canada

John Wiley & Sons (SEA) Pte Ltd, 37 Jalan Pemimpin   05-04,
Block B, Union Industrial Building, Singapore 2057

Library of Congress Cataloging-in-Publication Data:

Ammeraal, L. (Leendert)
    C for programmers : a complete tutorial based on the ANSI standard
    / Leendert Ammeraal. – 2nd ed.
        p. cm.
    Includes bibliographical references (p.   ) and index.
    ISBN 0 471 92851 8
    1. C (Computer program language) I. Title.
QA76.73.C15A46 1991
005.13'3-dc20   90-13077

British Library Cataloguing in Publication Data:

Ammeraal, L. (Leendert)
  C for programmers : a complete tutorial based on the ANSI
  standard. – 2nd ed.
  1. Computer systems. Programming : C language
  I. Title
  005.13

  ISBN 0 471 92851 8

Printed and Bound by Courier International Limited
East Kilbride

Contents

Preface

There are two reasons why C can be called a portable programming language. First, its original version already had so many good facilities that language extensions were not as badly needed as they were for some other languages, and second, such extensions as were highly desirable have been streamlined by the American National Standards Institute, or ANSI, for short. An advantage of ANSI C is that some common programming errors in the types of function arguments can now be dealt with much more satisfactorily. Another improvement is the definition of a standard library: a high degree of portability is obtained if we are prepared to use non-standard libraries only when there are very good reasons to do so.

Now that many ANSI C compilers are available, we should seriously consider the use of the new language version in academic and technical education. The language revision is at least as helpful for beginners as it is for experienced programmers. All who decided some years ago that C was no good as a programming language for students because of its pitfalls should now seriously reconsider that decision: ANSI has made C a good programming language for those who want to teach practical subjects.

This book is entirely different from its first edition, in which the programs were not presented in the style recommended by ANSI. They are in this second edition. It is intended as a text book, although Chapter 10 (Standard Library) may look more like a technical reference. There are many exercises, both at the end of each chapter and in Appendix A. Most examples are very simple and clarify just the language elements discussed. However, you will also find some more interesting programs, including those which deal with sorting, permutations, combinations, linear lists, binary trees and systems of linear equations.

I am grateful to all who commented on the first edition of this book. Any reactions to the second will be equally welcome.

Leendert Ammeraal

CHAPTER 1

Introduction

1.1 GETTING STARTED

The C programming language was designed and implemented by D. M. Ritchie, and it was published in the book *The C Programming Language* by B. W. Kernighan and D. M. Ritchie in 1978. In its first years, C was popular only in connection with the UNIX[1] operating system. Later, it turned out to be a very good programming language for microcomputers as well, and these days C can be used with almost any computer type. With its proliferation, it became very desirable for C to be standardized. In 1983 the American National Standards Institute, abbreviated ANSI, formed a committee (X3J11) to provide such a standard, and the result, known as ANSI C, is the subject of this book. ANSI C offers some important extensions to the original version of C. Many compilers already conform to the new standard, and it is to be expected that others will follow.

Since we write C programs in *source code*, that is, in readable form, we can use them in this form on a given computer only if we have a C compiler for that computer. A compiler transforms source programs into object programs, or, more technically, it transforms *source modules* into *object modules*. Then we need a *linker* to link the object modules together with library routines (termed library *functions* in C), which gives the *executable version* of the program. For future users of the program the executable version is all that is needed: the C compiler, linker and function library (collectively called the C *implementation*) is needed only during program development. Thanks to the ANSI standard, the C language as presented in this book is *implementation independent*: the programs we will be discussing are accepted by any C compiler that conforms to the ANSI standard. A great advantage of C over some other programming languages is that differences in C implementations are mainly restricted to their function libraries; except for these, this book discusses C as it is used in practice.

---

[1]   UNIX is a trademark of Bell Laboratories.

The C language is a very professional language. It supplies us with everything we need to write programs that are easy to use. This does not imply that the C language itself should be easy to use; nor is every realistic C program easy to understand. Fortunately, we can also write very simple C programs, as the following example shows. This complete program, EXAMPLE1, reads two integers a and b from the keyboard to compute both $u = (a + b)^2$ and $v = (a - b)^2$:

```
/* EXAMPLE1: A program to compute the squares of both the sum
            and the difference of two given integers.
*/
#include <stdio.h>

main()
{ int a, b, sum, diff, u, v;
  printf("Enter two integers: ");
  scanf("%d %d", &a, &b); /* a and b are read */
  sum = a + b; diff = a - b;
  u = sum * sum; v = diff * diff;
  printf("\nResults: %d and %d.\n", u, v);
}
```

When you run this program, the following text appears on the screen of your computer:

```
Enter two integers:
```

You can now enter, for example,

```
100 10
```

After your pressing the Enter key, the following appears:

```
Results: 12100 and 8100.
```

We can easily check this: with $a = 100$ and $b = 10$, it follows that $sum = 110$ and $diff = 90$, so the computed squares of sum and $diff$ are 12100 and 8100, respectively.

We can write C programs only if we are familiar with the 'grammar rules' of the C language. Let us now briefly discuss these rules as far as they apply to our example.

It is good practice to start any program with *comment*. In C comment always begins with the two characters

```
/*
```

and it ends with the same characters in reverse order:

```
*/
```

These two character pairs may or may not be on the same program line. Both types of comment can be found in program EXAMPLE1.

After the final characters ***/** of the comment at the top of this program, we find the following *include line*:

```
#include <stdio.h>
```

We say that this line 'includes' the file **stdio.h,** which is a so-called *header file* (hence the file-name extension **.h**) for standard input/output (abbreviated **stdio**). The contents of this header file logically replace this include line. Such lines always begin with **#include** and they require a program line of their own. For example, you cannot write **main( )** at the end of this line.

In this regard include lines form an exception to a general rule that says that, as far as the C compiler is concerned, program text may be split up over several lines as we please. For example, we can replace the line

```
sum = a + b; diff = a - b;
```

with the following two lines:

```
sum = a + b;
diff = a - b;
```

We can even split these lines further, but that would obviously not improve readability. When splitting a line into two new lines, we say that we insert a *new-line character*. Similar characters are the *blank* (that is, the *space character*) and the *tab*. Collectively, these three characters are called *white-space characters*.

Every C program contains one or more *functions*, one of which is called **main**. (In C the term *function* is not used in the abstract, mathematical sense; instead, it denotes a concrete program fragment.) In our example, the **main** function is the only one. It has the form

```
main()
{ ...
  ...
}
```

Functions may or may not have parameters. If they have, we write them between parentheses, as we will see later. If not, we still use the parentheses, with nothing in between, as is done here. The 'body' of every function is surrounded by braces {}. It is good practice to write every pair of braces either on the same line, or in the same (vertical) column, with everything in between indented as shown in EXAMPLE1.

After the open brace ({) of a function, we normally *declare* one ore more variables. Here we declare the variables **a**, **b**, **sum**, **diff**, **u**, **v**, using the following *declaration*:

```
int a, b, sum, diff, u, v;
```

It says that these five variables have type **int**, which means that they denote integers. Their range is limited: depending on the machine and the C-compiler we are using, they can have, for example, 32767 as their maximum value. The next program line is

```
printf("Enter two integers: ");
```

This is a call to the standard output function **printf**. This function is a very complex one, but here we have used it in a very simple way. It causes the text between the double quotes " " to be displayed on the screen. Instead of text being *displayed*, we often say that it is *printed*. With the *f* at the end denoting *formatted*, the name **printf** now makes sense. A call to a function, followed by a semicolon (;) is a special case of a *statement*. A similar statement is given on the next program line:

```
scanf("%d %d", &a, &b);
```

When executing this statement the machine will wait for input, so we can now enter the two integers as requested. We write **"%d %d"** because the numbers to be entered will be integers in decimal form. The character **&**, occurring twice in this statement, means *the address of*. To understand this, remember that **scanf** has the task of placing the integers read from the keyboard into the memory locations of **a** and **b**, and this can be done only if it knows what these locations are. Each memory location has a unique number, called its *address*, so it is the addresses of **a** and **b** that **scanf** needs to know. Without the character **&**, we would have given the old *values* of **a** and **b** to **scanf**, instead of their addresses. In the next two program lines

```
sum = a + b; diff = a - b;
u = sum * sum; v = diff * diff;
```

we compute **sum**, **diff**, **u**, and **v**, in that order. The asterisk ***** denotes multiplication. After computing **u** and **v** this way, we display these results on the screen by means of

```
printf("\nResults: %d and %d.\n", u, v);
```

This call to **printf** is more interesting than the previous one. In general, a function call contains arguments, separated by commas. Here we have three arguments, namely **"\nResults: %d and %d.\n"**, **u**, and **v**. The first of these is a *format string*, which contains two essentially different types of data:

1. Text, to be printed literally
2. Conversion specifications

Conversion specifications always begin with **%**. They specify how the internal format of numbers (and other data items) are to be converted to the external format that will appear in the output. The conversion specifications correspond to subsequent arguments, given in the same order: the first conversion specification belongs to the first of these arguments, and so on. Here we have the conversion specification **%d**; it is used if a decimal representation of a given integer is required. It occurs twice: the first corresponds to **u**, the second to **v**. Everything in the format string that is not a conversion specification is text to be printed. The pair **\n** is an escape sequence, which actually denotes the newline character. The values of **u** and **v**, in their converted forms, replace the corresponding conversion specifications in the format string. Since the format string begins with **\n**, a newline character is printed at the beginning. After the user of this program has entered two integers, the Enter key is pressed, which sends another newline character to the screen, so that there will be a blank line. As a result, a demonstration (showing both input and output data) of program EXAMPLE1 is

```
Enter two integers: 100 10

Results: 12100 and 8100.
```

Note the period at the end, which also occurs in the format string. Because of **int** in the declaration of the variables, program EXAMPLE1 works correctly only if we enter integers that are not too large. This word **int** is an example of a *data type* (or, more briefly, of a *type*). The range of values that can be assigned to a program variable depends on the type of that variable. In the next chapters we will discuss many other types.

1.2 MEMORY ORGANIZATION AND BINARY NUMBERS

Both compiled programs and data are stored in (the computer's) *memory*. In addition to this, many computers have registers, which can *temporarily* contain data. In most cases we can regard the memory as a long sequence of *bytes*, each consisting of eight binary digits or *bits*. A bit can only have two values, 1 and 0. There are also computer types with memories that primarily consist of *words*, each of which contains, for example, 16 bits. These two types of memory organization are often combined: every word of 16 bits then consists of two bytes. Conversely, if from a technical point of view the memory consists of bytes, every two (or four) bytes are grouped together to form a word of 16 (or 32) bits. The reason for this dualistic approach is that we need bytes to store characters, while words are more suitable for integers.

The contents of memory locations (either bytes or words) are variable: they can frequently change during program execution. In contrast to this, each location has a fixed number, its *address*, to indicate its position. In high-level languages we do normally not know the addresses of our variables. This also applies to C, but in this language we use a symbolic notation for such addresses. For example, **&a** denotes the address of variable **a**, as we have seen in the previous section.

Let us, for convenience, assume that our computer has words of 16 bits. We number these bits $0, \cdots, 15$, from right to left, as shown in Fig. 1.1.

15	14	13	12	11	10	9	8	7	6	5	4	3	2	1	0
0	0	0	0	0	0	0	0	0	1	0	1	0	0	1	1

Fig. 1.1. A word of 16 bits

This machine word contains the following bit sequence:

00000000 01010011

We can interpret these 16 bits in (at least) two ways: either as two characters (each represented by 8 bits) or as one integer of 16 bits. Which of these interpretations applies depends on the program that manipulates this word. If the word should be regarded as an integer, we use the 1 bits to compute its value.

Omitting leading zeros, we have 1010011 here, which is the binary representation of 83. This value can be computed as follows:

$$1 \times 2^6 + 0 \times 2^5 + 1 \times 2^4 + 0 \times 2^3 + 0 \times 2^2 + 1 \times 2 + 1 = 83$$

Instead of 'the binary representation of a number', the shorter (but less precise) term *binary number* is more often used, and we will conform to this usage. The value of a decimal number is found by using powers of 2, as this example shows. We say that 2 is the *base* or *radix* of the binary number system. Similarly, 10 is the radix of the usual decimal number system. For example, we can compute the value of the 'decimal number' 8241 as follows:

$$8 \times 10^3 + 2 \times 10^2 + 4 \times 10 + 1$$

If we use all 16 bits of a (16 bit) word the same way, the 2^{16} numbers that we can represent are

```
00000000 00000000 = 0
00000000 00000001 = 1
00000000 00000010 = 2
00000000 00000011 = 3
        ...
11111111 11111111 = 2^16 - 1 = 65535
```

We use the term *unsigned int* (or, briefly, *unsigned*) for this representation. In many cases we also want to use negative numbers. The usual way of doing this is by means of the two's-complement method. Using 16 bits, we can in this way represent the integers $-32768, \cdots, 32767$ as follows:

```
10000000 00000000 = -2^15 = -32768
10000000 00000001 = -(2^15 - 1) = -32767
        ...
11111111 11111110 = -2
11111111 11111111 = -1
00000000 00000000 = 0
00000000 00000001 = 1
        ...
01111111 11111111 = 2^15 - 1 = 32767
```

If the numbers we are dealing with can also be negative, as is the case here, the type of these numbers is *signed int*. As integers are signed by default, we usually write **int**, rather than **signed int**. On computers other than micros, the word length is often 32 instead of 16. The maximum values are then $2^{32} - 1 =$

4 294 967 295 for type **unsigned (int)** and $2^{31} - 1 = 2\ 147\ 483\ 647$ for type **(signed) int**.

We conclude this section with another important way of interpreting bit sequences, namely by means of *hexadecimal* numbers. We can then divide the machine word into groups of four bits. In the hexadecimal number system, the radix is 16, so there are 16 distinct digits, which, along with their binary representations, are given below:

```
0000 = 0
0001 = 1
    ...
1001 = 9
1010 = A (= 10)
1011 = B (= 11)
1100 = C (= 12)
1101 = D (= 13)
1110 = E (= 14)
1111 = F (= 15)
```

Now consider, for example, the following word of 16 bits, divided into groups of four bits:

1111 0000 1010 0011

These groups, in the given order, correspond to the following hexadecimal number:

F0A3

Recalling that we have F = 15 and A = 10, we can use this to compute

$$15 \times 16^3 + 0 \times 16^2 + 10 \times 16 + 3 = 61603$$

This is another way of computing the value of the given 16-bits word, when interpreted as an unsigned binary number.

Exercises

1.1   Write a program that prints your name and address. Compile and run this program on your computer.

1.2 Write a program that prints your age (or rather the age you hope to achieve at the end of this year). The program should request you to enter both the current year and your year of birth.

1.3 What numbers do the following bit sequences represent, with two's-complement method and 16 bits word length?

a. 00000000 00001111
b. 11111111 11110000
c. A sequence of $16 - k$ zeros followed by k ones ($0 \leq k \leq 15$).
d. A sequence of k ones followed by $16 - k$ zeros ($1 \leq k \leq 16$).

1.4 Use a word length of 16 bits and the two's-complement method to write the following numbers in the binary number system:

a. 19
b. -8

CHAPTER 2

Some Language Rules

2.1 IDENTIFIERS

As we quite often use names, technically known as *identifiers*, in our programs, we need to know how to spell them. An *identifier* is a sequence of characters in which only letters, digits and underscores (_) may occur. Its first character must not be a digit. Upper case and lower case letters are different, so there are 52 distinct letters. In ANSI C, at least the first 31 characters are significant, except for identifiers that have 'external linkage'. The latter means that not only the compiler but also the linker has to deal with those identifiers, as we will discuss in more detail in Section 4.6. The linker may be more restricted as regards the number of significant digits and may also ignore case distinctions. Here are some examples of valid identifiers:

```
a
largest_element
table1
```

2.2 KEYWORDS

A number of identifiers are reserved for use as *keywords*, so we must not choose them for our own purposes, such as for variable names. They are

```
auto, break, case, char, const, continue, default,
do, double, else, enum, extern, float, for, goto,
if, int, long, register, return, short, signed,
sizeof, static, struct, switch, typedef, union,
unsigned, void, volatile, while.
```

Besides these keywords, we had better also avoid using identifiers that begin with underscores, since many compiler use such identifiers for special purposes.

2.3 CONSTANTS

Besides variables, there are also *constants*, an example of which is the number
123 in the following statement:

```
x = a + 123;
```

There are various types of constants:

Integer constants

Here are four examples of integer constants:

123	(decimal)
0777	(octal)
0xFF3A	(hexadecimal)
123L	(decimal, long)

If the first character of a constant is **0** and this is immediately followed by
another digit, the constant is interpreted as an octal number (with radix 8); only
the digits 0, ···, 7 may then occur in it. If the constant begins with **0x** or **0X**, it
is taken to be a hexadecimal integer. We use **A**, ···, **F** (or **a**, ···, **f**) as
hexadecimal digits with values 10, ···, 15. A letter **L** (or **l**), which means *long*,
at the end of the constant is a *suffix*. We can also use the suffix **U** (or **u**), which
means *unsigned*. The order of **L** and **U** is irrelevant if they both occur. The
unsigned suffix means that the number in question has type *unsigned*. As we have
seen in Section 1.2, the value of an unsigned type can be about twice as large as
a value of the corresponding *signed* type but cannot be negative. A suffix **U** does
not increase the *size*, that is, the number of bytes it needs. This may be different
for a suffix **L**. With most microcomputers, the types **int** and **unsigned** take two
bytes, whereas the types **long int** and **unsigned long** take four bytes.

If no suffix **L** or **U** occurs in a very large integer constant, the type of that
constant may yet be **long**, **unsigned**, or **unsigned long**. The precise decision rules
for these cases are rather tedious, and it is unlikely that we will really need them
because they have been carefully devised so that they are in accordance with what
is both convenient and efficient. Nevertheless, they are included here for the sake
of completeness:

- If a *decimal* integer constant without any suffix is too large for type **int**, it has type **long**, unless it is even too large for that type: in that case its type is **unsigned long**.

- If a *hexadecimal* or *octal* integer constant without any suffix is too large for type **int**, its type is **unsigned**, if possible. If its value is too large for **unsigned** its type is **long**, if possible. If this is not possible, its type is **unsigned long**.

Let us assume, for example, that the types **int** and **long** take two and four bytes, respectively. Then 32767 is the maximum **int** value, so **32768** has type **long** and therefore takes four bytes. On the other hand, **0x8000** (which also has 32768 as its value!) has type **unsigned** and therefore takes only two bytes.

Character constants

We use single quotes at the beginning and at the end of a character constant, as, for example in ´**A**´. A character constant has type *int*, and its value is simply the numerical value of its internal representation. For most machines this is the value that can be found in an ASCII table, as included in this book in Appendix B. For ´**A**´ we find the value 65, or 41 in hexadecimal. The latter is useful if you want to write down the actual bit string quickly: 41 hex = 0100 0001 binary (= 65 dec.). In C the notations **65** and ´**A**´ are really equivalent, so the expression ´**A**´ + ´**A**´ is allowed and (with ASCII) has the value 130. A more sensible thing to do is to compute ´**A**´ + **i** in a loop, where **i** runs from 0 to 25. In this way we successively obtain the values 65, 66, ···, 90, or, in other words, ´**A**´, ···, ´**Z**´.

Some special characters can be represented by *escape sequences*, in which the backslash character (\) occurs:

'\n'	newline, go to the beginning of the next line
'\r'	carriage return, back to the beginning of the current line
'\t'	horizontal tab
'\v'	vertical tab
'\b'	backspace
'\f'	form feed
'\a'	audible alert
'\\'	backslash
'\''	single quote
'\"'	double quote
'\?'	question mark
'\\ooo'	octal number
'\\xhh'	hexadecimal number

In the last two cases, *ooo* and *hh* denote at most three octal and two hexadecimal digits, respectively. We can use these forms conveniently if actually bit strings are given. For example, we can write ´\x4F´ to denote the bit string 01001111. However, we must be careful if the leftmost bit of such a bit string (of length 8) is 1. Remember that character constants actually have type **int**, so the bit string is extended to the left to the size of type **int**, which is at least 16 bits. If the compiler regards characters as 'signed', the leftmost bit is used as a 'sign bit'. The value of ´\80´ may therefore be − 128 instead of 128, because extending the corresponding bit string 1000 0000 to 16 bits may give 1111 1111 1000 0000 instead of 0000 0000 1000 0000. If we insist on extending the bit string to the left with zero bits, we had better use a hexadecimal integer constant, such as **0x80** in our example. Fortunately, the problem just discussed does not apply to 'normal' characters, since their leftmost bit (when stored in eight bits) is always 0.

An important special case is ´\0´, the so-called *null character*, which consists of only zero bits. Note that ´\0´ is equivalent to the integer constant **0**, but different from the character constant ´0´. As the ASCII table in Appendix B shows, the latter character is equivalent to **48**.

Floating constants

A *floating constant* represents a real number. It can have a fractional part, and its value can be much greater than integer values. However, in its internal format it normally only *approximates* the real number it represents. For example, the constant **0.1** may be stored internally as a value that is actually closer to 0.0999999999999999 than to 0.1. When writing a floating constant, we always have to use a period or the letter **E** (or **e**), as, for example, in

```
82.347
.63
83.
47e-4
1.25E7
61.e+4
```

These constants have type **double**, which means 'double-precision floating point'. We can insist that they be (single-precision) **float**, by writing a letter **F** (or **f**) at the end of the constant. By contrast, we can write **L** (or **l**) at the end as a request for more precision than that of type **double**. If this is done the constant has type **long double**. Most current compilers ignore such requests and deal with type **long double** in exactly the same way as with type **double**.

String constants

A *string constant* (or, briefly, a *string*) is a sequence of characters written between double quotes, as, for example, in

```
"How many numbers?"
"a"
```

The string constant "a" must not be confused with the character constant ´a´. As we will see in Chapter 6, a string constant is, technically speaking, an array of characters. Internally, a null character ´\0´ is always stored after the final character written in the string constant. We will see that this null character is essential in detecting the end of the string.

If we want to write a double quote inside a string, it must be preceded by a backslash, so we write \". We can also use other escape sequences, as has been done in

```
printf("The character\n\\\nis called a \"backslash\".");
```

This statement produces the following output:

```
The character
\
is called a "backslash".
```

Without special measures, we cannot write a string on more than one program line. However, two or more successive string constants, possibly with white-space characters in between, are logically pasted together. For example, writing

```
"ABC"    "DEF""GHI"
"JKL"
```

literally in our program is just another way of writing the following string:

```
"ABCDEFGHIJKL"
```

As we will see later in this book, we normally use indentation when writing our program, so it may happen that a long string constant, which starts, say, at the middle of a program line, does not fit into that line, especially if we want our program lines to be rather short. Then we can simply use two double quotes in the same way as those between **I** and **J** in the above example.

The facility just mentioned was introduced only in ANSI C. In the original version of C there was another method, which is also valid in ANSI C. It consists of writing a backslash at the end of the line that is to be continued, as, for example, in

```
printf("This is a string that is regarded \
as being on one line.");
```

A drawback of this older method is that we must not indent the second of these two lines: any blanks preceding the word 'as' in this example are inserted between this word and the preceding word 'regarded', in addition to the blank that there is already after the latter word. The newer method is therefore to be preferred. For example, the following two program lines have the same effect as those just shown:

```
printf("This is a string that is regarded "
        "as being on one line.");
```

2.4 COMMENT

As we have seen in Section 1.1, comment always has the following form:

```
/* ... */
```

It is not restricted to one program line. Since the first occurrence of */ is seen as the end of the comment, comment must not be nested. Comment cannot occur inside a string, so the statement

```
printf("/* ABC */");
```

causes the following to be printed:

```
/* ABC */
```

Exercises

2.1   Find the errors in the following program, and correct them:

```
include <stdio.h>

main();
{ int i, j
  i = 'A';
  j = "B";
  i = 'C' + 1;
  printf("End of
          program")
}
```

2.2   Use only one **printf** statement to print the following lines, including the
       double quotes:

```
One double quote: "
Two double quotes: ""
Backslash: \
```

2.3   Use a hexadecimal constant to assign the following binary number to a
       variable **i**:

   01010101 01010101

       Print the value of **i** in the normal way, that is, as a decimal number.

2.4   What does the following statement print?

```
printf("Single quote: \'\nDouble quote: \"\n"
        "Backslash: \\\nThe End.\n");
```

CHAPTER 3

Simple Expressions and Statements

When writing C programs, we must be familiar with some more language rules than those dealt with in Chapter 2. We can discuss these rules in a clear and efficient way only if we are familiar with some technical terms. For example, each of the following three forms is an *expression*:

```
a + b
1
x = p + q * r
```

It may make sense for an expression, such as the last of these three, to be immediately followed by a semicolon (;). Then the result is no longer an expression but a *statement*. The characters +, *, and =, as used here, are called *operators*. In the first of the above three expressions the variables **a** and **b** are *operands*.

3.1 ARITHMETIC OPERATIONS

As we have seen in Chapter 1, we use the plus and minus operators + and − to add and subtract. In the expression

```
a - b
```

the minus operator has two operands (**a** and **b**). It is therefore called a *binary* operator. The situation is different with the minus sign in

```
(-b + D1)/(2 * a)
```

where we say we have a *unary* minus operator, because it has only one operand (**b**). In contrast to the original version of C, ANSI C also allows us to use + as a unary operator, so we can now write, for example,

```
neg = -epsilon;
pos = +epsilon;
```

which, for reasons of symmetry, looks nicer than without the plus sign.

With the binary operators +, −, and *, the result of the computation is integer if both operands are integer; if at least one of the operands has floating-point type, so has the result. There is no automatic detection of *integer overflow*. For example, if the largest **int** value is 32767, the program fragment

```
int i=1000, j;
 j = 100 * i;
```

will give the variable **j** some value in the range −32768, ···, 32767 instead of expected value 100000. There will be no error message.

Except for integer overflow, the results of +, −, and * will be what anyone would expect. This may not be the case with the division operator /. As with the three previous operators, the result of

```
a / b
```

has integer type only if both **a** and **b** have integer type, and floating type if **a** or **b** has floating type. This implies, for example, that

```
39 / 5        is equal to 7,
39. / 5       is equal to 7.8.
```

We see that there are in fact two essentially different division operators, one for integer and one for floating type. It depends on the operand types which one is taken. Beginning C programmers often make the mistake of writing, for example, **1/3** (which is equal to 0) instead of **1.0/3.0** with the intended value 0.333···. Instead of **1.0/3.0** you can also write **1.0/3** or **1/3.0**, and in each of these three expressions the zeros may be omitted.

When using integer division, we are sometimes interested not only in the *quotient* (obtained by /), but also in the *remainder*, which we obtain by using the operator %. For example:

```
39 % 5        is equal to 4.
```

The % operator must not be applied to floating types.

The three operators *****, **/**, **%** have the same precedence, which is higher than that of **+** and **−**. If addition or subtraction should precede a multiplicative operation, we must use parentheses:

```
(8 - 1) * 2        is equal to 14;
8 - 1 * 2          is equal to 6.
```

Very often we want to increase a variable by some value. Instead of doing this by means of, for example,

```
x = x + a
```

we can write the following shorter and more efficient expression:

```
x += a
```

Once we are used to this new notation, we prefer the latter expression to the former also because it is more closely related to the way we think and speak: we say that we 'increase **x** by **a**', not that we 'assign the sum of **x** and **a** to **x**'.

Note that the above two forms are expressions. They would have been statements if they had been followed by a semicolon. Both expressions not only perform an assignment to **x**, but also yield a value, which is equal to the value assigned to **x**. For example, this whole line is an assignment statement, while **x += a** is an assignment expression with the value assigned to **x** as its value:

```
y = 3 * (x += a) + 2;
```

Assignment expressions perform the same actions as assignment statements. It depends on the context which of them is required.

Combining arithmetic operations with assignments is by no means confined to the adding operator. We can also use the following expressions, the meaning of which is obvious:

```
x -= a
x *= a
x /= a
x %= a
```

It often occurs that the value 1 is to be added to (or subtracted from) a variable. For these special cases there is an even more compact notation. Instead of, for example,

```
i += 1          and           i -= 1
```

we can write

```
++i            and            --i
```

The unary operators **+ +** and **− −** are called *increment* and *decrement* operators, respectively. We can also write these operators *after* the operand, as in

```
i++            and            i--
```

Although the variable **i** is updated in this way as was done before, there is an important difference: the value of the whole expression is now equal to the old value of **i**. In other words, if we write such an operator before its operand, it is applied before its value is taken; if we write it at the end, it is applied only after its value has been taken. For example, after the execution of the statements

```
i = 0; j = (i++);
m = 0; n = (++m);
```

the four variables used have the same values they would have by executing:

```
i = 1; j = 0;
m = 1; n = 1;
```

The parentheses in the above statements can be omitted. They were used here to illustrate the fact that those surrounding **i+ +** do not cause **i** to be incremented before its value is taken, as is sometimes thought.

If we use **i+ +** or **+ +i** *only* to increment **i**, ignoring the values of these expressions, it does not matter which form is used: the statements **i+ +;** and **+ +i;** (with semicolons!) are equivalent.

3.2 TYPES, VARIABLES, AND ASSIGNMENTS

In C the equal sign **=** always indicates *assignment*: we use it to assign a value to a variable. If that variable has been assigned a value previously, that value is lost. Every variable has a fixed *size*, which is the number of bytes it occupies in memory. With a given C implementation, the size of a variable depends on its *type*. Here are the elementary types, along with realistic examples of their sizes:

Type	Size
char	1
short (or short int)	2
int	2 or 4 (depending on the implementation)
enum	2 or 4
long (or long int)	4
float	4
double	8
long double	8 or 10

The types **char**, **short**, **int**, and **long** may be preceded by the keyword **unsigned**. Writing only **unsigned** is equivalent to writing **unsigned int**. We will discuss the keyword **unsigned** in more detail in Section 4.3.

If each of the types **short, int** and **enum** (to be discussed shortly) takes two bytes, the values of these three types are stored in the same way. (This is the case, for example, with current MS-DOS compilers.) With other machines (the VAX, for example) type **int** takes four bytes, as does type **long**. We can inquire the size of a type by using **sizeof**. This is a unary operator, which can be applied either to a type name (written between parentheses) or to an expression. It is a good idea to use parentheses anyway, so that we need not bother about which case applies.

The following program shows how **sizeof** can be used, and many other things besides:

```
/* TYPES: Types, variables, and assignments.
*/
#include <stdio.h>

main()
{ char ch;
  float f;
  double ff;
  int i, j;
  ch = 'A';  ch++;
  f = 5.0/3;
  ff = 5.0/3;
  j = 2 * (i = 5.0/3);  /* i = 1 */
  printf("ch = %c   ASCII value: %d\n\n", ch, ch);
  printf("f = %20.17f   ff = %20.17f\n", f, ff);
  printf("i = %20d   j = %20d\n\n", i, j);
  printf("Type 'double' takes %d bytes.\n", sizeof(double));
}
```

Although this is not a practical program, it demonstrates some important new language aspects. First the five variables **ch**, **f**, **ff**, **i**, and **j** are declared. The variable **ch** is first given the value ´A´, or 65, and is then increased by 1, so its final value will be ´B´, or 66. We want this value to be printed both as ´B´ and as 66. Therefore **ch** occurs twice in the **printf** statement, with corresponding conversion specifications %c and %d. It seems that the three variables **f**, **ff**, and **i** are assigned the same value, namely **5.0/3**. Yet these variables assume different values: because of their types the exact value of 5.0/3 is approximated reasonably by **f**, very well by **ff**, and very badly by **i**. This program also demonstrates that an *assignment expression*, such as **i = 5.0/3**, may occur in a more complicated expression. Since **i** has type **int**, the computed value 1.66··· is truncated to the integer 1. The output of this program (when using Turbo C 2.0) is as follows:

```
ch = B   ASCII value: 66

f =  1.66666662693023682   ff =  1.66666666666666674
i =                    1   j  =                    2

Type 'double' takes 8 bytes.
```

Field width and precision

The values of **f**, **ff**, **i**, and **j** in program TYPES are printed in 20 positions, and the fractional parts of **f** and **ff** consist of 17 decimal digits. This is done by using %20.17f and %20d instead of simply %f and %d. In the following general forms, *m* and *k* are called the *field width* and the *precision*, respectively. They can only be integer constants, not variables:

    %*m.k*f   Converts a value of type **float** (or **double**) to *m* decimal positions, with *k* digits after the period.

    %*m*d   Converts an **int** value to *m* decimal positions.

If the field width *m* is larger than is needed, blank space is added at the left; if it is smaller, as many positions are used as are needed.

Initialization

When declaring a variable to allocate memory for it, we can *initialize* it, that is, we can give it an initial value, as is done, for example, in:

```
int i=27, j=25*38;
char ch='A';
```

(Although equal signs are used, these declarations do not contain assignment expressions, nor do we call **j=25*38;** an assignment statement in this example.)

Enumeration types

The keyword **enum**, which occurs in the table of types at the beginning of this section, is new in ANSI C. It is normally used when we need some constants with names that say what they mean and with values that are irrelevant. For example, we can write

```
enum days
{ Sunday, Monday, Tuesday, Wednesday, Thursday, Friday, Saturday
} yesterday, today, tomorrow;
```

After this declaration, we can use

- The *enumeration type* **enum days**. We can declare some more variables with it, as, for example, in:

    ```
    enum days the_day_after_tomorrow, my_birthday;
    ```

- The symbolic integer constants **Sunday, Monday, ⋯, Saturday**, which have the values 0, 1, ⋯, 6, respectively; these are the values of type **enum days**.

- The variables **yesterday, today**, and **tomorrow**, which can be assigned values of type **enum days**.

Enumeration types are compatible with type **int**: their values can be assigned to **int** variables. Conversely, an **int** value can be assigned to an enumeration-type variable, provided that it is equal to one of the enumeration-type values, such as 0, ⋯, 6 in our example. If it is not, there may be an error message, but for reasons of efficiency many compilers do not perform the 'range checks' that would be required, so such error messages do not normally appear.

We can also specify numerical values ourselves for enumeration constants. The following example demonstrates this. It also shows that the declaration of variables (**great, greater, greatest**) can be separated from the declaration that specifies the enumeration type (**enum mathematician**) itself:

```
enum mathematician    /* Numerical value = Year of birth */
{ Cauchy=1789,
  Euler=1707,
  Fourier=1768,
  Gauss=1777,
  Hesse=1811,
  Hilbert=1862,
  Kronecker=1823,
  Laplace=1749
};
enum mathematician great, greater, greatest;
```

If we specify a value for a constant, and none for some that follow, that value is repeatedly incremented for these constants that follow. For example, after

```
enum example {aaa, bbb, ccc=48, ddd, eee, fff=1, ggg};
```

we have

```
aaa = 0, bbb = 1, ccc = 48, ddd = 49, eee = 50, fff= 1, ggg = 2
```

This example also shows that two constants of an enumeration type may have the same value, as is the case here with **bbb** and **fff**. However, all constant names must be distinct, even if they belong to different enumeration types, for it would otherwise not be possible to tell the value and the type of a given constant name.

Register variables

As mentioned in Section 1.2, computers usually have some *registers* and can work faster with registers than with memory locations. It may therefore be advantageous for some variables, which are used very frequently, to be kept only in registers, not in memory. We can ask the compiler to do this by using the keyword **register** when we declare the variables in question, as, for example, in

```
register int i;
```

The compiler will then use a register instead of a memory word for **i**, if this is possible. If not, the keyword **register** is ignored. You may wonder why not always use this keyword. The first reason is that the number of registers is normally very small, and they are also used for all kinds of other work, which we do not want to be slowed down because of too few free registers being available. Second, only memory locations have addresses, registers have not. Therefore the 'address of' operator **&** must not be used for register variables. This implies that after the above declaration of **i** the call **scanf("%d", &i)** would be illegal.

The 'const' and 'volatile' keywords

ANSI C offers the possibility of using the *type qualifier* **const** for an initialized variable that will never be changed. Here is an example:

```
const int weeklength=7;
```

At the end of Section 6.5, we will see that we can use **const** also when specifying formal parameters of functions.

Another new keyword is **volatile**. It is used syntactically in the same way as **const,** but we can regard it as its opposite. In principle, it is possible for a **volatile** variable to be changed by hardware or by system software. Since the use of **volatile** is implementation dependent, we will not discuss it any further.

3.3 COMPARISON AND LOGICAL OPERATORS

When programming decisions and repetitions, we often need the following operators:

Operator	*Meaning*	
<	<	(less than)
>	>	(greater than)
<=	$\leq$	(less than or equal to)
>=	$\geq$	(greater than or equal to)
==	=	(equal to)
!=	$\neq$	(not equal to)
&&	*AND*	(logical *and*)
||	*OR*	(logical *or*)
!	*NOT*	(logical *not*)

The operators **<**, **>**, **< =**, **> =** are known as *relational* operators, while **= =** and **!=** are called *equality* operators. The former have higher precedence than the latter. We may collectively use the term *comparison* operators for these two operator classes. A comparison, such as **a < b**, is an expression with two possible values, which we would intuitively identify with *true* and *false*. In C the integers 1 and 0 are used for this purpose:

  1   means *true*;
  0   means *false*.

Comparisons (and logical expressions in general) have type **int**: there is no such thing as a 'Boolean' or 'logical' type in C, as there is in some other languages. As a result of this,

```
(3 < 4) + (7 < 9)
```

is a valid integer expression, and its value is 2. A very funny example is

```
5 < 4 < 3
```

This is interpreted as

```
(5 < 4) < 3
```

or as

```
0 < 3
```

so that its value is 1.

The unary operator **!** is normally used to turn 'true' into 'false', and vice versa. For example, the values of the following two expressions are equal for any x and y:

```
x < y
! (x >= y)
```

We can express the effect of **!** more technically as follows. The value of **!i** is 1 if **i** is equal to 0, and it is 0 if **i** is unequal to 0. Not only 1 but any nonzero value can be used as *true*. For example, the value 2 (like 1) denotes *true*, so **!2** should denote *false* and is therefore equal to 0. Note that we can write

```
i = !!i;
```

if we want **i** to be 1 if **i** $\neq 0$, and to be left unchanged if **i** = 0.

We can combine comparisons (and other logical expressions) by using the logical operators **&&** and **||**, as is done in, for example, in the test

```
x > a && x < b
```

to check that x lies between **a** and **b**. (The example **5 < 4 < 3** above shows why we cannot write **a < x < b** here.) With the two forms

```
operand1 && operand2
operand1 || operand2
```

it is guaranteed that the *operand2* will not be evaluated if the value of the result is already known after the evaluation of *operand1*. After all, for any value of *operand2*,

```
0 && operand2        is equal to 0, and
1 || operand2        is equal to 1.
```

This behavior of **&&** and **||** is important not only because (with complicated *operand2*) it may save computing time, but also because it may prevent undesirable actions, such as division by zero. For example, in the following expressions the division by **n** will not take place if **n** happens to be zero:

```
n != 0  &&  q < 1.0/n
!(n == 0  ||  q >= 1.0/n)
```

(Note that these two expressions are equivalent!)

Beginning C programmers often make the mistake of writing one equal sign instead of two. Doing this in the last example would *cause* dividing by zero instead of preventing it! Remember that **n = 0** is an expression, which, after assigning 0 to **n**, also yields a value. As this value, 0, means *false*, the second operator in

```
n = 0 || q >= 1.0/n
```

will be evaluated, which will cause a division by zero.

If you are familiar with Pascal, the following table may be useful:

C-operator	Pascal notation
=	:=
==	=
!=	<>

3.4 CONDITIONAL STATEMENTS

It will by now be clear that *statements* describe actions; in contrast to expressions, they do not yield values. The simplest statement is the *null statement*, which consists only of a semicolon. Normally, an expression precedes the semicolon:

```
scanf("%d", &n);
x = a + b;
printf("The End.");
```

We can use *braces* { } to build complex statements from simpler ones, just as we can use parentheses ( ) to build complex expressions. For example, the line

```
{x = a + b; y = c + d; z = e + f;}
```

contains a *compound statement*, built from three simpler statements. We often use compound statements in syntactic positions that allow only one statement, whereas we want to write more than one. We will apply this idea shortly.

We often want the execution of a statement to depend on a condition. In C we use the term *expression* rather than *condition*, and we want the given statement to be executed if that expression is nonzero. This is achieved by a *conditional statement* (also called *if-statement*) of the following form:

```
if (expression) statement1
```

We can also use this extended form of the conditional statement:

```
if (expression) statement1 else statement2
```

If *expression* has a nonzero value (which means *true*), *statement*1 is executed and *statement*2, if present, is ignored. In the opposite case, with *expression* equal to 0, *statement*1 is ignored and *statement*2, if present, is executed. The following examples should be studied carefully:

Example 1

In this example, *statement*1 is a compound statement and there is no *statement*2. It swaps the values of **a** and **b** if **a** is greater than **b**:

```
if (a > b)
{ w = a;
  a = b;
  b = w;
}          /* Now a <= b */
```

Example 2

The statements in a conditional statement can again be conditional statements, as is the case here with *statement2*:

```
if (x > 0) printf("Positive"); else
if (x < 0) printf("Negative"); else printf("Zero");
```

A pair of (superfluous) braces clarifies this example:

```
if (x > 0) printf("Positive"); else
{ if (x < 0) printf("Negative"); else printf("Zero");
}
```

Example 3

We can also take a conditional statement for *statement1*, as in

```
if (x <= 0) if (x < 0) printf("Negative"); else printf("Zero");
```

In this example we have two **if** keywords, and at first sight it is not clear to which of these the **else** keyword belongs. This ambiguity is resolved by the rule that, in case of doubt, the **else** belongs to the most recent **if**. Therefore the above line should be read as

```
if (x <= 0)
{ if (x < 0) printf("Negative"); else printf("Zero");
}
```

not as

```
if (x <= 0)
{ if (x < 0) printf("Negative");
} else printf("Zero");
```

Note that the only essential difference between the last two versions consists of the position of the closing brace }. The difference in layout, however important it may be for us humans, is ignored by the compiler.

Example 4

This example shows that even in complicated situations we can make a program readable by paying attention to the layout and, in particular, to the way indentation is used:

```
if (a >= b)
{ x = 0;
  if (a >= b+1)
  { xx = 0;
    yy = -1;
  } else
  { xx = 100;
    yy = 200;
  }
} else
{ x = 1;
  xx = -100;
  yy = 0;
}
```

The indentation method used in this book, with each brace pair in the same column, is based on the way ALGOL60 programs were written as early as 1960 (with **begin** and **end** instead of { and }). This style is also frequently applied to Pascal programs, which are generally regarded as very readable.

Example 5

When developing large programs, we normally want to see a good many statements on one screen of, say, 25 lines or on one page. It may therefore be good practice to write a rather short conditional statement on one line, as is done in:

```
if (a < b) {w = a; a = b; b = w;}
```

This form is as readable as the equivalent form in Example 1, which was written on five lines. Let us use this example for a brief discussion about where to insert semicolons. If you are familiar with Pascal, you will know that in that language statements are separated by semicolons. The **end** keyword of a Pascal compound statement is therefore followed by a semicolon if another statement follows, and it need not be preceded by a semicolon. In C a semicolon at the end of a statement is part of that statement. Not every statement ends with a semicolon: its final character may also be a closing brace (}). This explains that a closing brace of a statement is never followed by a semicolon but may be preceded by one.

Example 6

```
if (i) i = 1;
```

Not only 1, but any nonzero value means *true*. This if-statement is therefore equivalent to the following one, which is slightly less efficient:

```
if (i != 0) i = 1;
```

In both cases **i** is assigned the value 1, unless it is equal to 0, in which case its value is not altered. As we have seen in Section 3.3, there is an essentially different way of obtaining the same effect:

```
i = !!i;
```

3.5 ITERATION STATEMENTS

There are three types of *iteration statements*, also called *repetition statements*, or, more briefly, *loops*:

While-statement:

```
while (expression) statement
```

Do-statement:

```
do statement while (expression);
```

For-statement:

```
for (expression1; expression2; expression3) statement
```

To see how they work, let us use all three of them for the same purpose, namely to compute the sum

$$s = 1 + 2 + \cdots + n$$

without using the equality $s = \frac{1}{2} n(n + 1)$. Supposing that **s**, **n**, and **i** have been declared as integer variables, we can compute **s** as follows:

With a *while*-statement:

```
s = 0; i = 1;
while (i <= n)
{ s += i;  i++;
}
```

With a *do*-statement (to be used here only if **n** > 0):

```
s = 0; i = 1;
do
{ s += i;
  i++;
} while (i <= n);
```

With a *for*-statement:

```
s = 0;
for (i=1; i<=n; i++) s += i;
```

In all three solutions, the process of repeatedly increasing both s by i and i by 1 continues as long as the test **i** < = **n** succeeds. In the *while*-statement this test is done at the beginning of the loop, before s is increased. The latter is important, because **n** may be 0 (or negative). In that case the eventual value of **s** will be equal to 0, as will probably be expected.

In the *do*-statement, on the other hand, that test takes place after the inner part of the loop has been executed. The first time, s is increased by i regardless of the value of **n**. So if **n** is zero, s will be equal to 1, which is undesirable. We should therefore use the do-statement (also called *do-while-loop*) only if we know **n** to be positive. The inner part of a do-while-loop is always executed at least once, but the inner part of a while-statement may not be executed at all.

The given solution with the *for*-statement works exactly like that with the while-statement. We can describe the effect of

```
for (expression1; expression2; expression3) statement
```

by means of the following, equivalent form with **while**:

```
expression1;
while (expression2)
{ statement
  expression3;
}
```

(At the moment, we ignore the continue-statement; if this occurs inside the loop, the two forms are not completely equivalent, as we will see in the next section.) The given general form of the for-statement contains three expressions, separated by two semicolons. We see that *expression*1 is executed (or, rather, 'evaluated') only once, at the beginning; *expression*2 is evaluated each time just before a possible execution of the inner part of the loop, and it determines whether or not the loop is to be continued. Finally, *expression*3 is evaluated each time at the end of the inner part of the loop; it is often (but not necessarily) used to update some 'running' variable, such as i in our example.

Each of the three expressions just discussed may be omitted; the two semicolons, however, must be present. We can, for example, write the following solution to our summation problem; it only illustrates the point we are discussing and is not meant as an improvement:

```
s = 0; i = 1;
  for ( ; i<=n; ) s += i++;
```

If *expression*2 (here $i<=n$) is omitted, we have an endless loop, unless we use some other means of loop termination, to be discussed in the next section.

Let us now turn to a more realistic example. The following program produces a table with two columns x and $f(x)$, where

$$f(x) = x^2 + x + 1/x$$

We want x to run from 2.0 to 4.0, with step 0.2. (If this particular function and these x values are not really what you need, you can easily replace them.) The following program shows how to produce the desired table:

```
/* TABLE: This program produces a table. */
#include <stdio.h>
main()
{ int i; double x;
  printf("  x            f(x)\n\n");
  for (i=20; i<=40; i+=2)
  { x = i/10.0; printf("%3.1f %15.10f\n", x, x*x+x+1/x);
  }
}
```

Note the use of the conversion specifications %3.1f and %15.10f, each with a field width and a precision, as discussed in Section 3.2. We really need these in programs that produce tables: with so many numbers in the output, it is very important that we can specify exactly how they are to be printed. The output of this program is as follows:

x	f(x)
2.0	6.5000000000
2.2	7.4945454545
2.4	8.5766666667
2.6	9.7446153846
2.8	10.9971428571
3.0	12.3333333333
3.2	13.7525000000
3.4	15.2541176471
3.6	16.8377777778
3.8	18.5031578947
4.0	20.2500000000

The C language does not require the 'running variable' in a for-statement to have integer type, so it seems more natural to use a floating-point variable instead of the **int** variable **i** for this purpose, as is done in

```
#include <stdio.h>

main()
{ double x;
  printf("  x          f(x)\n\n");
  for (x = 2.0; x <= 4.0; x += 0.2)
    printf("%3.1f %15.10f\n", x, x*x+x+1/x);
}
```

However, this version is not correct. Floating-point values are only approximated: the values actually stored in memory may slightly differ from the theoretically correct values. In this example, this may not really affect the final digits in the above table, but yet there may be something wrong. The condition x < = 4 in the for-statement says that this statement is to terminate as soon as x is greater than 4. Now the problem here with the floating-point variable x is that this variable may be slightly greater than 4 at the moment that it should be exactly equal to 4. If this happens (which with Turbo C, Version 2.0, is indeed the case!), the last line of the above table is omitted. In our original program, TABLE, there is no such problem, because rounding errors do not apply to the integer running variable **i**. It is true that the problem in the last program can easily be remedied by writing, for example, **4.1** instead of **4.0** in the for-loop, but it is wise always to use integer running variables. In this way we avoid *cumulating* rounding errors. This example shows that besides knowledge of the C language itself we should also have some idea about how numbers are stored inside the computer.

3.6 BREAK, CONTINUE, GOTO, SWITCH

The break-statement

The execution of a loop terminates immediately if in its inner part the following statement is executed:

```
break;
```

If this *break-statement* occurs inside some nested loops, only the innermost enclosing loop is terminated. Here is a program which demonstrates this statement:

```
/* BREAK: Demonstration of the break-statement.
*/
#include <stdio.h>

main()
{ double s=0, x;
  printf("Enter numbers, separated by blanks.\n");
  printf("They are added up as long as they are positive.\n\n");
  for ( ; ; )
  { scanf("%lf", &x);
    if (x <= 0) break;
    s += x;
  }
  printf("Sum of the positive numbers that have been read: %f\n", s);
}
```

The interesting point about this program is that the test for loop termination is placed neither at the beginning nor at the end but in the middle of the loop. This is a very natural thing to do: we can test a number only after reading it, so inside the loop the **scanf** statement should precede the test. On the other hand, if the loop is not terminated, s is to be increased by x, so it is logical to write s + = x; after the test.

Instead of

```
for ( ; ; )
```

we might have written

```
while(1)
```

But for the break-statement, we would have endless loops in both cases.

You may have noticed the letter **l** used in **"%lf"**. This is needed here because **&x** denotes the address of a **double** variable. Similarly, **scanf** requires **"%ld"** for a **long int** variable. Note that we use the letter **l** for this purpose with **scanf** only, not with **printf**, because in the latter case the conversion specifications **"%f"** and **"%d"** correspond to the values to be printed, not to addresses.)

The continue-statement

The *continue-statement* looks similar to the break-statement, but it works essentially differently. We simply write it (inside a loop) as

```
continue;
```

Normally the continue-statement is executed conditionally, as in

```
while (...)
{ xxx
  if (condition) continue;
  yyy
}
```

where ..., xxx, yyy stand for valid program text. The meaning of this loop is given by the following, equivalent form:

```
while (...)
{ xxx
  if (!(condition))
  { yyy
  }
}
```

This shows that the continue-statement causes an immediate jump to the test for continuation of the (smallest enclosing) loop. Note that in the former fragment we have only one brace pair, whereas there are two in the latter. This shows that continue-statements can reduce the number of compound-statements, nested inside each other.

With **continue** in the for-statement, the 'running variable is updated' before the test for continuation is performed. More precisely, we can replace the form

```
for (expression1; expression2; expression3)
{ xxx
  if (condition) continue;
  yyy
}
```

with the following while-construction, which is equivalent to it:

```
expression1;
while (expression2)
{ xxx
  if (!(condition))
  { yyy
  }
  expression3;
}
```

Note that *expression*3 is evaluated even if the *yyy* fragment is skipped. Due to the continue-statement, it would not be correct here to apply the principle discussed in our explanation of the for-statement in Section 3.5. If we did, we would replace the above for-statement with the following program fragment, but this would cause *expression*3 to be skipped whenever *yyy* was skipped.

```
expression1;
while (expression2)        /* Not equivalent to the above for-statement. */
{ xxx
  if (condition) continue;
  yyy
  expression3;
}
```

The goto-statement

As we have seen, continue-statements can sometimes be used to reduce the number of nested compound statements: with many nested brace pairs it is not always easy to see which closing brace belongs to a given opening brace, especially if (in large programs) they are very far apart. However, in most cases it is the other way round: properly indented nested compound statements makes a program considerably more readable than programs written in the style of 'unstructured' languages, such as assembly languages, where 'jump' or 'branch' instructions are frequently used. C programmers can use something similar, namely the *goto-statement*. Its use is not recommended.

Let us consider two programs, EVEN1 and EVEN2, one without and one with goto-statements. They solve the same problem: positive integers are to be read from the keyboard, and the sum of those which are even is to be computed. Odd integers are ignored; the first negative integer signals the end of the input data:

```
/* EVEN1: Solution without goto-statements.
*/
#include <stdio.h>

main()
{ int x, s=0;
  for ( ; ; )
  { scanf("%d", &x);            /* Read x.                      */
     if (x <= 0) break;         /* Exit if x is negative.       */
     if (x % 2 == 0) s += x;    /* Use x only if it is even.    */
  }
  printf("Sum of even integers: %d\n", s);
}
```

```
/* EVEN2: Solution with goto-statements.
*/
#include <stdio.h>

main()
{   int x, s=0;
l1: scanf("%d", &x);            /* Read x.                      */
     if (x <= 0) goto l2;       /* Exit if x is negative.       */
     if (x % 2 == 0) s += x;    /* Use x only if it is even.    */
     goto l1;                   /* Back to start of program.    */
l2: printf("Sum of even integers: %d\n", s);
}
```

These two programs are equivalent, but the style of EVEN2 is old-fashioned. Its readability is not as good as that of EVEN1, because we can not immediately see its loop structure. Program EVEN2 may not be a striking example, because it is very short and simple. Generally, programs with goto-statements become far less readable if they grow larger and more complicated. Curiously enough, the trouble with the goto-statement is that we can do too much with it: we can use it to jump to positions where we should not jump to. The higher-level control constructs for loops and conditional execution are more restricted and therefore safer.

The switch-statement

The *switch-statement* can be regarded as a (very restricted and therefore innocent) kind of goto-statement. The place we jump to depends on the value of an integer expression. Its general form is

```
switch (expression) statement
```

with one ore more so-called *case-labels* in the statement.

In the following example, the variable **y** is increased by 1 if **x** is equal to one of the integers that occur in the case-labels, and left unchanged otherwise:

```
switch (x) case 100: case 150: case 170: case 195: y++;
```

The switch-statement is more often used in a somewhat different way, as the following example demonstrates. It shows another application of the **break**-statement, which may be used not only in loops but also in switch-statements:

```
switch (letter)
{ case 'N': case 'n': printf("New York\n"); break;
  case 'L': case 'l': printf("London\n"); break;
  case 'A': case 'a': printf("Amsterdam\n"); break;
  default: printf("Somewhere else\n"); break;
}
```

For example, let us assume **letter** to be equal to ´**L**´ (or ´**l**´). Then a jump to the statement that prints **London** takes place. The break-statement that follows causes immediate exit from the switch-statement. Without it, **Amsterdam** would also have been printed. If **letter** is not equal to one of the letters in the case-labels, a jump to the default-label takes place, so that **Somewhere else** is printed. If the line starting with **default** had been omitted, nothing would have been printed in that case. Only one default-label is allowed. The values in the case-labels must be constant expressions of integral type, and they must all be different. (Remember, character constants have type **int**.) Note that the colon after case labels may be followed by any number of statements, which need not be enclosed in braces. Beginning C programmers who use switch-statements often forget to insert break-statements, and are then surprised that the computer does more than they expect.

Exercises

3.1   Write a program to read a sequence of positive integers and to print the greatest of these. Use a negative integer to signal the end of the input data.

3.2   Write a program that reads a sequence of positive real numbers and computes their average. A negative number signals the end of the input data.

3.3   Write a program that reads an integer (into a variable of type **int**) and computes the sum of its final two decimal digits.

3.4   Write a program that reads 20 integers and counts how often a larger integer is immediately followed by a smaller one.

3.5   Write a program to read 10 integers and to find the second smallest of them.

3.6   Write a program that reads a decimal digit d and prints a table with two columns: one for positive integers x, less than 100, and one for their squares x^2. Only those lines in which the digit d occurs both in x and in x^2 are to be printed.

3.7   With a positive integer s read from the keyboard, find all sequences of consecutive integers (such as 13, 14, 15, 16) whose sum is equal to s.

3.8   Write a program that reads the (small) positive integers n and k, and uses these to print a board of $n \times n$ squares, similar to a chessboard. The white squares are blank and the black ones consist of $k \times k$ asterisks (*). As with a chessboard, there must be a black square in the lower-left corner.

CHAPTER 4

More Operators

4.1 CONDITIONAL EXPRESSIONS

Besides the conditional *statement* (beginning with **if**) there is also the *conditional expression*. Not the keyword **if**, but, instead, the two characters **?** and **:** are used in it. It has the following form:

  *expression*1 **?** *expression*2 **:** *expression*3

First, *expression*1 is evaluated. Its purpose is similar to that of the parenthesized expression after **if** in a conditional statement. If its value is nonzero, *expression*2, and otherwise *expression*3, is evaluated. In other words, on the basis of *expression*1 a choice is made between *expression*2 and *expression*3, and the value of the chosen expression is taken as the value of the whole conditional expression. The conditional statement and the conditional expression are different not only in their appearance but also in the way they are used, that is, they are used in different contexts. A conditional expression, possibly surrounded by parentheses, can occur in any expression; a conditional statement cannot. Here is an example in which a conditional expression is used in this way:

```
z = 3 * (a < b ? a + 1 : b - 1) + 2;
```

With a conditional statement we would have to write

```
if (a < b) z = 3 * (a + 1) + 2; else z = 3 * (b - 1) + 2;
```

or, with the temporary variable **t**:

```
if (a < b) t = a + 1; else t = b - 1;
z = 3 * t + 2;
```

The form with the conditional expression is shorter and more elegant than these two program fragments with conditional statements. Conditional expressions are also useful as arguments of functions. We will not discuss functions in more detail

41

until Chapter 5, but we already know some standard functions, such as **printf**. We can, for example, write

```
printf("The greater of a and b is %d", a > b ? a : b);
```

Again, an equivalent program fragment without a conditional expression is longer and less elegant:

```
printf("The greater of a and b is ");
if (a > b) printf("%d", a); else printf("%d", b);
```

Besides, the former solution corresponds more closely to the way we think and speak, since we normally say: 'we print the greater of *a* and *b*', using the word *print* only once. We therefore also prefer using the name **printf** only once for this purpose in our program.

Here is a third example of using the conditional expression:

```
printf(u == v ? "Equal" : "Unequal");
```

Although the first argument of **printf** must be a string, it need not be a string *constant*, but it may be any expression the value of which is a string. (In Section 6.4 we will see that something more can be said about this subject.)

Now that we have seen so many cases in which a conditional expression is to be preferred to a conditional statement, you may wonder if there are also cases in which we need or prefer the latter. This is indeed the case. First, we should bear in mind that in a conditional statement the 'else part' may be absent, whereas in a conditional expression there must always be a colon, followed by an expression. The effect of the conditional statement

```
if (a < b) c = 0;
```

can therefore not be obtained with a conditional expression, unless we write something that is both contrived and inefficient, such as

```
c = (a < b ? 0 : c);
```

or

```
a < b ? (c = 0) : 0;
```

Second, the statements that are part of a conditional statement can be quite complex; for example, they can be compound statements in which loops occur. In such cases we cannot use conditional expressions. The conditional statement is therefore by no means a superfluous element in the C language.

4.2 THE COMMA-OPERATOR

Two expressions, separated by a *comma-operator*, as indicated in

*expression*1 , *expression*2

form a *comma-expression*. The two expressions are evaluated in the given order, and the value of the whole comma-expression is equal to that of *expression*2. This language construct is useful only if *expression*1 does something more than just yielding a value (since that value is ignored). Here is an example in which this is the case:

```
/* SUM1: Solution based on comma-operator. */
s = 0;
while (scanf("%d", &i), i > 0) s += i;
```

This program fragment computes the sum of positive integers entered on the keyboard and followed by an integer that is zero or negative. The comma-expression used here is

```
scanf("%d", &i), i > 0
```

The call to the standard function **scanf**, preceding the comma-operator, is an *expression*. We will discuss the value returned by **scanf** shortly; here we ignore it, as we do when writing the *statement*

```
scanf("%d", &i);
```

(with emphasis on the semicolon at the end). The interesting point of program fragment SUM1 is that a call to **scanf** occurs between the parentheses that follow the **while** keyword: a statement would not be allowed there. The comma-operator is needed here, because we want another expression, **i > 0**, for the loop test. Note that this test is done between two actions that are also in the loop, as Fig. 4.1 shows.

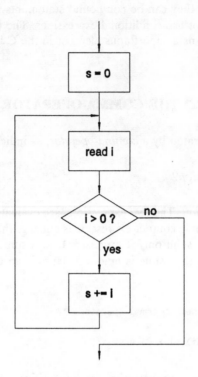

Fig. 4.1. Loop with test in the middle

This diagram also applies to program fragment SUM2, which is another way of writing a loop with the test in the middle, discussed in Section 3.6:

```
/* SUM2: Solution based on the break-statement. */
s = 0;
for ( ; ; )
{ scanf("%d", &i);
  if (i <= 0) break;
  s += i;
}
```

We now see that in C we have at least two ways of programming a loop with the test in the middle. If we had none, which is the case in Pascal (supposing that we do not want to use the goto-statement), we would probably have used the following solution to the same problem:

```
/* SUM3: Solution in the spirit of Pascal. */
s = 0;
scanf("%d", &i);
while (i > 0)
{ s += i;
  scanf("%d", &i);
}
```

Version SUM3 does not correspond to Fig. 4.1. A flow diagram for it would have two boxes with 'read i', one outside and one inside the loop. The program fragments SUM1 and SUM2 are more natural solutions to our summation problem than program fragment SUM3. When comparing SUM1, SUM2, and SUM3, most experienced C programmers will probably prefer the short solution SUM1.

The value returned by scanf

In our last example, the integer sequence read from the keyboard was terminated by a nonpositive integer. We often want to use some other means to signal the end of the input data, such as, for example, the word END. We can realize this in C in a very simple way, based on the value returned by the standard input function **scanf**. This value is an integer equal to the number of data items (such as numbers) that are read. For example, we can write the following assignment statement:

```
n = scanf("%f %f %f", &x, &y, &z);
```

If this call to **scanf** is successful, that is, if three numbers can be read, the returned value is 3, so this is the value assigned to **n**. If only two can be read because of some nonnumerical character following the second number in the input, **n** will be given the value 2, and so on. If we now modify our summation problem in that the word END (or some other nonnumerical characters) signals the end of the input data, a solution to this new problem is

```
/* SUM4: Input data terminated by the word END, for example.  */
s = 0;
while (scanf("%d", &i) == 1) s += i;
```

Note that SUM4 is even slightly shorter than SUM1. When **scanf** has to read an integer, as is the case in SUM4, it begins by skipping any leading white-space characters. If then a correct integer follows, its characters are read until a character is encountered that does not belong to the integer. That character is not regarded as being read. The same applies when the above call to **scanf** is unsuccessful because some nonnumeric character is encountered before the first character of

an integer. It is important to know this, because after SUM4 some more calls to
scanf may follow; we then have to skip the nonnumerical characters in the input
stream before we can read another number. If we know that there is only one
such character, we can use a **char** variable **ch** and write either

```
ch = getchar();
```

or, equivalently,

```
scanf("%c", &ch);
```

Now that we have used **getchar**, to read one character, we may as well mention
the analogous way of writing one character. For the latter purpose we can write

```
putchar(ch);
```

which is equivalent to

```
printf("%c", ch);
```

4.3 BIT MANIPULATION

We can apply the following operators for bit manipulation to integer operands:

&	Bitwise AND
|	Bitwise OR
^	Bitwise XOR (exclusive OR)
~	Inversion of all bits
<<	Shift left
>>	Shift right

The term *bitwise*, used above, means that the operation in question applies to all
pairs of bits in the same positions. This will be clear from the examples that
follow. Let us again assume **sizeof(int)** to be equal to 2, so that type **int** has 16
bits. (You can easily construct similar examples for other word lengths.)

The operator & gives a 1 in a bit position of the result only if the two bits of the
operands in the same position are also 1. For example, we can find the value of
0x3A6B & 0x00F0 as follows:

```
0x3A6B              = 0011 1010 0110 1011
0x00F0              = 0000 0000 1111 0000
─────────────────────────────────────────  &
0x3A6B & 0x00F0 = 0000 0000 0110 0000 = 0x0060
```

As this example shows, we can use the operator & to extract some bits from a word of 16 bits. Counting the bits from right to left, starting at 0, we have extracted the bits 4, 5, 6, 7 in this example. In the result they have the same values as these bits in the first operand, 0x3a6B, have; this is so because the bits 4, 5, 6, 7 in the second operand (called a *mask*) are 1 and all others are 0.

We have an analogous situation with |. This operator gives 0 for all positions in which the two corresponding operand bits are 0, as the following example shows:

```
0x3A6B              = 0011 1010 0110 1011
0x00F0              = 0000 0000 1111 0000
─────────────────────────────────────────  |
0x3A6B | 0x00F0 = 0011 1010 1111 1011 = 0x3AFB
```

This illustrates that we can use the operator | to set some bits (that is, to make them equal to 1) and leave the others unaltered.

The operator ^ gives 1 for all positions in which the two corresponding operand bits are different, and it gives 0 if they are equal:

```
0x3A6B              = 0011 1010 0110 1011
0x00F0              = 0000 0000 1111 0000
─────────────────────────────────────────
0x3A6B ^ 0x00F0 = 0011 1010 1001 1011 = 0x3A9B
```

We can see that ^ inverts the selected bits and leaves the others unaltered.

With the operator ~ each bit in the result is the inverse of the corresponding bit of its operand. It has only one operand, that is, it is a unary operator. Here is an example:

```
 0x3A6B = 0011 1010 0110 1011
~0x3A6B = 1100 0101 1001 0100 = 0xC594
```

With < < the result is obtained by shifting the first operand as many positions to the left as the second operand specifies. We lose bits at the left of the word, and zero bits are inserted at the right, as the following example shows:

```
0x63B7      = 0110 0011 1011 0111
0x63B7 << 4 = 0011 1011 0111 0000 = 0x3B70
```

We can shift to the right in a similar way by using > >:

```
0x63B7      = 0110 0011 1011 0111
0x63B7 >> 4 = 0000 0110 0011 1011 = 0x063B
```

Here the leftmost bit of the first operand is 0. Unfortunately, things are not so easy if that bit happens to be 1. As mentioned in Section 2.3, we can distinguish between the types

unsigned int   (or **unsigned**, for short) and
signed int   (or, briefly, **int**).

With an **unsigned** first operand, it is guaranteed that zeros will be shifted into the word on the left-hand side. This is also the case if the first operand has type **int** and its leftmost bit is 0, as is the case in the above example. In the remaining case, with an **int** operand the leftmost bit of which is 1, the result is system dependent: some machines will use zeros and others ones (that is, 'sign bits') to shift into the word on the left-hand side. If the first operand is a hexadecimal constant, as in the above example, we are certain that zeros are inserted on the left, because such a constant is taken as **unsigned**. In practice, however, we normally use variables rather than constants; if we want zeros to be inserted on the left, we should declare such variables as **unsigned**, not as **int**.

Bit operations combined with assignments

Not only the arithmetic operators +, −, *, /, and %, but also the bit operators &, |, ^, <<, and >> can be combined with assignment, which gives the following new operators:

```
&=   |=   ^=   <<=   >>=
```

For example, we can shift the contents of the **int** variable i one bit to the left by writing

```
i <<= 1;
```

instead of

```
i = i << 1;
```

(As we will see in Section 4.6, < < has higher precedence than =.)

Output and input of hexadecimal numbers

Now that we are frequently using hexadecimal constants, it is useful to know that the format string for **scanf** and **printf** accepts hexadecimal conversion specifications. We use these by writing %···X instead of %···d. Note that if we want we can use different number bases in conversion specifications and constants, as, for example,

```
printf("%04X", 255);
```

This gives the following output:

```
00FF
```

The 0 in %04X causes padding on the left with zeros instead of with spaces. We can also use this principle with decimal conversion specifications, but that is normally not desirable. If we had written %04x, with lower case **x**, the output would have been

```
00ff
```

If we want to *read* hexadecimal numbers we can simply use %X (or %x) with **scanf**. This gives us complete freedom in the way the hexadecimal numbers are spelled in the input data. For example, the forms **0xFF**, **0Xff**, **FF**, **00ff** will all be accepted. The following program may be useful if you are given a hexadecimal constant and want to know its value (written, as usual, in the decimal number system):

```
#include <stdio.h>
main()
{ int i;
  printf("Enter a hexadecimal integer: ");
  scanf("%X", &i);
  printf("This is written in the decimal number system as: %d.\n", i);
}
```

4.4 SIMPLE ARRAYS

Each variable used so far corresponds to only one number (or one character). With many programming problems we want to use sequences of numbers (or other objects), the elements of which have the same name and are distinguished by an integer 0, 1, 2, ···. We can do this by using *arrays*. Here we will only deal

with the most elementary aspects of arrays; they will be discussed in more detail
in Chapter 6. The array declaration

```
int a[100];
```

enables us to use the following variables:

```
a[0], a[1], ..., a[99]
```

Although in the declaration 100 is given as the number of array elements, the
final element is **a[99]**, not **a[100]**. In this example the elements have type **int**, as
indicated in the declaration. This may be any other type instead. When, after
having *declared* an array, we are *using* it, we can write any integer expression
between the square brackets, as is done, for example, in the statement

```
k = 50 * a[3 * i + j/2] - 1;
```

provided that the expression **3 * i + j/2** has a value that is less than 100 and not
negative. The value denoted between brackets is called a *subscript*. It must have
type **int** (or **unsigned**), no matter what the array-element type is. This example
also illustrates that array elements can be used in the same way as the simple
variables we have been using so far.

In the declaration, the *dimension* 100 is only given as an example, but we must
always write array dimensions as constants, or, in general, as *constant expressions*.
For example, if **n** is a variable, **int a[n]** is incorrect, but **int a[3 * 75 + 1]** is
correct. So much for array declarations.

It is possible to denote constants by symbolic names (that is, by identifiers). If
we write, for example,

```
#define LENGTH 100
```

at the top of the program, the symbolic constant **LENGTH** can be used instead
of 100. As it is a constant, we cannot assign other values to **LENGTH** later, but
we *can* write

```
int a[LENGTH];
```

which would not have been allowed if **LENGTH** had been a variable. With this
new way of declaring **a**, we would consistently use **LENGTH** instead of 100, and
write, for example,

```
for (i=0; i<LENGTH; i++) a[i] = 0;
```

if all elements of **a** are to be set to zero. If later we want to replace 100 with some other value, only the above **#define** line need to be modified. Another advantage of symbolic constants is that we can use names that tell something about the meaning of these constants. Such a style of programming, with emphasis on readability and documentation, is highly recommended. We will discuss other interesting possibilities with **#define** lines in Section 5.8. For this moment, remember that, like **#include** lines, they should really be separate lines (not ending with semicolons).

Let us now have a look at a complete program that uses both an array and a symbolic constant. It reads 30 integers from the keyboard and prints them in reverse order, that is, we use the principle 'last in, first out':

```
/* LIFO: This program reads 30 integers and prints them
         in the reverse order (Last In, First Out).
*/
#include <stdio.h>
#define LENGTH 30

main()
{ int i, a[LENGTH];
  printf("Enter %d integers:\n", LENGTH);
  for (i=0; i<LENGTH; i++) scanf("%d", &a[i]);
  printf("\nThe same integers, in reverse order:\n");
  for (i=0; i<LENGTH; i++)
    printf("%6d%c", a[LENGTH-i-1], i % 10 == 9 ? '\n' : ' ');
}
```

Notice the conditional expression

```
i % 10 == 9 ? '\n' : ' '
```

whose value is a blank in most cases but is a newline character when **i** is equal to 9, 19, or 29. In this way we obtain three lines of ten integers each in the output. (In the input the integers may be distributed over several lines any way the user likes.)

In Section 6.6 we will discuss a way of using certain variables as arrays, except that their dimensions need not be constants but may depend on variables.

4.5 ASSOCIATIVITY

It is obvious that the expression

```
a - b - c - d
```

is equivalent to the first of the following two expressions:

```
((a - b) - c) - d                    a - (b - (c - d))
```

This is expressed in a technical way by saying that the operator − *associates from left to right*. We see that this phrase means that the expression in question is equivalent to one in which parentheses, *starting from the left*, have been inserted. Each operator always associates in the same way: either from left to right or from right to left. This characteristic of an operator is called its *associativity*.

Since most operators, like + and −, associate from left to right, the most efficient way of discussing associativity is to focus on the exceptions. All operators associate from left to right except those mentioned in the following rules:

(i)   All unary operators (with only one operand) associate from right to left.

(ii)   The operator ?:, used in conditional expressions, associates from right to left.

(iii)   The assignment operators = += −= *= /= %= &= |= ^= <<= >>= associate from right to left.

Here is a (not very practical) example of (i):

```
- ! 0
```

Since − and ! are used here as unary operators, they associate from right to left, so when inserting imaginary parentheses we must start on the right, which gives −(!0). This means that the given expression is equal to −1.

Let us also consider a more interesting example of (i). Unlike mathematics, the C language has some unary operators that follow their operands. This is the case with ++ in

```
-n++
```

Since both operators in this expression are unary, they associate from right to left, which means that we have to read this expression as −(n++), not as (−n)++. Again, we should think of inserting parentheses, starting on the right.

Incidentally, $(-n)++$ would not have been a valid expression, because $-n$ is not a variable and can therefore not be incremented. This is, however, not the proper way of explaining the meaning of $-n++$ but we should really use rule (i) for this purpose.

As for (ii), here is an example, which without any explanation would be difficult to read:

```
a < b ? x : c == d ? y : z
```

Since the operator ?: associates from right to left (and because this operator has lower precedence than the others, as we will see in the next section), we should read this as

```
a < b ? x : (c == d ? y : z)
```

Let us illustrate rule (iii) by means of a complete program:

```
#include <stdio.h>

main()
{ int i, j, k, l, m;
  i = 20;
  j = 10;
  k = l = i += j += m = 1;
  printf("m=%d  j=%d  i=%d  l=%d  k=%d\n", m, j, i, l, k);
}
```

Since all operators in $k = l = i += j += m = 1$; associate from right to left, imaginary parentheses should be inserted starting on the right, which gives

```
k = (l = (i += (j += (m = 1))));
```

If we like, we may really use this statement to replace the third line from below in the program. Whether or not we do this, the output is as follows:

```
m=1  j=11  i=31  l=31  k=31
```

(Because we have assignment *expressions* in C, with operators that associate from right to left, there is no need for a special language concept called 'multiple assignments', as there is in some other languages.)

4.6 PRECEDENCE OF OPERATORS

In the following table, all operators are listed in order of decreasing precedence, including those which we have not yet discussed. The operators on the first line have the highest precedence, those on the second line the second highest, and so on; operators on the same line have the same precedence.

Operator (see Section 4.5 for the associativity)

```
()   []   .    ->
!    ~    ++   --   +    -   (type)   *   &   sizeof   (all unary)
*    /    %
+    -
<<   >>
<    <=   >    >=
==   !=
&
^
|
&&
||
?:
=    +=   -=   *=   /=   %=   &=   |=   ^=   <<=   >>=
,
```

Each operator occurs in the following list once again, along with a brief indication of its meaning and a section in this book where you can find more about it. Note that the characters *, &, +, and −) occur twice: each of them is used both for a binary and a unary operator:

()	Function calls (Section 5.1)
[]	Subscripting (Sections 4.4 and 6.1)
.	Selecting a component of a structure (Section 7.1)
->	Selecting a structure component by means of a pointer (Section 7.2).
!	*NOT*, unary operator (Section 3.3)
~	Inversion of all bits, unary operator (Section 4.3)
++	Increment, unary operator (Section 3.1)
--	Decrement, unary operator (Section 3.1)
+	Plus, unary operator (Section 3.1)
+	Addition, binary operator (Section 3.1)
-	Minus, unary operator (Section 3.1)
-	Subtraction, binary operator (Section 3.1)
(type)	Cast, unary operator (Section 4.7)

*	'Contents of address', unary operator (Section 5.3)
*	Multiplication, binary operator (Section 3.1)
&	Bitwise *AND*, binary operator (Section 4.3)
&	'Address of', unary operator (Section 6.1)
sizeof	Number of bytes in memory, unary operator (Section 3.2)
/	Division, either floating point or integer (Section 3.1)
%	Remainder with integer division (Section 3.1)
<<	Shift left (Section 4.3)
>>	Shift right (Section 4.3)
<	Less than (Section 3.3)
>	Greater than (Section 3.3)
<=	Less than or equal to (Section 3.3)
>=	Greater than or equal to (Section 3.3)
==	Equal to (Section 3.3)
!=	Unequal to (Section 3.3)
^	Bitwise *Exclusive OR (XOR)* (Section 4.3)
|	Bit*wise OR* (Section 4.3)
&&	Logical *AND* (Section 3.3)
||	Logical *OR* (Section 3.3)
?:	Conditional expression (Section 4.1)
=	Assignment (Section 3.2)
+=	Addition combined with assignment. The following operators have similar meanings: - =, *=, /=, %=, < < =, > > =, &=, |=, ^= (Sections 3.1 and 4.3)

4.7 ARITHMETIC CONVERSIONS; THE CAST

In Section 3.1 we have dealt with the arithmetic operators +, −, *, /, and %. We will now discuss in more detail how the type of the expression

*operand*1   *operator*   *operand*2

(in which *operator* is one of the five operators just mentioned) depends on the types of *operand*1 and *operand*2. Now that we are familiar with associativity and precedence of operators, it will be clear that this general form applies not only to very simple expressions, such as **a + b**, but also to more complicated ones, such as

```
a * b - c * d - e * f,
```

According to Sections 4.5 and 4.6 we should read this as:

```
((a * b) - (c * d)) - (e * f)
```

This has indeed the general form just shown, with $((a * b) - (c * d))$ as *operand*1, and $(e - f)$ as *operand*2.

The precise rules to find the type of an expression may seem rather complicated, but fortunately we will seldom need them, because they have been devised in such a way that the type in question is just what we intuitively expect. If you think the following discussion tedious, don't worry. It is included here because it is important to know that every arithmetic expression has a type that can be derived from those of its operands, and this book might be considered incomplete if I did not show how this can be done.

First, *integer promotion* may take place: any operands that have type **char** or **short** are 'promoted' to type **int**. (Things are more complicated if there are any operands of type **unsigned short**. These are promoted to type **int** if **sizeof(int)** is greater than **sizeof(short)** but to type **unsigned** if these two **sizeof** values are equal.)

Type conversion (to be discussed below) is now applied to the operands to ensure that their types will be the same. The common type thus obtained is then used as the type of the result. This operand type conversion is done by applying at most one of the seven rules listed below. These rules are to be considered *in the given order*, and only one of them is to be applied; as soon as the two operands have the same type, any remaining rules are ignored. For brevity, the phrase 'an operand is converted to a given type' will include the case that this operand already has that type. For example, rule 1 includes the case that both operands are **long double**:

1. If either operand is **long double**, the other is converted to this type.
2. If either operand is **double**, the other is converted to this type.
3. If either operand is **float**, the other is converted to this type.
4. If either operand is **unsigned long**, the other is converted to this type.
5. If either operand is **long** and the other is **unsigned**, it depends on the computer system which of the following two cases applies:
   A. If **sizeof(long)** is greater than **sizeof(unsigned)**, the **unsigned** operand is converted to **long**.
   B. If **sizeof(long)** is equal to **sizeof(unsigned)**, both operands are converted to **unsigned long**.
6. If either operand is **long**, the other is converted to this type.
7. If either operand is **unsigned**, the other is converted to this type.

Note that very often none of these rules apply because both operands have type **int** (possibly due to integer promotion, discussed earlier in this section).

Signed and unsigned char types

Depending on the implementation, type **char** can mean either **signed char** or
unsigned char (although the former choice seems to be more fashionable than
the latter these days). If we use **char** variables only to store 'real' characters, the
distinction is not important, because these use only seven bits so that the 'sign
bit' is zero; in other words, the normal characters have positive values between
0 and 127. Things are different if we assign other values, such as, for example,
'\xFF' to a **char** variable. In this case we had better write **signed char** or
unsigned char, instead of just **char**, to avoid machine dependence. Program
SIGNEDCH examines, for the machine on which it runs, which of the two
possibilities (signed or unsigned) applies to type **char**:

```
/* SIGNEDCH: This program finds out whether characters are
             signed or unsigned.
*/
#include <stdio.h>
main()
{ signed char s_ch='\xFF';
  unsigned char u_ch='\xFF';
  char ch='\xFF'; /* Binary: s_ch = u_ch = ch = 11111111          */
  int s, u, i;
  s = s_ch;        /* Conversion from signed char to int          */
  u = u_ch;        /* Conversion from unsigned char to int         */
  i = ch;          /* Conversion from char to int (system dependent!) */
  printf("It was found that, for this C implementation,\n");
  printf(
  i == s ? "type 'char' is identical with type 'signed char'.\n" :
  i == u ? "type 'char' is identical with type 'unsigned char'.\n" :
          "something is wrong.\n");
}
```

Assuming that 16 bits and the two's complement system are used for type **int**, we
can write the binary representations of **s** and **u**, along with their values, as
follows:

```
s = 11111111 11111111 = -1  (= s_ch)
u = 00000000 11111111 = 255 (= u_ch)
```

The value of **i**, on the other hand, is system dependent. It is equal to either **s** or
u. Note that the values of **s_ch**, **u_ch**, and **ch** are a matter of interpretation: they
have the same internal representation, namely 11111111. The difference between
signed and unsigned character types becomes apparent only after these types are
converted to type **int**. In program SIGNEDCH this is done by using assignment

statements. As discussed in this section, conversion to type **int** (known as *integer promotion*) also takes place in expressions, such as in **s_ch + 1** and **u_ch + 1**; the values of these expressions are 0 and 256, respectively, despite the fact that **s_ch** and **u_ch** are represented by identical bit strings.

You may think this discussion about signed and unsigned characters rather theoretical and perhaps even useless. However, character variables are in practice used not only for normal characters but also for any byte values and for 'very short' integers. Especially in the latter case it is very important for the keyword **char** to be preceded by either **signed** or **unsigned**.

The cast operator

Forced type conversion, also known as *coercion*, can be achieved by means of a special operator, the *cast*. We can simply write the desired type between parentheses, in front of the expression to be converted, as, for example, in

```
(float) n
```

Casts are useful for many purposes; one is to convert a signed type to the corresponding unsigned type or vice versa. Let us use our example about signed and unsigned characters once again. If we write

```
signed char s_ch='\0xFF';
int i;
i = (unsigned char) s_ch;
```

then the value of **i** will be 255, while it would be −1 if the cast had been omitted.

A very useful application of the cast is a division operation that, although applied to integers, is to yield a real quotient. For example, in

```
int i=14, j=3;
float x, y;
x = i/j;
y = (float)i/(float)j;
```

we have **x** = 4.0 and **y** = 4.666⋯. According to the conversion rules discussed in this section, we could have omitted one of the two casts in the last statement. It is important to know that the cast has the second highest precedence (as we have seen in Section 4.6), so instead of the latter statement we could have written

```
y = (float)i/j;   /* y = 4.666... */
```

Here the cast is applied before the division by **j**, which is essential. By contrast, the following statement performs integer division (with integer 4 as its result!) before the cast is applied:

```
y = (float)(i/j);   /* y = 4.0     */
```

In the last example, the result would have been the same if we had omitted the cast, since conversion is performed automatically if an integer value (4) is assigned to a floating-point variable (**y**).

Conversion can really alter values, as is the case in

```
int i;
float x = -6.9;
i = x;
```

Here **i** is given the value −6. Using a cast is highly recommended here, not to make the computer do some additional work for us, but rather for the sake of documentation. By writing

```
i = (int)x;
```

we can see more clearly than in the last fragment that **i** will be obtained by truncating **x**.

Exercises

In Exercises 4.1, 4.2, 4.3 a sequence of integers is to be read from the keyboard, followed by some nonnumeric code to signal the end of the sequence. The sequence may have any length, so you cannot store all integers that are read into an array.

4.1   Read in a sequence of integers. Find out what is the largest of these and how many times this largest integer occurs in the sequence.

4.2   Read in a sequence of integers (some of which may be equal). Count how many distinct integers are given. You may assume that there will be no more than 100 (although the sequence length is unlimited).

4.3   Read in a sequence of integers. From each integer, its least significant six bits are taken, which forms a small integer (less than 64). The program is to produce a table with all small integers obtained in this way, along with their frequencies.

4.4   Write a program which reads a date given as three positive integers (day,
       month, year), as, for example,

       31 12 1990

       Your program is to compute the day number of this date, counted from
       January 1st of that year. So in the given example, that day number would
       be 365. Take into account that the year may be a leap year. This is the
       case if the given year number is a multiple of 4 but not a multiple of 100.
       There is one exception: it is also a leap year if it is a multiple of 400.

4.5   Show that by means of bit operations you can store four nonnegative
       integers, each less than 16, into a **short int** variable x. Write a program
       which first reads four such integers, a_0, a_1, a_2, a_3, and stores them into the
       variable x. Then the user is asked to enter an integer i ($0 \leq i \leq 3$) to find
       a_i (in x) and to print its value.

4.6   Show how you can efficiently multiply an integer that is read from the
       keyboard (and that is not too large) by 100, without using the operator **∗**.
       Use the operator < < several times.

4.7   Read a hexadecimal integer from the keyboard (using the conversion
       specification %x). In its binary representation we count the bits 0, 1, ···,
       starting on the right. Swap the following bits, and print the result as a
       hexadecimal integer:

           bit 0 and bit 7,
           bit 1 and bit 6,
           bit 2 and bit 5,
           bit 3 and bit 4.

4.8   As exercise 4.7, but now the bits 0 to 7 are to be rotated one position to
       the left (instead of being swapped):

           bit 0 moves to bit 1;
           the original bit 1 moves to bit 2;
                              ···
           the original bit 6 moves to bit 7;
           the original bit 7 moves to bit 0.

4.9   Read in the following numbers

$$n \quad x \quad a_n \quad a_{n-1} \quad \ldots \quad a_1 \quad a_0$$

to compute

$$y = a_n x^n + a_{n-1} x^{n-1} + \ldots + a_1 x + a_0$$

by means of *Horner's method*. This means that, for example, with $n = 3$, the following identity is used

$$a_3 x^3 + a_2 x^2 + a_1 x + a_0 \equiv ((a_3 x + a_2) x + a_1) x + a_0$$

With values of n other than 3 the method works analogously. Use type **double** (with **%lf** in calls to **scanf**) for all numbers except for n, which is an integer.

CHAPTER 5

Functions and Program Structure

In some languages there is a distinction between functions and procedures, there are several ways of parameter passing, and functions are either local or global. In C all this is much simpler: there are only functions, no procedures, there is only 'call by value' parameter passing, and all functions are global. Remarkably enough, when dealing with functions in C we do not miss anything.

5.1 BASIC CONCEPTS

Let us begin with a function **fun** with four parameters, **x**, **y**, **i**, and **j**, where **x** and **y** have type **float**, and **i** and **j** have type **int**. We will define this function in such a way that **fun(x, y, i, j)** is equal to

$$\frac{x - y}{i - j}$$

if $i \neq j$. If $i = j$, we cannot compute this quotient because in a division the denominator must not be zero. In that case, **fun** is to return the value 10^{20}, preceded by the sign of the numerator **x − y**, unless this is also zero: if that happens, **fun** is to return the value 0. Program FDEMO1 shows how this can be done. It consists of two functions, **main** and **fun**. As you can see in this program, the following occurs twice:

```
float fun(float x, float y, int i, int j)
```

We say that **fun** is *declared* inside the **main** function and *defined* after it. The function *definition* is the function itself, whereas the function *declaration* is only an announcement of it.

```
/* FDEMO1: Demonstration program with a function in the new style.
*/
#include <stdio.h>

main()
{ float fun(float x, float y, int i, int j), xx, yy;
  int ii, jj;
  printf("Enter two float and two int values: ");
  scanf("%f %f %d %d", &xx, &yy, &ii, &jj);
  printf("Value returned by function: %f\n", fun(xx, yy, ii, jj));
}

float fun(float x, float y, int i, int j)
{ float a = x - y;
  int b = i - j;
  return b != 0 ? a/b :
         a > 0 ? +1e20 :
         a < 0 ? -1e20 : 0.0;
}
```

The technical term for an expression such as

```
fun(xx, yy, ii, jj)
```

is a (function) *call*; **xx, yy, ii,** and **jj** are called *arguments*. A function call implies the execution of the actions described by the function, after which the program is resumed immediately after the call. The *parameters* (**x, y, i, j**) are used as local variables in the function, with the values of the corresponding arguments (**xx, yy, ii, jj**) as their initial values. The term *local variables* is more often used for variables such as **a** and **b** in our example. They do not exist outside the function.

A *return-statement* of the form

```
return expression;
```

causes a jump back to the calling function (**main** in our example), with the evaluated *expression* as the *return value*. In FDEMO1 we have used a rather complicated conditional expression in the return-statement.

Here is a demonstration of program FDEMO1, which computes 80.0/16 = 5.0:

```
Enter two real numbers followed by two integers:
100.5 20.5
20 4
Value returned by function: 5.000000
```

You may have noticed the term *new style* in the comment of program FDEMO1. This version is indeed 'new' in the sense that a very important new facility of ANSI C has been used. In the 'old' version of C, as originally published by Kernighan and Ritchie (K & R), function declarations did not contain any information about parameters, and the beginning of functions was written differently, as the following program shows:

```
/* FDEMO2: Demonstration program with a function in the old style.
*/
#include <stdio.h>

main()
{ float fun(), xx, yy;
  int ii, jj;
  printf("Enter two float and two int values: ");
  scanf("%f %f %d %d", &xx, &yy, &ii, &jj);
  printf("Value returned by function: %f\n", fun(xx, yy, ii, jj));
}

float fun(x, y, i, j) float x, y; int i, j;
{ float a = x - y;
  int b = i - j;
  return b != 0 ? a/b :
         a > 0 ? +1e20 :
         a < 0 ? -1e20 : 0.0;
}
```

Note the differences in both the declaration and the definition of **fun**. In many existing programs and books the old style is used. ANSI C is tolerant: although the new style is recommended, the old style is also accepted. As FDEMO2 shows, a function declaration in the old style only specifies the type of the return value. If that type is **int**, the function declaration can even be completely omitted: if a function is called without being declared in the preceding program text, it is assumed to return an **int** value.

As we will see in Section 5.6, a function can be called in a module different from the one in which it is defined, so when a compiler is dealing with a call to a function, there is not always a definition of that function with detailed information about it. This explains why each call to a function should (in the same module) preferably be preceded by a complete declaration of that function, written in the new style. If it is not, the compiler has no information about the parameters, so when compiling a function call it cannot check the arguments, let alone convert these to the required parameter types. This means in practice that programming errors in old-style programs may not cause the compiler to complain. Instead, the errors will turn up only during execution, which is very undesirable. (An incorrect function call, accepted by the compiler, may occur in a portion of the program that is rarely executed; it would be very unfortunate if that error were detected only long after the program has been tested and released for production.)

It will now be clear that the new style is to be preferred to the old one, and that every call to a function should be preceded by a declaration of that function. The latter applies not only to functions of our own, but also to standard library functions, such as **scanf** and **printf**. This explains the importance of the line

```
#include <stdio.h>
```

The compiler knows where to find the file **stdio.h**, which contains the declarations of **scanf** and **printf** (along with those of many other functions). As the contents of this file logically replace the #include-line, we see that this line provides for the desired function declarations.

Instead of a combined declaration, such as in

```
int m, n, k;
```

we may, of course, write separate declarations for each variable that is to be declared. Similarly, we can in program FDEMO1 replace the line

```
float fun(float x, float y, int i, int j), xx, yy;
```

with

```
float fun(float x, float y, int i, int j);
float xx, yy;
```

A function declaration such as the first of these two lines is often called a *function prototype*. It is identical with the first line of the function definition, except for the semicolon at the end, which is written in the declaration but must be absent in the definition. We may omit the parameter names in a function declaration, as, for example, in

```
float fun(float, float, int, int);
```

However, we prefer including such names: first they may be useful for documentation purposes, and, second, the compiler may use them in error messages for any incorrect function calls. (For each function definition we can obtain the corresponding function prototype in a very simple way, namely by copying its first line and writing a semicolon at its end.)

A function (such as **fun** in our example) may be declared either inside a function (such as **main**) that contains a call to it, or before it, at the global level. The latter is the case in

```
...
float fun(float x, float y, int i, int j);

main()
{ ...
```

When declared at the global level, the declaration is valid until the end of the program module, that is, the end of the file. A declaration inside a function is valid only in that function. A function may be defined only once, but may be declared as often as we like. Suppose that besides **main**, there is another function, **f**, that also calls **fun**. Then if we declare **fun** inside **main** we also have to declare it inside **f**; we need not do this if **fun** is declared globally, before **main** and **f**.

So far, we have discussed function definitions and function declarations as if they were always distinct entities. However, this need not be the case. Remember, a function definition also counts as a function declaration. This is interesting because we can write functions in any order. In our example, defining **fun** before **main** means that this function is defined before it is called, so that no separate declaration is needed. Therefore the following program is completely equivalent to FDEMO1: in contrast to FDEMO2, FDEMO3 is in accordance with the new style:

```
/* FDEMO3: Demonstration program with a function (in the new style).
          Function definition acts also as function declaration.
*/
#include <stdio.h>

float fun(float x, float y, int i, int j)
{ float a = x - y;
  int b = i - j;
  return b != 0 ? a/b :
         a > 0 ? +1e20 :
         a < 0 ? -1e20 : 0.0;
}
```

```
main()
{ float xx, yy;
  int ii, jj;
  printf("Enter two float and two int values: ");
  scanf("%f %f %d %d", &xx, &yy, &ii, &jj);
  printf("Value returned by function: %f\n", fun(xx, yy, ii, jj));
}
```

As you can see, **fun** is not declared on the second line of the function **main**, as it was in FDEMO1; such a declaration is not needed here because of the order of the functions **fun** and **main**.

5.2 USING THE VOID KEYWORD

Functions not returning a value

The function **fun** of Section 5.1 returned a **float** value, as the keyword **float** at the beginning of both its declaration and its definition shows. Instead, functions may return values of other types, or no value at all. Functions that do not return values are similar to what we call *procedures* in Pascal and *subroutines* in Fortran or assembly language. Instead of a normal type keyword, such as **float**, we write **void** at the beginning of such functions, as the following program illustrates:

```
/* MAX3: A function that prints the maximum of three integers.
*/

#include <stdio.h>

main()
{ int i, j, k;
  void max3(int x, int y, int z);
  printf("Enter three integers: ");
  scanf("%d %d %d", &i, &j, &k);
  max3(i, j, k);
}

void max3(int x, int y, int z)
{ if (y > x) x = y;
  if (z > x) x = z;
  printf("The maximum of these three is: %d\n", x);
}
```

Note that **max3** does not contain a return statement; we may write

```
return;
```

at the end of this function, but this would be superfluous and very unusual, since a function, when its end is reached, returns to its caller anyway . Yet this simple form of the return-statement may be useful if it is executed conditionally and is followed by other statements, as in

```
void test(int x)
{ if (x < 0) return;
  ...
}
```

As for function **max3**, its parameter x is really used as a local variable: its value is altered. This will not affect the corresponding argument **i**. (If we wanted to alter **i** in this way, an essentially different approach would be required, as we will see in Section 5.3.)

If we call a function when it has not (yet) been declared, the compiler assumes that it returns an **int** value. It does so even if the call does not suggest that the function should return a value at all, as is the case with the call to **max3**. In programs written in the old style, this principle is often used. Thus, in programs written some years ago, the following style is quite usual, and, though not recommended, it is still valid in ANSI C:

```
main()
{ ...
  f(123);
  ...
}

f(i) int i;
{ ...
}
```

Since the first occurrence of the function name **f** is in the call **f(123)**, the compiler assumes **f** to return an **int** value. (If **f** really did, by means of a return-statement, that value would simply be ignored: any C function may be called in the way a procedure is called in Pascal.) In the function definition in the above program, no type keyword is written at its beginning. As mentioned in Section 5.1, the compiler will therefore once again assume **f** to return an **int** value (even though there is no return-statement). Therefore the call to **f** is consistent with the definition of this function, and everything works fine. Now suppose that we want to modernize the above program by replacing the first line of the function **f** with

```
void f(int i)
```

If we leave the rest of the program unchanged, the compiler will give an error message, since the assumption about type **int**, made when compiling the call to **f**, is inconsistent with the keyword **void** that we have added. We must correct this error, either by changing the order of the functions **main** and **f** or by writing a separate declaration for **f**. Including such a declaration in the **main** function gives

```
main()
{ void f(int i);
   ...
   f(123);
   ...
}

void f(int i)
{ ...
}
```

Functions without parameters

The keyword **void** is also used for another purpose, namely to state that a function has no parameters. Program NOPAR contains such a function, which reads in a real number. As mentioned in Section 4.2, we can use the value returned by **scanf** to check whether or not a read attempt has succeeded: that value says how many data items (such as numbers) have been read and stored into variables, the addresses of which are arguments of **scanf**. So far, we have usually omitted such checks on correct input, but in practice it is wise to include them in our programs. In a large program, we may want to read input data at a great many places; it would then be rather tedious if we had to write both a call to **scanf** and a check for correct input each time we wanted to read a number. Instead, we can write a function of our own to perform these two tasks. Program NOPAR shows how this can be done:

```
/* NOPAR: Using a function without parameters.
*/
#include <stdio.h>
double readreal(void);
```

```
main()
{ double xx;
  float x;
  printf("Enter a real number: ");
  xx = readreal();
  printf("Another one, please:  ");
  x = readreal();
  printf("The following numbers have been read: %f %f\n", xx, x);
}

double readreal(void)
{ double x;
  char ch='\0';
  while (scanf("%lf", &x) != 1) scanf("%c", &ch);
  if (ch != '\0')
    printf("Skipped over invalid character(s).\n");
  return x;
}
```

The word **void** is used both in the declaration and in the definition of **readreal**. It denotes that this function has no parameters. The program line that precedes **main( )** is a function declaration in the new style. It would have been one in the old style if we had written

```
double readreal();
```

This declaration should not be confused with one in which the keyword **void** occurs between the parentheses, as in program NOPAR. It merely says that **readreal** returns a **double** value. According to this declaration in the old style, **readreal** may have any number of parameters. Function declarations in the old style are still valid in ANSI C, but if we use them, neither the number of arguments nor their types will be checked. Suppose, for example, that we mistake **readreal** for a different function type and write

```
readreal(&xx);
```

instead of

```
xx = readreal();
```

If we make this mistake in a program that, like NOPAR, contains a function prototype for **readreal**, the compiler will give an error message. This will not be the case if we omit **void** and write the declaration of **readreal** in the old style: the program will then seem correct when it is compiled but cause trouble during execution. We see that again we had better not omit the keyword **void**.

Note that our function **readreal** has the advantage that we can use it to read the values of both **float** and **double** variables. Although its return value is **double** we can write x = **readreal**( ), where x has type **float**.

As we have already seen, a function that returns a value may also be called like one that does not. For example, if we want to skip three numbers in the input, ignoring their values, we can write

```
readreal(); readreal(); readreal();
```

In program NOPAR, **getchar** is also used in this way: at the end of Section 4.2 we have seen that it returns a character, which we are now ignoring. Another very well known example is **scanf**, whose return value we often ignore (although it has been used in program NOPAR in the way discussed in Section 4.2).

The notation 'main( )'

It is very usual to use the old style, rather than the new one, for the **main** function. Many people write the first line of this function as

```
main()
```

As we know, omitting a return type implies type **int** (not **void**!). Since we have been using **main** without any parameters, the equivalent new-style notation for its first line would be

```
int main(void)
```

Writing **int** here is an aesthetic improvement only if we also include a return-statement. Depending on our operating system, this may make sense, in which case we can write, for example,

```
return 0;
```

at the end of the function **main** if the program terminates normally. Since this subject is system dependent, we will not discuss it in detail. This book is similar to many others in that both the **int** keyword at the very beginning of the function **main** and the return-statement at its end are omitted. It must be admitted, however, that there are arguments in favor of the opposite practice of including both: first, your operating system may use the return value, and, second, that practice is consistent with the new style and may become fashionable.

So much for the value returned by the **main** function. Another point to be mentioned here is about the keyword **void** that we may or may not write between parentheses after **main**. On the basis of what we have seen so far, you may not have the impression that a **main** function can have parameters. However, we will see in Section 6.10 this is really the case. Neither the traditional notation **main( )** nor the very modern form **int main(void)** can therefore be used at the beginning of *all* C programs.

Global variables

The variables that we use in a function can be either *local* or *global*. We call them *local* if they are declared and used only in that function. As a rule, we use local variables, unless this has serious drawbacks. The alternative, *global* variables, are declared (or, more specifically, *defined*) outside functions, at the same level as functions are defined. Here is a very simple (and therefore unrealistic) example:

```
#include <stdio.h>
int i;

void print_i(void)
{ printf("%d\n", i);
}

main()
{ i = 123;
  print_i();
}
```

Because we have defined **i** prior to **print_i** and **main**, we can use this variable in both functions. Note that function **print_i** does not have parameters, nor does it return a value. Although, in principle, functions like this can do all kinds of useful work, this programming style is not recommended. We should be very careful with functions that have *side effects*, that is, functions that change the values of global variables. For example, if we had assigned a new value to **i** in function **print_i**, the call **print_i( )** would have been confusing, because the function name does not suggest any side effects: we expect **i** to have still the value 123 after the call.

5.3 FUNCTIONS THAT ALTER VARIABLES VIA PARAMETERS

As we have seen in Section 5.1, we can regard parameters of functions as local variables, in each call initialized with the values of the corresponding arguments. This makes it impossible to write a function **swap** in such a way that the statement

```
swap(i, j);
```

should interchange the values of the variables **i** and **j**: this call passes only the *values* of these variables to **swap**, and these values are only used to initialize the corresponding parameters. Yet we badly need a way of writing functions that use their parameters to give values back to the calling function. The solution to this problem lies in supplying addresses as arguments. Associated with addresses are the following unary operators, which are inverse to each other:

Operator	Meaning
&	The address of
*	The contents of

An *address* is a number permanently associated with a memory location. As ***** is the inverse operator of **&**, the expression ***&i** is just a complicated way of writing **i**. We are normally interested only in the *value* of a variable, not in its *address*, that is, we are not interested in where a variable is located in memory. Yet we often use the operator **&**, as we have already done very often in calls such as

```
scanf("%d", &n);
```

Since **scanf** is given the address of **n**, it can place a value into this variable. Similarly, the function **swap** that we need will be called as follows:

```
swap(&i, &j);
```

From this call and from the fact that arguments supply the corresponding parameters with initial values, it follows that the parameters of **swap** must be variables whose values are addresses. If these parameters are **p** and **q**, the values of **p** and **q** are addresses of certain locations, and we must write ***p** and ***q** to denote the contents of these locations. As we are dealing with addresses of **int** variables, ***p** and ***q** have type **int**, which explains why p and q are declared as

```
int *p, int *q
```

in the following function definition, which is the solution to our swapping problem:

```
void swap(int *p, int *q)
{ int temp;
  temp = *p; *p = *q; *q = temp;
}
```

Remember, in each call to **swap** we must not forget to supply addresses as arguments, as we have done in the call **swap(&i, &j)**. This function **swap** can interchange the values of any two variables. Let us, for example, consider the case that these are elements of array **a**, declared as

```
int a[100];
```

If we want to interchange the values of the first and the last elements, we can write

```
swap(&a[0], &a[99]);
```

Pointers

We have seen that in the function **swap** the expressions ***p** has type **int**. However, the first parameter itself is **p** (not ***p**). We know that inside a function a parameter is in fact a local variable, so we may wonder what type this variable has. In C, variables that have addresses as their values are called *pointers*, so **p** is a *pointer*, and its type is *pointer-to-int*. We will discuss pointers in more detail in Section 6.3.

5.4 TYPE PROBLEMS IN FUNCTIONS

Argument types

With function declarations in the old style, the types of arguments must be the same as those of the parameters, except for two kinds of differences that are allowed: with a **float** parameter, the argument may be **double** and vice versa, and, similarly, if either is **int** the other may be **char**. This is so because in the old style **float** arguments are always converted to type **double**, even if the parameter types have been specified as **float**; analogously, **char** arguments are always converted to type **int** in the old style. We will not discuss all this in more detail, because it is far better to use the new style, with arguments automatically converted to the required parameter types, if possible. If not, an error message is given. For example, the call **f(5)** in the following program is correct, even though **5** has type **int** and **f** has a **float** parameter. Thanks to the new-style definition of **f** (which also counts as a declaration), this call is in fact equivalent to **f(5.0)**, and the output of this program is 26.0.

```
#include <stdio.h>

float f(float x)
{ return x * x + 1;
}

main()
{ printf("%4.1f\n", f(5));
}
```

The conversion from **5** to **float**, the type of parameter **x**, is possible because such a conversion is also possible in the assignment statement

```
x = 5;
```

This is a general rule: with the new style, any conversions from argument types to parameter types are similar to analogous conversions that may take place in assignments; if the latter is possible, so is the former, and vice versa. With the above function **f**, the call to **f** in the following **main** function is incorrect:

```
main()
{ float t=5;
  printf("%4.1f\n", f(&t));   /* Error */
}
```

The address argument **&t** is incompatible with the float parameter **x**. The error made here is analogous to the one in the assignment statement

```
x = &t;   /* Error */
```

where both **x** and **t** have type **float**. In either case the C compiler will print an error message.

Types of return values

The conversion rules for assignments can also be used as a model for conversions in return-statements. Here is an example:

```
int g(double x, double y)
{ return x * x - y * y + 1;
}
```

Although the keyword **int** at the beginning of this function says that **g** will return
an integer, the expression in the return-statement has type **double**. The compiler
will accept this, and perform the same conversion as it does when compiling the
following assignment statement, where **i** has type **int**:

```
i = x * x - y * y + 1;
```

In either case truncation takes place, so 7.9, for example, is converted to 7. As
discussed in Section 4.7, a cast is to be recommended in this assignment
statement, so that we may see more clearly what actually happens. The same
applies to the return-statement: although not required by the compiler, the cast
in the following version of the return-statement is very welcome as a reminder
that, because of conversion from **double** to **int**, the values before and after
conversion may be different:

```
return (int)(x * x - y * y + 1);
```

5.5 INITIALIZATION

It is often convenient to *initialize* variables, that is, to give values to them when
we are declaring them. We have done this several times already, but we have not
yet discussed all aspects of this subject. When initializing variables, we should
bear in mind the following rules:

(i)   Variables may be initialized only when memory locations are assigned to
        them.

(ii)   In the absence of explicit initialization, the initial value 0 is assigned to
        all variables that are global or static.

As we already know, the term *global* in (ii) refers to variables that are declared
outside functions. The new term *static* is used for all variables in the declaration
of which the keyword **static** is used. Global and static variables have in common
that their memory locations are *permanent*, whereas nonstatic, local variables are
assigned memory locations temporarily, on a 'stack'. As the latter variables are
automatically assigned memory locations when the functions in which they are
declared are entered, they are called *automatic* variables, and we may use the

keyword **auto** for them. Memory for automatic variables is released when the functions in which they are declared are left. This discussion about memory allocation for variables is relevant with regard to both rules (i) and (ii). Because of (i), static variables local to a function are initialized only the first time this function is called.

For example, in the following program the variable **i** is set to 1 only once (either by the compiler or by the linker). The first call prints that value and increments **i**. The second call is more interesting in that **i** is not initialized once again: it still has its last value, 2, because the keyword **static** causes its memory space to be permanent. Consequently, this program prints the values 1 and 2.

```
#include <stdio.h>

void f(void)
{ static int i=1;
  printf("%d ", i++);
}

main()
{ f(); f();
}
```

If we had separated the declaration and the assignment (by writing **static int i;** **i=1;** instead of **static int i=1;**) the output would have been **1 1**, as it would have been if we had simply omitted the keyword **static**.

According to rule (ii), the declarations

```
static int i;
```

is equivalent to

```
static int i=0;
```

where **i** can be either a global or a local variable. If we omit **static** in these two lines, the resulting declarations are equivalent only if **i** is a global variable.

So far, we have not discussed why static variables might be useful. As for *global* static variables, they are useful for programs that consist of more than one file, as we will see in the next section. A simple, but interesting application of a *local* static variable is its use as a 'flag' that indicates whether a function is called for the first time. Sometimes we want some special action to take place during the first call. Here is very simple example, which you can easily replace with a more practical one yourself:

```
void f(void)
{ static int firsttime=1;
  if (firsttime)
  { printf("This is printed only the first time f is called.\n");
    firsttime = 0;
  }
  printf("This is printed each time f is called.\n");
}
```

We can also initialize *arrays*, by writing their initial values within a pair of braces. Again, the rules (i) and (ii) apply. There must not be more initial values between the braces than there are array elements. If there are fewer, the trailing elements are initialized to 0. For example, with

```
float a[100] = {23, 41.5};
```

we have:

```
a[0] = 23; a[1] = 41.5; a[2] = ... = a[99] = 0.
```

If, for an initialized array, we omit the array length, the number of initial values is taken as that length, as, for example, in

```
int b[] = {95, 34, 72};
```

which is equivalent to

```
int b[3] = {95, 34, 72};
```

So far, we have been writing (numerical) initial values as constants, which is allowed for any variable that is initialized. We can generalize this as follows. First, we may write *constant expressions* (such as **123 * 4 - 3 * 30**) whenever constants are allowed. For simple automatic variables, we can go further than that and initialize them with any expression of a suitable type. But remember, global and static variables (with permanent memory) and arrays may only be initialized with constant expressions.

If we want to initialize arrays of characters, we can write a list of character constants between braces, as is done in:

```
char str[16] = {'C', 'h', 'a', 'r', 'l', 'e', 's', ' ',
                'D', 'i', 'c', 'k', 'e', 'n', 's', '\0'};
```

However, this way of initializing is very tedious for long strings, as in this example. Fortunately, a much more convenient way is available; we can abbreviate the declaration just given by:

```
char str[16] = "Charles Dickens";
```

We will discuss arrays of characters, or *strings*, in Section 6.4.

5.6 SEPARATE COMPILATION

Large C programs are preferably split up into several program files, also called program *modules*. Although its small size does not make splitting it up worthwhile, the following program shows how this can be done:

```
/* MODULE 1 */
#include <stdio.h>

main()
{ void f(int i), g(void);
  extern int n;    /* Declaration of n (not a definition) */
  f(8);
  n++;
  g();
  printf("End of program.\n");
}
```

```
/* MODULE 2 */
#include <stdio.h>
int n=100;        /* Definition of n (also a declaration) */
static int m=7;

void f(int i)
{ n += i+m;
}

void g(void)
{ printf("n = %d\n", n);
}
```

These two modules, separated here by a horizontal line, are independent units; we can compile them one by one, and link them together afterwards. An interesting point about variable **n** is that it is used in both modules. We say that the variable **n**, like the functions **f** and **g**, is *defined* in module 2 and *declared* in module 1. If a variable declaration begins with the keyword **extern**, it is not at the same time a variable definition. Without this keyword, it is a definition. Every variable definition is at the same time a variable declaration; as the latter term is more common than the former we have often used it for declarations that were, more specifically, definitions. We may use a variable only after it has been declared (in the same file). Only variable definitions allocate memory and may therefore contain initializations. We define a variable only once but we may declare it as often as we like. A variable declaration at the global level (outside functions) is valid from that declaration until the end of the file; a declaration (such as that of **n** in module 1) inside a function is valid only in that function. In this regard, definitions and declarations of global variables are similar to those of functions; the main difference is that we normally omit the keyword **extern** in function declarations.

Another interesting variable is **m**, defined in module 2 as

```
static int m=7;
```

As we know, *local* static variables have permanent memory, as have global variables. Since **m** is a global variable, its memory location is already permanent, so the keyword **static** seems superfluous here. However, **static**, when used for a global variable, makes this variable 'private property' of the module in which it occurs, that is, other modules cannot have access to it. Note that this is somewhat similar to *local* static variables, which, although having permanent memory, are 'private property' of the functions to which they are local. If we had written

```
extern int m;
```

in module 1, the linker would have given an error message because the static variable **m** of module 2 is not published to the linker. Figure 5.1 shows that the linker can build an executable program, using object modules each of which is obtained by compiling a source module. You can easily verify the following output of the program consisting of modules 1 and 2:

```
n = 116
End of program.
```

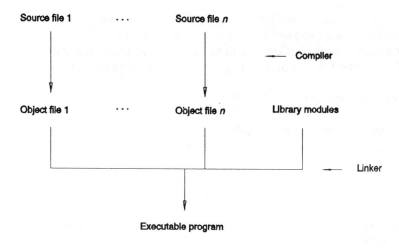

Fig. 5.1. Separate compilation

Although not demonstrated in this program, the keyword **static** can also be applied to *function* definitions. We then write it at the very beginning, before the type of the return value. That function will then not be published to the linker, so that other modules have no access to them. The keyword **static**, both for global variables and for functions, is useful to avoid conflicts of names and to prevent accidental use of them. Imagine a very large program, consisting of a great many modules, in which we have to look for an error caused by a global variable that at some moment obtains a value that we did not anticipate. If that variable is static, we can restrict ourselves to the module in which it is defined; if not, we have to extend our investigation to all other modules in which it is declared (with the keyword **extern**).

As a rule, we prefer local variables to global ones. If it is really necessary or desirable for some variables to be global, we preferably make them static, which means that they are 'local with regard to the file in which they are defined'. As we know, all C functions are global: we cannot define a function inside another function. However, by using the keyword **static** for them, their scope is restricted to the file in which they occur, which makes them 'less global' than nonstatic functions.

5.7 SOME MATHEMATICAL LIBRARY FUNCTIONS

We can successfully use the C language for a great variety of application fields, including science and engineering. For these purposes we often need to use some well-known mathematical functions, available in the C standard library. The easiest and safest way of including their declarations in our program is by writing

```
#include <math.h>
```

Except for some rather technical functions (to be discussed in Section 10.6), these declarations are listed below, along with some comment which says what these functions are about. This comment and some explanations that follow will be sufficient for those who want to use them. Remember, thanks to our including **math.h**, we need not actually write these declarations in our programs:

```
double cos(double x);              /* cos x  (x in radians)      */
double sin(double x);              /* sin x                      */
double tan(double x);              /* tan x                      */ ·
double exp(double x);              /* exp x                      */
double log(double x);              /* ln x                       */
double log10(double x);            /* log x (base 10)            */
double pow(double x, double y);    /* x to the power y           */
double sqrt(double x);             /* the square root of x       */
double floor(double x);            /* floor(4.9) = 4.0 etc.      */
double ceil(double x);             /* ceil(8.1) = 9.0 etc.       */
double fabs(double x);             /* absolute value             */
double acos(double x);             /* arccos x                   */
double asin(double x);             /* arcsin x                   */
double atan(double x);             /* arctan x, range (-pi/2, pi/2) */
double atan2(double y, double x);  /* see explanation below      */
double cosh(double x);             /* cosh x                     */
double sinh(double x);             /* sinh x                     */
double tanh(double x);             /* tanh x                     */
```

The functions **atan2** comes in very handy if, in the xy-plane, a point $P(x, y)$, not coinciding with the origin O, is given and we want to know the (positive or negative) angle φ between OP and the positive x-axis. This angle φ is equal to atan(y/x) if x is positive. However, the latter expression is undefined for zero x and is different from φ for negative x. For any x and y (not both zero) the angle $\varphi = \text{atan2}(y, x)$ is defined, and it satisfies:

$$\cos \varphi = x/\sqrt{(x^2 + y^2)}, \quad \sin \varphi = y/\sqrt{(x^2 + y^2)}, \quad -\pi < \varphi \le \pi.$$

5.8 PREPROCESSOR FACILITIES

Program lines that begin with # are usually regarded as being processed (by the *preprocessor*) before the normal compiling activities start. The actions the preprocessor performs are much like those of a text processor, and completely different from those done later by the compiler.

Macro substitution

As we have seen in Section 4.4, we can write

```
#define LENGTH 100
```

after which we can write the symbolic constant **LENGTH** instead of 100. This line is a simple example of a *macro definition*. It is of the following form:

```
#define identifier text
```

Each occurrence of *identifier* is replaced with *text*. This text need not be a constant, such as 100, but it may also be a longer and more complicated sequence of characters. At the end of the line we may use the backslash for continuation on the next line, as in

```
#define TITLE Interactive 3D \
Computer Graphics
```

The replacement of each occurrence of *identifier* with *text* takes place only if the identifier is a *token*, that is, if it is not part of another identifier: our last example does not apply to the identifier **TITLE1**, although **TITLE** occurs in this longer identifier. (The term *token* is used for small basic units: identifiers, keywords, constants, operators and other separators; they may be separated by white-space characters.)

Parameters

Macros are more interesting if they have parameters, as this one has:

```
#define funmac(x, y) x * x + y * y
```

This macro **funmac** is similar to a function. (As we will see, this similarity is no equivalence.) After this macro definition, we can use it by writing, for example,

```
funmac(a, b)
```

The preprocessor will conceptually (that is, without actually modifying the source file) replace this *macro call* with the following text:

```
a * a + b * b
```

In general, the text given in the macro definition replaces the macro identifier, but, at the same time, all occurrences of the parameters (**x** and **y**) in it are replaced with the corresponding arguments (**a** and **b**).

Our above definition of **funmac** is not very useful, because it will not do what we want in more complicated macro calls, such as

```
3 * funmac(a + 1, b + 2)
```

This will lead to the macro expansion

```
3 * a + 1 * a + 1 + b + 2 * b + 2
```

which is not likely to be the intended one. To obtain what we want in cases like this, we must insert a good many parentheses in the macro definition:

- we enclose each parameter (**x** and **y**) in parentheses, and
- we enclose the whole replacement text in parentheses.

This gives the following new version:

```
#define funmac(x, y) ((x) * (x) + (y) * (y))
```

Thanks to all these parentheses, the expansion of the macro call in question will now be:

```
3 * ((a + 1) * (a + 1) + (b + 2) * (b + 2))
```

Macros can have any number of parameters. As for our examples, **LENGTH** has none and **funmac** has two. Remember, we must not write a space immediately after the macro name, as is done immediately after the name **funmac** in

```
#define funmac (x, y) ((x) * (x) + (y) * (y))
```

This 'incorrect' macro definition is regarded as a macro without parameters, since it has the form

```
#define funmac text
```

which causes the name **funmac** to be replaced with the *text*

```
(x, y) ((x) * (x) + (y) * (y))
```

In our (correct) example, the argument expressions **a + 1** and **b + 2** occur twice in the expansion and will therefore be evaluated twice, which is not efficient. This would not have been the case if, instead of a macro, we had used the following function:

```
float funmac(float x, float y)
{ return x * x + y * y;
}
```

On the other hand, very short macros can be faster than functions in that they do not require arguments to be passed during execution time, nor are there any subroutine jump instructions to be executed. As for memory space, we should always bear in mind that each macro call is expanded. At first sight macros looks more expensive than function calls, but if a macro expansion is short, the code it produces may be less than that produced by the corresponding function call. Another interesting aspect of macros is that, unlike functions, we do not need different versions for different parameter types. For example, with our macro **funmac** and with the declarations

```
int i, j;
float u, v;
```

both expressions **funmac(i, j)** and **funmac(u, v)** are simply equivalent to

```
((i) * (i) + (j) * (j))
```

and

```
((u) * (u) + (v) * (v))
```

respectively. This means that **funmac(i, j)** results in pure integer arithmetic so that on most machines it will be much faster than the floating-point computations performed by the expansion of **funmac(u, v)**. This would not be possible if **funmac** were a function.

Problematic error messages

Since macro calls are expanded by the preprocessor, they do no longer exist during the later syntax checking. Therefore any messages of syntax errors apply to the expanded text. For example, if by mistake we write a semicolon at the end in

```
#define f(x) ((x)*(x)+(x)+1);
```

then the apparently correct line

```
y = f(a) * f(b);
```

will produce the following expansion:

```
y = ((a)*(a)+(a)+1); * ((b)*(b)+(b)+1);;
```

Most compilers will not display this expansion but will give an error message that refers to the shorter, correct line with the two macro calls. To make things worse, the compiler will not recognize * in the middle of the expanded expression as a multiplication operator, but rather regard this character as the 'indirection operator', to be discussed in detail in the next chapter. We may therefore obtain a very confusing error message in this example, such as *Invalid indirection*.

Special situations

If in a macro definition we use the names of earlier defined macros, these will be expanded as well; in other words, a macro may call other macros. However, unlike functions, macros cannot call themselves: if, in a macro definition, its own name is used, the latter is not expanded. For example, after

```
#define cos(x) (cos((x) * PI/180))
```

the macro call **cos(phi + a)** is expanded to **(cos((phi + a) * PI/180))**, and the identifier **cos** in this expansion is not expanded once again.

Another special situation arises if a macro is defined more than once. This is allowed provided the replacement text is identical in all these definitions. For example, the following two lines are contradictory and must therefore not occur in this combination:

```
#define LENGTH 100
#define LENGTH 1000
```

If in the latter line we replace 1000 with 100, these two identical lines may both be used. Curiously enough, this is a useful facility, as will be clear shortly in our discussion of header files.

The string-generating character

If, in a macro definition, a parameter is immediately preceded by the character #, that parameter is surrounded by double quotes in the macro expansion. For example, with

```
#define printtext(x) printf("%s\n", #x)
```

the macro call **printtext(Example)** will be expanded to

```
printf("%s\n", "Example")
```

The interesting point of this is that we can use the parameter in question several times, both with and without #, as this example shows:

```
#define printvalue(x) printf(#x " = %f\n", x)
```

Thanks to this slightly more complicated macro definition, we can simply use the macro call **printvalue(Temperature)** to obtain the following expansion:

```
printf("Temperature" " = %f\n", Temperature)
```

which in turn is equivalent to

```
printf("Temperature = %f\n", Temperature)
```

as we have discussed in Section 2.3.

The token-concatenation operator

In most programming languages there is no way of concatenating tokens to form new ones. In C this can be done with macros. For example, suppose we want to abbreviate these three lines:

```
table_entry[0] = table_entry0;
element[5] = element5;
article[9] = article9;
```

As you can see, a name and a number occur twice on each line, but the second time they are no longer individual tokens (such as **table_entry** and **0**), but rather combined into one token (**table_entry0**). Here is a macro definition that we can use for this purpose:

```
#define set(x, i) x[i] = x##i
```

The 'operator' **##** (to be used only in macro definitions!) concatenates **x** and **i**, or, rather, the corresponding arguments, used in macro calls such as

```
set(table_entry, 0);
set(element, 5);
set(article, 9);
```

Header files

Besides expanding macros, the preprocessor also expands #include-lines such as

```
#include <stdio.h>
#include "myfile.h"
```

The preprocessor will replace these two lines with the contents of the header files **stdio.h** and **myfile.h**. Notice the difference in notation between **<stdio.h>** and **"myfile.h"**, which is to indicate where the header file is to be found:

<...>   The header file is looked for (only) in the general include directories.
"..."   The header file is successively looked for
          1. in the current directory, and, if not found there,
          2. in the general include directories.

In practice, header files are frequently used to declare functions and to define macros (not functions). In particular with programs that consist of many modules, header files provide a convenient way of reducing the amount of source code: we often want to write calls to the same functions (and macros) in different modules, and we can now simply include the header files in which these functions are declared (and in which these macros are defined). Without the facility of using header files, it would be necessary to duplicate program text, which, in case of program modifications, would be a potential source of errors. It is possible to write #include lines in header files: if the header file **a.h** contains the line **#include "aa.h"**, including **a.h** implies including **aa.h**.

Suppose that we have written two header files, say, **a.h** and **b.h**, which are used in many program modules. Sometimes we use only **a.h**, sometimes only **b.h**, and occasionally we include them both. It may then be desirable to write the definition of some macro in both **a.h** and **b.h**. This implies that, if we include both **a.h** and **b.h**, that macro will occur twice after the inclusion of **a.h** and **b.h**. Fortunately, such a duplication is allowed, provided the macro definitions are identical. We have mentioned this possibility of duplicated macros earlier in this section, but only now can we see its significance.

Conditional compilation

We can instruct the preprocessor to compile a program fragment only if a certain condition is met; if not, we can give another fragment to be compiled. Here is a very simple example of how this can be done:

```
#if constant expression
  Program fragment A
#else
  Program fragment B
#endif
```

Note that this is a *preprocessor statement*, not a normal conditional statement: it is executed during compilation time, not during execution time. We always write **#if** at its beginning and **#endif** at its end. The line **#else** (and program fragment B) is optional. The condition after **#if** must be a constant expression so that the compiler can evaluate it. If its value is nonzero, the compiler compiles program fragment A; otherwise it compiles program fragment B, if present.

Conditional compilation is interesting especially in combination with the use of header files. For example, if **MAX** is a symbolic constant defined (as a macro without parameters) in header file **a.h**, we can write

```
#include "a.h"
#define LENGTH 100

#if LENGTH < MAX
...    /* Program fragment A */
#endif
```

Whether or not program fragment A is compiled depends on how **MAX** is defined in **a.h**.

Preprocessor statements for conditional compilation may be nested. However, instead of doing this, we can often use a special construction with **#elif**, as, for example, in

```
#if LENGTH < 100
... /* Fragment A */
#elif LENGTH < 1000
... /* Fragment B */
#else
... /* Fragment C */
#endif
```

As its name suggests, **#elif** is a combination of **#else** and **#if**, but it does not requires an **#endif** (as **#if** would). This example is equivalent to the following, with two **#if**s and therefore also with two **#endif**s.

```
#if LENGTH < 100
... /* Fragment A */
#else
#if LENGTH < 1000
... /* Fragment B */
#else
... /* Fragment C */
#endif
#endif
```

With conditional compilation we can make the compiler temporarily ignore a portion of our program. We sometimes want to do this during program development. Most people would insert the comment tokens (/* and */) for this purpose, but this will cause a problem if the program fragment that is to be ignored already contains comment, because comments must not be nested. In that case we can simple use a line with **#if 0** at the beginning and one with **#endif** at the end (instead of /* and */). For example, the second and the third of the following lines are ignored by the compiler, and the comment on the second line causes no problems:

```
#if 0
  i = 123;  /* Some comment */
  j = i + 1;
#endif
```

Tests about names being known

The preprocessor can check whether or not a name has been defined, as the following example shows:

```
#if !defined(PI)
#define PI 3.14159265358979
#endif
```

Only if **PI** has not been defined will the second line be processed; if **PI** has already been defined, this line is ignored. This prevents any problems with conflicting definitions of **PI**: we may define symbolic constants more than once, but such multiple definitions must be identical. Therefore the above conditional definition of the constant **PI** is useful if (a) we do not know whether this constant is defined in a header file that we are using and (b) we do not know the precision used in such a definition, if any.

In combination with **defined(...)**, we can use the logical operators !, ||, and &&. These operators cannot be used in combination with the older alternative forms **#ifdef** and **#ifndef**:

`#ifdef` *name*	is equivalent to	`#if defined(`*name*`)`
`#ifndef` *name*	is equivalent to	`#if !defined(`*name*`)`

If we want to cancel the effect of

```
#define name text
```

we can 'undefine' *name* by writing

```
#undef name
```

Thus, to be complete, we should say that the operator **defined** and the preprocessor directives **#ifdef** and **#ifndef** apply to names defined with **#define**, *in so far as these names have not been undefined by means of* **#undef**.

It is not an error to use **#undef** for a name that has not been defined at all, so we may use it to cancel any previous definition of a name without being sure that there is one.

Numbering of program lines

Error messages from the compiler normally refer to line numbers (1, 2, ···). If for some reason or other we want the lines to be numbered, for example, 1001, 1002, ···, from some position in the program, we can write

```
#line 1001
```

in that position. If the compiler also mentions the name of the program file, we can instead supply a different name to be used. For example, if the desired new name is AAA.C and it is to be used after the new line number 1001, we can write

```
#line 1001 "AAA.C"
```

Making the compiler print error messages

We can use a line starting with **#error** to make the compiler give an error message. This is useful especially in connection with conditional compilation and with special information in header files. For example, suppose that we have various versions of a certain header file (say, **myfile.h**), and we want to check that its correct version (say, version B) is included. If in that header file the version number is defined as

```
#define V_B
```

(in which the replacement text is allowed to be empty) we can perform this check as follows:

```
#include "myfile.h"
#if !defined(V_B)
#error You should use Version B of myfile.h!
#endif
```

If a version of **myfile** is used that does not contain the definition of **V_B**, the compiler will display the error message given on the **#error** line, after which compilation terminates.

Instead of testing an identifier in a header file of our own, we can test one in a header file, say, **dos.h**, that belongs to a particular compiler. If that identifier is unique for that compiler, we can use this method to check whether the required compiler is being used, and make the compiler give a clear error message if that is not the case. This is very useful if compiler-dependent source text is distributed among programmers who may try to use the wrong compiler.

Pragmas

Although we prefer to restrict ourselves to language elements accepted by any (ANSI) C compiler, it may sometimes be necessary or desirable to deviate from this principle and to use facilities that depend on a particular compiler and on a particular machine. According to ANSI, such system dependent facilities should preferably be used only by means of a line of the following form:

```
#pragma ...
```

The three dots in this line denote some piece of text that causes the compiler, if it recognizes that text, to perform certain actions. If it does not recognize it, the **#pragma** line is simply ignored, after which compilation continues.

Predefined names

There are also some names that are immediately available and that can be used in 'constant expressions':

__LINE__   An integer indicating the current line number. (Note that the term *constant* is dubious here: if it is used on different program lines its value will not be the same throughout the program but rather depend on its position.

__FILE__   A string indicating the name of the file that is being compiled.

__DATE__   A string of the form "M*mm dd jjjj*", indicating the date of compilation (for example, "M12 31 1990" for December 31st, 1990).

__TIME__   A string of the form "*hh:mm:ss*", indicating the time of compilation (for example, "15:00:00" for 3 o'clock in the afternoon).

__STDC__   The constant 1, available only if the compiler conforms to ANSI C.

Remember, the values of these names are fixed at the moment of compilation. Therefore, if you write

```
printf(__DATE__);
```

and your program is compiled at December 31st, 1990, this statement is equivalent to

```
printf("M12 31 1990");
```

which means that the same date will be printed whenever you run the program. If you want to use the date of program execution (rather than that of program compilation) you need to use a different method, which will be discussed in Section 10.14.

Exercises

In the following exercises, whenever you are asked to write a function (or macro), this should be a general one; you should also demonstrate this function by a program (or, rather, a 'main module') that need not be general. In at least one of these exercises, use distinct modules for the main module and the function to practise the principle of separate compilation (or 'modular programming').

5.1   Write the function **rectangle(w, h)**, to print an open rectangle of asterisks (*). The parameters **w** and **h** are the width and the height of the rectangle, expressed in numbers of asterisks.

5.2   Write the function **digitsum(n)**, which computes and returns the sum of the decimal digits of the integer parameter **n**.

5.3   Write the function **sort4**, which has four parameters. If the integer variables **a**, **b**, **c**, and **d** are available and have been assigned values, we want to write

```
sort4(&a, &b, &c, &d);
```

to sort these four variables, so that, after this call, we have

$$a \leq b \leq c \leq d$$

5.4   In the following program, function **f** contains a call to itself, and is therefore said to be *recursive*. This program reads the integer k from the keyboard. With the values $k = 0, 1, 2, \cdots, 5$, investigate (first without and then with the computer) what the output of this program will be.

```
#include <stdio.h>

void f(int n)
{ if (n > 0)
  { f(n-2); printf(" %d", n); f(n-1);
  }
}

main()
{ int k;
  printf("\nEnter k: "); scanf("%d", &k);
  printf("Output:\n");
  f(k);
}
```

5.5 Write the function **gcd(x, y)** which computes the greatest common divisor of the integers x and y. These two integers are nonnegative and not both equal to zero. Use *Euclid's algorithm*, according to which we can write (using the C operator %):

$$gcd(x, y) = \begin{cases} x & \text{if } y = 0 \\ gcd(y, x \% y) & \text{if } y \neq 0 \end{cases}$$

Write a C function **gcd** that is recursive and therefore closely related to this formulation of Euclid's algorithm. (A function is said to be *recursive* if it calls itself; see also Exercise 5.4.) Write also a nonrecursive version, **gcd1**.

5.6 Write the macro **max2(x, y)**; its value (that is, the value of its expansion) is equal to the greater of **x** and **y**. Use **max2** to write another macro, **max3(x, y, z)**, the value of which is the greatest of **x**, **y**, and **z**.

5.7 Write a function which can be declared as follows:

```
unsigned int datecode(int day, int month, int year);
```

The task of **datecode** is to encode a given date in the (rightmost) 16 bits of an **unsigned int** value, and to return that value. From left to right we use

7 bits for the final two digits of the year ($\leq$ 99).
4 bits for the month number ($\leq$ 12),
5 bits for the day number ($\leq$ 31),

Take care that both the long and the short notations (for example, 1992 and 92) are allowed as the third argument of **datecode**.

5.8 Write a function declared as

```
unsigned char bcd(int n);
```

This function has the task to build a byte (of eight bits) containing the least significant two decimal digits of the argument, **n**, in 'binary coded decimal' format, and to return this byte. For example, if **n** is equal to 12345, the rightmost decimal digits, 4 and 5, are written 0100 and 0101 in four bits, so in this case the byte to be returned is represented by the bit sequence 0100 0101.

CHAPTER 6

Arrays, Pointers, and Strings

6.1 ADDRESS ARITHMETIC

This section is more important than it may seem at first sight. Although its title may suggest that it is about some technical subject that 'normal' users can safely ignore, the rest of this chapter, and in fact almost the whole C language, is based upon it.

In Section 5.3 we have discussed expressions such as **&x**, the values of which are addresses. There are other kinds of expressions, which when evaluated also yield addresses. One of these is the name of arrays, written without brackets; the address obtained in this way is that of the first element of the array in question. For example, after the declaration

```
char s[50];
```

we can use **s**, not followed by [···], as shorthand for **&(s[0])**, which, incidentally, we may write as **&s[0]**.

Another expression whose value is an address is **s + i**, where **i** is an integer; in this case that address is that of **s[i]**, so we have the following equivalences:

```
s        ≡     &s[0]
s + i    ≡     &s[i]
```

The addresses (yielded by the expressions) **s** and **s + i** lie **i** bytes apart. Note, however, that the byte is used here as a unit of length only because **s** is a **char** array, that is, because each element takes one byte. In general, address arithmetic takes into account the size of the object the address of which is given, and uses that size as a unit of memory space. This makes address arithmetic more convenient and more useful than it would otherwise have been. For example, let us use **int** array **a**, declared as

```
int a[10];
```

In this case the addresses **a** and **a + i** lie **i** integers (not **i** bytes) apart. Therefore the equivalence

```
a + i   ≡      &a[i]
```

also holds for **int** array **a** (and, in fact, for *any* array). The following two lines are therefore equivalent:

```
for (i=0; i<10; i++) scanf("%d", &a[i]);
for (i=0; i<10; i++) scanf("%d", a + i);
```

Besides the *address of* operator **&**, there is also the *indirection* operator *****, as we have seen in Section 5.3. We use it to find the contents of a given address. Now that we know which addresses **a** and **a + i** represent, the following equivalences will be clear:

```
*a      ≡      a[0]
*(a + i) ≡      a[i]
```

The following two lines are therefore equivalent:

```
for (i=0; i<10; i++) printf("%7d", a[i]);
for (i=0; i<10; i++) printf("%7d", *(a + i));
```

It is also possible to subtract an integer from an address, as is done in

```
&a[9] - 3
```

Recalling that **&a[9]** can be written as **a + 9**, we see that this subtraction gives **a + 6**, which can be written as **&a[6]**. We can also subtract an address from another address, as in

```
&a[9] - &a[6]
```

Rewriting this as

```
(a+9) - (a+6)
```

makes it evident that the result is 3. Other arithmetic operations on addresses are not allowed. For example, we cannot compute the sum of two addresses.

Suppose that **p** and **q** denote the addresses of two elements of the same array. We now want to find some address between **p** and **q**, preferably the one in the middle. If **p** and **q** were subscript values, we could write **(p + q)/2**, but we cannot use this expression now, because that would involve two illegal address operations (addition and division). The way to obtain the desired value is by using either of the following two expressions:

```
p + (q - p)/2
p + ((q - p) >> 1)
```

Here all operations are legal, for **q** − **p** has integer type, and so has **(q** − **p)/2**, which may therefore be added to **p**. Instead of **/2**, we can write **> >1** if we like: for signed integers, shift right means division by 2 and may be faster.

6.2 ARRAYS AND FUNCTION ARGUMENTS

It follows from the previous section that we can find all elements of an array if we are given its begin address. There is therefore no need in C for any special parameter-passing mechanism for arrays. Instead of the array itself, we use the address of its first element as an argument; in the function that is called we can compute the addresses of the other elements by means of address arithmetic. This principle is very convenient: the fact that the name of an array denotes its begin address makes array arguments very simple. The following program demonstrates a function that finds the smallest element of a given integer array:

```
/* MINIMUM: Finding the smallest element of an integer array.
*/
#include <stdio.h>

main()
{ int table[10], i, minimum(int *a, int n);
  printf("Enter 10 integers: \n");
  for (i=0; i<10; i++) scanf("%d", table + i); /* See Section 6.1 */
  printf("\nThe minimum of these values is: %d\n", minimum(table, 10));
}

int minimum(int *a, int n)
{ int small, i;
  small = *a;
  for (i=1; i<n; i++) if (*(a+i) < small) small = *(a+i);
  return small;
}
```

Recalling Section 5.3, we know that

```
int *a, ...
```

in the first line of function **minimum** means that **a** denotes the address of an integer. The corresponding argument, **table**, is the address of **table[0]**, so the following two calls are equivalent:

```
minimum(&table[0], 10)
minimum(table, 10)
```

As the latter is shorter and clearer, we prefer it to the former.

The above version of function **minimum** makes it very clear that address arithmetic is applied. As an alternative, we can write a version that does not do this to the same extent but may, on the other hand, be considered more readable because it uses conventional array notation. In the last section we have seen that we may replace **a[i]** with ***(a + i)**. These two expressions are really equivalent: we can also replace the latter with the former, which leads to

```
int minimum(int *a, int n)
{ int small, i;
  small = a[0];
  for (i=1; i<n; i++)
    if (a[i] < small) small = a[i];
  return small;
}
```

We can emphasize the array nature of **a** even more by replacing the first line of this function with

```
int minimum(int a[], int n)
```

Note that the array length is omitted in **a[ ]**; if we had written it, it would have had to be a constant, which would have made the function less general and elegant.

Although not demonstrated here, it is also possible to *alter* the array elements in question instead of only *using* their values. Any assignment to **a[i]** or to ***(a + i)** implies the modification of array **table** in the **main** function.

6.3 POINTERS

If we declare

```
int *p;
```

then **p** is a *pointer variable*, or *pointer*, for short. We use pointers to store addresses, like we use arithmetic variables to store numbers. In Sections 5.3 and 6.2, we have already been using pointers, since a parameter, such as **a** in

```
int minimum(int *a, int n)
```

can be used as a local variable. We will now also use pointers that are normal variables, not parameters. For example, we can use such a variable **p** in yet another version of **minimum**:

```
int minimum(int *a, int n)
{ int small, *p;
  small = *a;
  for (p=a+1; p<a+n; p++)
    if (*p < small) small = *p;
  return small;
}
```

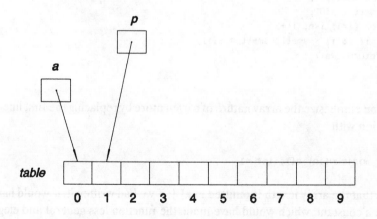

Fig. 6.1. Situation immediately after p = a + 1

The value of **p** is an address, the contents of which is denoted by ***p**. Initially, **p** is assigned the value **a + 1**, that is, the address of **a[1]**. This is shown in Fig. 6.1, where it is assumed that **minimum** has again been invoked by the call

```
minimum(table, 10)
```

By repeatedly incrementing **p**, we move each time to the next element, until **p** is equal to **a + n**. Then **p** is equal to the address of the memory location that follows the final element, **table[n − 1]**. Incidentally, this example shows that the 'less than' operator < can be applied to addresses. (The latter also holds for the operators >, < =, > =, = =, and ! =.)

Our last version of **minimum** is not intended to be an improvement of the version in Section 6.2, but it only illustrates the use of pointers. Our next example has the same purpose; however, it has nothing to do with arrays and it shows that pointers can lead to very compact code. Suppose that we know that **i** is equal to 1, 2, or 3. Depending on this, it is required to assign a number, read from the keyboard, to **x**, **y**, or **z**, respectively. Then that variable is to be divided by 5, and, finally, the resulting value must be printed. It is required that the other two variables remain unaltered. The use of a pointer enables us to decide only once which of the variables **x**, **y**, or **z** is to be used:

```
float x, y, z, *p;
int i;
...
p = i == 1 ? &x : i == 2 ? &y : &z; /* Assign &x, &y, or &z to p */
scanf("%f", p);                      /* Read x, y, or z          */
*p /= 5;                             /* Divide x, y, or z by 5   */
printf("New value: %f", *p);         /* Print x, y, or z         */
```

Since the value of **p** is already an address, we must not use the 'address of' operator **&** in the above call to **scanf**. Conversely, the second argument of **printf** must have type **float**, not 'pointer-to-float', hence the use of the indirection operator * in the call to this function.

The importance of assigning values to pointers

After declaring a pointer, say **p**, we must not use ***p** before assigning a value to **p**. If we do, we make a mistake similar to using, for example, − **i** immediately after declaring the **int** variable **i** without initializing it. Thus the following program shows an error:

```
main()
{ char *p, ch;
  *p = 'A';
}
```

This error is very serious: the undefined value of **p** is used and interpreted as an address; then the contents of this address are altered. This may destroy some important piece of information in memory. What makes things worse, you may get away with it on one machine and run into all kinds of trouble on another. In this example, it is very easy to correct it by inserting the statement

```
p = &ch;
```

before

```
*p = 'A';
```

After this correction, the latter statement has the effect of assigning the value ´A´ to the variable **ch**.

We can use a pointer as an array, but, again, this is possible only after we have given it a suitable value. If it is a function parameter, such an initial value is automatically provided for by the corresponding argument, but for other pointer variables we have to take care of this ourselves, as is done in the following program:

```
main()
{ char s[10], *p;
  p = s;
  p[9] = 'A';
}
```

In this program, the declaration of **s** allocates a block of ten bytes for it. By contrast, only one location (for an address) is allocated by declaring **p**, and its initial value is undefined. By executing the statement **p = s;**, the address of **s[0]** is assigned to **p**, after which we can use **p[0], p[1], ⋯, p[9]** in the same way as **s[0], s[1], ⋯, s[9]**: the variables **p[i]** and **s[i]** denote the same memory location. If the statement **p = s;** had been omitted, the statement **p[9] = ´A´;** would have been incorrect and as dangerous as the statement ***p = ´A´;**, discussed in our previous example.

Pointer conversion and void-pointers

We sometimes feel a need for a general kind of pointer, to which we can assign the address of any object, irrespective of its type. Suppose we declare **i** and **p_char** as follows:

```
int i;
char *p_char;
```

Since the address of an integer has the same internal format as the address of a character, you may wonder if the following statement is allowed:

```
p_char = &i;          /* Incorrect */
```

This is not the case. The expression **&i** has type 'pointer to **int**', while **p_char** is of type 'pointer to **char**'. In an assignment statement such as this one, these two types are incompatible, which means that this statement is invalid. However, we can easily correct it by using a cast:

```
p_char = (char *)&i;  /* Correct   */
```

Note the asterisk in **(char *)**. It says that **&i** is to be converted to type 'pointer to **char**, not to type **char**.

In the original version of C this type 'pointer to char', combined with casts from one pointer type to another, was normally used as a substitute for a general pointer type. In ANSI C we can instead use *void-pointers*, also known as *generic pointers*. We can write, for example,

```
void *p_void;
```

We do not need a cast to assign the address of an object of any type to **p_void**, or, conversely, to assign the value of **p_void** to another pointer variable, so the following statements are correct:

```
p_void = &i;
p_char = p_void;
```

Generic pointers may also be used in comparisons. For example, here is a valid and an invalid comparison:

```
int *p_int;
char *p_char;
void *p_void;
...
if (p_int == p_char) ... /* Invalid */
if (p_void == p_int) ... /* Valid   */
```

Address arithmetic must not be applied to void-pointers. After all, the value of **p_void** can be the address of any type, so, if **p_void + 1** yielded an address, it would not be clear how many bytes this address should lie apart from the address stored in **p_void**. Therefore **p_void + 1** is not a valid expression. In Section 6.6 we will see that the new, general pointer type applies to the important standard function **malloc**.

6.4 STRINGS

We already know the concept of *address* as it appears in three forms, namely:

(i)   An expression that begins with the operator &, such as **&table[0]**.
(ii)   The name of an array, such as **table**.
(iii)   A pointer, such as **p**.

There is another important form, which we will discuss now:

(iv)   A string (also called a *string constant* or *string literal*), such as **"ABC"**.

If the string **"ABC"** occurs in a program, the three characters ´A´, ´B´, and ´C´, extended with the null character, ´\0´, are stored somewhere in memory, similar to the way a character array with the same four elements would be stored. We may therefore regard **"ABC"** as an array of four elements. The actual value of this string is the address of its first character, and its type is 'pointer to **char**'. Applying the operator ***** to an object of this type yields the character that forms its contents; it is also possible to use address arithmetic with strings:

```
 *"ABC"            is equal to       'A'
 *("ABC" + 1)      is equal to       'B'
 *("ABC" + 2)      is equal to       'C'
 *("ABC" + 3)      is equal to       '\0'
```

As we have seen, not only array names but also pointers may be *subscripted* (that is, they may be followed by an integer expression in brackets). Array names and pointers have in common that they have type 'pointer to ⋯' (where ⋯ can be any type) or, in other words, that their values are addresses. This can be generalized to all other expressions with these characteristics. A string is an example of such an expression, so instead of the above four expressions in the left column we can write

```
"ABC"[0]
"ABC"[1]
"ABC"[2]
"ABC"[3]
```

Only if we know that **"ABC"** yields an address can we understand how the following program works:

```
/* POINTER */
#include <stdio.h>

main()
{ char *p;
  p = "ABC";
  printf(p);
}
```

First, it would be wrong to imagine that the assignment statement in this program should copy characters. Instead, only the start address of the character sequence **ABC**, stored somewhere in memory, is assigned to **p**. So much for this assignment statement. As for the next statement, we see that pointer **p** is used as an argument in the call to **printf**, which seems to be essentially different from more usual calls, such as

```
printf("ABC");
```

However, these two calls are in fact very similar. In both cases, **printf** is supplied with an address as its argument, which is exactly what it expects. After all, both **p** and **"ABC"** are expressions the values of which are addresses and with type 'pointer to **char**'. As expected, the output of program POINTER is

```
ABC
```

You can now easily verify that the output would have been

```
BC
```

if the call to **printf** had been replaced with either of the following calls:

```
printf(p + 1);
printf("ABC" + 1);
```

'String variables'

Instead of a special type of variable to store strings, we simply use arrays of characters for this purpose. With such arrays we have to distinguish between what we may call their physical and their logical length. The former is simply the length of the array; for example, it is 11 in array **s**, declared as

```
char s[11];
```

By convention, the sequence of characters stored in **s** is extended with a null character (´\0´). For example, we can say that the four assignment statements

```
s[0] = 'A'; s[1] = 'B'; s[2] = 'C'; s[3] = '\0';
```

store **"ABC"** in **s**. The logical length of this string is 3. Note that actually four elements of **s** are used in this case. We see that the logical length is always less than the physical length and is therefore at most 10 in our example. After the execution of these four assignment statements, the following call to **printf** will again print ABC:

```
printf(s);
```

6.5 STRING OPERATIONS

It would be very unfortunate if assigning a string such as **"ABC"** to array **s** always had to be done by means of a sequence of assignment statements, as we did at the end of the last section. The practical way of doing this and many other string operations is by calling standard functions declared in **string.h**. We therefore write

```
#include <string.h>
```

after which the task mentioned is performed by the statement

```
strcpy(s, "ABC");
```

Those who are not familiar with C may be inclined to write

```
s = "ABC";  /* Incorrect */
```

to achieve this, but this is wrong for two reasons. First, the right-hand side would yield an address, so if the statement were valid then an address would be copied (as was done in program POINTER) instead of the characters themselves. Second, the name of an array, such as **s**, is not really a variable and must therefore not be used as the left-hand side of an assignment. Besides names of variables, we can also write more complicated expressions that are allowed as the left-hand side of an assignment. Collectively, we call them *lvalues*. The name of an array is not an lvalue, which is why the above program line is incorrect. This lvalue concept is also relevant to some other operators, such as **+ +** and **+ =**, which combine assignments with other operations. With the declarations

```
char ch, *p, s[100];
int i, j;
```

the distinction between expressions that are lvalues and those which are not will be clear by carefully comparing the left and the right columns below:

Lvalue	*No lvalue*
ch	&ch
p	s
*p	ch + 1
*(s + 99)	s + 99
s[99]	5
*"ABC"	"ABC"
i	-i
*&i	&*p
*(i<j ? &i : &j)	i<j ? i : j
*p++	p++

For example, if the smaller of the two variables **k** and **m** is to be set to zero and the other is to be left unchanged, we can do this as follows:

```
*(i < j ? &i : &j) = 0;
```

Note that the following construction would be incorrect:

```
(i < j ? i : j) = 0;   /* Incorrect */
```

Any expression that begins with the indirection operator ***** is an lvalue; any expression that begins with the 'address of' operator **&** is not. On the other hand, the latter operator can only be applied to lvalues. Thus, in the following form the *operand* that follows **&** must be an lvalue, but the whole expression is not.

   & *operand*

Let us now revert to the function **strcpy**. We call it with two arguments, which can be any expressions of type 'pointer to **char**'. In other words, the expressions that we write as *destination* and *source* in the call

```
strcpy(destination, source)
```

must yield addresses. Bytes are copied from the source area to the destination area until the null character has been copied. It is our responsibility to take care that the destination area is large enough for all characters to be copied, the null character included. As we have seen at the beginning of Section 6.4 and elsewhere, there are all kinds of expressions whose values are addresses, which implies that the destination need not be the beginning of an array, as the following program shows:

```
#include <stdio.h>
#include <string.h>

main()
{ char s[100]="Program something.", t[100];
  strcpy(t, s);
  strcpy(t + 8, "in C.");
  printf(s); printf("\n");
  printf(t);
}
```

Its output is

```
Program something.
Program in C.
```

The expression **t + 8** yields the address of the **s** in **Program something.** This is the start position of the destination, to which the characters of **"in C."** of the source are copied. After copying these five characters, the null character (actually present in the source) is copied as well, which causes the copying process to terminate. It is essential that this null character is included in the copying process, because its presence in array **t** is the only means to prevent **printf(t)** from printing any 'garbage' characters that in this array may follow the null character.

As we have seen, we cannot use an assignment statement to place a string into a character array. The *initialization* of array **s** in the above program seems to contradict this. However, initialization is a language concept entirely different from assignment, even though they look similar because of the equal sign being used in both cases. Recall that we have discussed array initialization at the end of Section 5.5.

This is perhaps a good opportunity to mention another subtle point in connection with this subject. In the following two lines, **s** is an array with four elements; it is just large enough for the string **"ABC"**, the null character included.

```
char s[4]="ABC";
char *p="DEF";
```

During initialization, the four characters of this string are copied to **s**; we can, of course, place other characters into this array later, but its (physical) length will always remain 4. Things are essentially different with the pointer variable **p**. Here the address of **"DEF"**, not the character sequence itself, is copied to **p** (not to ***p**). Note that we can split up the last line into a declaration and an assignment:

```
char *p; p="DEF";
```

We cannot do this with the declaration of **s** (unless we use **strcpy**). Another point in which **p** is different from **s** is that **p** is by no means restricted to an array of only four characters, as is the case with **s**. In **p** only an address is stored, and we can write, for example,

```
p = "ABCDEFG";
```

later, to use **p** for the address of a larger string. Now that we have focused on their differences, we must also remember that **s** and **p** are similar in many respects; for example, the following four expressions are all valid:

```
s[i]        *(s + i)
p[i]        *(p + i)
```

Substrings

Although **strcpy** is quite a useful function, copying everything from the given source until the null character is encountered may not be what we want. We often want to replace only some portion (sometimes called a *substring*) in the middle of a given string. This can be done by means of the function **strncpy**. This has not only the letter **n** in the middle of its name but also a third parameter, which says how many characters are to be copied at most: the call

```
strncpy(destination, source, n)
```

copies *n* characters from *source* to *destination*, unless in *source* a null character is encountered before *n* characters have been copied. In that case, the null character is copied and the copying process terminates. For example, after

```
char s[100];
strcpy(s, "This is positive.");
```

we can use the statement

```
strncpy(s + 8, "nega", 4);
```

to give array **s** the following new contents:

```
This is negative.
```

After copying the letters, **n**, **e**, **g**, and **a**, the given maximum number of characters to be copied has been reached, so copying stops; this implies that the null character is not copied. If the final argument had been greater than 4, precisely five characters (**n**, **e**, **g**, **a**, and ´**\0**´) would have been copied. The characters in **"tive."** would then no longer have been considered to belong logically to the string stored in **s**.

The results of **strcpy** and **strncpy** are undefined if the destination and the source overlap. For example, if we want to insert the string **"The "** at the beginning of the string stored in **s** after

```
char s[100] = "programming language C",
     temp[100];
```

we should use the temporary variable **temp**, by writing, for example,

```
strcpy(temp, s);
strcpy(s, "The ");
strcpy(s + 4, temp);
```

Return values

The functions **strcpy** and **strncpy** return the start address of the destination. We often ignore these returned values, but we can use them if we like, as is done in

```
printf(strcpy(s, "William Shakespeare"));
```

which can be used instead of

```
strcpy(s, "William Shakespeare"); printf(s);
```

String length and concatenation

The standard function **strlen** (declared in **string.h**) returns the length of a string, so we can write, for example:

```
#include <string.h>
...
int length;
char s[100]="ABC";
length = strlen(s);
```

That length is 3 in this example: it says how many characters precede the null character. We can also say that it indicates the position of the null character: in our example, the null character can be found in **s[3]**. Because of this null character the number of characters logically used in **s** is equal to **strlen(s) + 1**.

If we want to append a string **t** with string **s**, we might do this as follows:

```
strcpy(t + strlen(t), s);
```

However, there is a special function, **strcat**, for this *concatenation* operation, which in this case we would use as follows:

```
strcat(t, s);
```

Again, it is possible to limit the number of characters to be copied, by using a related function, **strncat**. If we write

```
strncat(t, s, n);
```

then the first **n** characters of **s** are copied, unless a null character is encountered (and copied). In the latter case, the copying process terminates immediately.

It is the programmer's responsibility that there is enough memory available in the 'target' **t** to contain the concatenation result, consisting of both its old value and the characters copied from the 'source' **s**.

String comparison

If we want to compare two strings, we normally should not use the relational operators == , !=, <, <=, >, >=, because, if we do, *start addresses* are compared, not the characters stored there. For example, the test in

```
strcpy(s, "ABC");
if (s == "ABC") ...
```

will fail: although **s** contains the string **"ABC"**, the address of **s** is different from the address of the constant **"ABC"** that in the program follows the equality operator == . Instead of the operator == , we should use the function **strcmp** (declared in **string.h**). The last program line should be replaced with

```
if (strcmp(s, "ABC") == 0) ...
```

It may seem curious for **strcmp** to return 0 in case of equality, but the reason for this is that this function can also be used for the other relational operations, which here refer to the alphabetical order of words as these appear, for example, in a telephone directory. For example, we have

```
strcmp("Walker", "Wood")              < 0
strcmp("Morrison", "Morris")          > 0
strcmp("Johnson", "Johnson")          = 0
```

When we use the call **strcmp(s, t)**, first the characters **s[0]** and **t[0]** are compared. If these are equal, **s[1]** and **t[1]** are compared, and so forth. This process can terminate in two ways. Either

- two unequal characters **s[i]** and **t[i]** are encountered, or
- the null character is encountered in both **s[i]** and **t[i]**.

In either case, the value returned by **strcmp** is **s[i]** − **t[i]**. Note that this also gives the correct result if **s[i]** or **t[i]** is the null character (which is equivalent to integer 0).

Again, there is a special version, **strncmp**, to limit the number of characters to be compared. For example, if two character arrays **s** and **t** are given and we want to know if the characters stored in **s[7]**, **s[8]**, and **s[9]** are equal to those in **t[0]**, **t[1]**, and **t[2]**, we can write

```
if (strncmp(s + 7, t, 3) == 0) ...
```

The keyword 'const'

The string functions we have been discussing are declared in **string.h** as follows:

```
int strlen(const char *s);
int strcmp(const char *s1, const char *s2);
int strncmp(const char *s1, const char *s2, int maxlen);
char *strcpy(char *dest, const char *src);
char *strncpy(char *dest, const char *src, int maxlen);
char *strcat(char *dest, const char *src);
char *strncat(char *dest, const char *src, int maxlen);
```

Notice the use of the keyword **const**, briefly discussed in Section 3.2. The advantage of this keyword is that we can immediately see the distinction between what we may call 'input' and 'output' parameters. For example, the second parameter, **src**, of **strcpy** denotes the source area; it is used only to copy characters from, so this area will not be modified. The keyword **const** can therefore be used for it. We may call it an 'input parameter' because the function 'receives' data through it. In contrast to this, the first parameter, **dest**, of **strcpy** is the destination area, which will be overwritten. We must not use **const** for it. We may call it an 'output parameter' because data is written in the destination area, to be used later by the caller of **strcpy**. If you are familiar with other languages, such as Pascal, remember that there are only 'value parameters' in C: the arguments themselves are never altered by a function call. The keyword **const** does therefore not apply to the arguments themselves but only to the memory areas denoted by them.

6.6 DYNAMIC MEMORY ALLOCATION

When declaring an array, we have to specify its length as a constant expression, as is done with length 100 in

```
char s[100];
```

Sometimes we would rather use a variable, or some expression containing variables, for this purpose, if that were possible, so that we would have, for example,

```
int n;
...
scanf("%d", &n);
char s[n];          /* Error */
```

There are two errors in this program fragment. First, we cannot write declarations immediately after statements, and, second, we cannot use variables, such as **n**, in array declarations. Surprisingly enough, what is aimed at here can very well be achieved, namely as follows:

```
#include <stdlib.h>
int n;
char *s;
...
scanf("%d", &n)
s = malloc(n);
```

This method is based on the fact that we can use a pointer as an array, provided that we have assigned a suitable address to it. The latter can be done by means of the function **malloc**, short for (dynamic) *memory allocation*. We can now really use the 'array elements'

```
s[0], s[1], ..., s[n-1]
```

that is, if the call to **malloc** in the last statement is successful. (We will see shortly how to inquire whether or not that is the case.) The line

```
#include <stdlib.h>
```

is used because the function **malloc** is declared in it. This declaration may read as follows:

```
void *malloc(unsigned nbytes);
```

The argument of **malloc** is the number of (contiguous) bytes to be allocated. Its return value is the start address of this block of memory. Its type is 'pointer to void' (discussed in Section 6.3), so that the address can be assigned to any pointer, without using a cast. For example, we can use **malloc** to allocate memory for a **float** array with 1000 elements as follows:

```
#include <stdlib.h>

main()
{ float *a;
  a = malloc(1000 * sizeof(float));
  ...
```

Note that **malloc** requires the size of the memory block to be expressed in bytes, regardless of what these bytes will be used for. As one **float** object takes **sizeof(float)** bytes, the argument of **malloc** in this example will be clear. If this call to **malloc** succeeds, the 'array elements'

```
a[0], a[1], ..., a[999]
```

are available as if we had written

```
float a[1000];
```

Success and failure of 'malloc'

If enough memory room is available, **malloc** works as we have discussed in the above examples. If not, **malloc** returns the value 0. This is possible because of a special language rule, not yet discussed, which says that, unlike other numeric values, the special integer value 0 may be assigned to pointers and may also be compared with them. Furthermore, it is guaranteed that any 'real' address in C is nonzero. Instead of 0, it is customary to use the symbolic constant **NULL**, defined as 0 in the header file **stdlib.h** (and in **stdio.h**). The fact that **malloc** returns the special value **NULL** if the call to this function fails due to lack of memory enables us to take whatever action we like. The simplest way to cope with this problem is to test if **NULL** is returned, and, if so, to print an error message and terminate program execution:

```
s = malloc(n);
if (s == NULL)
{ printf("Not enough memory.\n");
  exit(1);
}
```

The function **exit**, used here, is also declared in **stdlib.h**. It terminates program execution and returns its argument to the operating system. It is customary to use argument 0 for 'normal' and 1 for 'abnormal' program termination. It depends on the operating system being used what can be done with this argument value. The main point to remember is that it would be very unwise not to test the value returned by **malloc**. If this value happens to be **NULL**, the effect of ignoring this using **NULL** as a real address may be very unpleasant and similar to using undefined pointers or to storing data outside array boundaries.

Some functions related to 'malloc'

There are some more useful functions for memory allocation; like **malloc**, they are declared in **stdlib.h**. If we want the allocated memory to be initialized with zero values, we can use **calloc** instead of **malloc**. Another new point of **calloc** is that it takes two arguments, the number of data elements and the number of bytes required for one data element. Clearly the product of these two arguments is the number of bytes that **malloc** would require as an argument. For example, if we want to allocate memory for an 'array' of **n** integers, with 0 as their initial values, we can write:

```
#include <stdlib.h>
...
int *p;
...
p = calloc(n, sizeof(int));
if (p == NULL) ...
```

Memory allocated by **malloc, calloc,** or **realloc** (to be discussed shortly) can be released by calling the function **free**. The argument of this function is an address previously obtained by a call to one of the three allocation functions just mentioned. We often use something of the following form:

```
...
s = malloc(...);
xxx
free(s);
...
```

It goes without saying that the memory locations s[0], s[1], ⋯ can be used
only in program fragment *xxx*. There is no point in calling **free** if, after this call,
program execution terminates immediately or very soon, since in that case
memory will be released anyway. Calling **free** is particularly important at the
end of a function that is called a great many times. If we call **malloc** in such a
function and omit calling **free**, the amount of memory in use cumulates
unnecessarily. This is a rather tricky point, since with a normally defined array
we are used to the fact that its memory space is automatically released on return
from the function. For memory allocated with **malloc** (or **calloc** or **realloc**) we
should not forget to do this ourselves.

We sometimes want to alter the size of the block of memory previously allocated
by **malloc** or **calloc**; for example, it may turn out that more room is needed than
we had anticipated. The function to use for this purpose is **realloc**. It takes two
arguments: the address previously obtained by **malloc** or **calloc**, and the new
length of the block of memory, expressed in bytes. It can be used as follows:

```
#include <stdio.h>
#include <stdlib.h>
...
char *s;
...
s = malloc(1000);  /* Anticipated length: 1000 bytes      */
if (s == NULL) {printf("malloc fails with n = 1000"); exit(1);}
...
/* Here s[0], ..., s[999] can be used. */

scanf("%d", &n);   /* New length n, possibly greater than 1000 */
s = realloc(s, n);
if (s == NULL) {printf("realloc fails with n = %d", n); exit(1);}
...
/* Here s[0], ..., s[n-1] can be used. */
```

If, in the call to **realloc**, the argument **n** is greater than 1000, then after this call
s[0], ⋯, s[999] have the same contents as before, which means that we have
added the elements s[1000], ⋯, s[n−1] at the end. All **n** bytes are again
contiguous, that is, they form one block. To achieve this, it may be necessary to
move the previously allocated block, which means that frequent use of **realloc**
may be very time consuming. If **n** is less than 1000, the 'array size' is decreased.

In this case, only the elements s[0], ···, s[n−1] are available after the call to **realloc**, and we must no longer use s[n], ···, s[999]. The most drastic way of reducing previously allocated memory is by writing **realloc(s, 0)**, which we can use instead of **free(s)**.

6.7 INPUT AND OUTPUT OF STRINGS

When we are reading a string from the keyboard, it must be clear when the end of the string is reached. In most cases we want to read entire lines, that is, pressing the Enter key should signal the end of the input. We can do this by writing

```
gets(s);
```

in which **s** is an expression whose value is the start address of the area in memory where the string is to be placed. It is obvious that there must be enough memory be available. For example, after

```
char s[30], *p;
```

the above call to **gets** is correct only if the user enters at most 29 characters before pressing the Enter key. Remember, a null character will be stored at the end, so only 29 bytes are left for the real characters. The newline character entered is not stored.

Immediately after the above declaration, the following call would be incorrect:

```
gets(p);
```

We may use this call only after assigning a suitable address to **p**. This could be done, for example, by means of

```
p = malloc(100);
```

or

```
p = s;
```

The function **gets** is declared in the header file **stdio.h** as follows:

```
char *gets(char *s);
```

As this declaration shows, **gets** also returns a value, which is of type 'pointer to **char**'. This is normally equal to **s**, the address given as an argument, except when 'end of file' occurs; in that case the return value is **NULL**. As we will see in Chapter 8, a *file* is normally an area on disk in which data is stored. When reading from it, we must have a means of detecting the end of the file. Now that we are reading from the keyboard, all this may be irrelevant. However, with some machines we can use a special key combination, such as Ctrl-Z, with the effect of 'end of file'. The following program demonstrates this:

```
/* LINLEN: This program determines the length of the longest line that is
           read from the keyboard. It works only if you can use a special
           key combination, such as Ctrl-Z, to indicate 'end of file'.
*/
#include <stdio.h>
#include <string.h>

main()
{ int longest=0, len;
  char s[100];
  printf("Enter some lines. After the final one, type Ctrl-Z,\n"
         "or some other key combination, to indicate 'end of file':\n");
  while (gets(s) != NULL)
  { len = strlen(s);
    if (len > longest) longest = len;
  }
  printf("Length of the longest line: %d.\n", longest);
}
```

Here is a demonstration of this program. The program was run on an MS DOS machine. As you can see below, it displays ^Z when the letter **Z** is typed with the Ctrl key pressed down.

```
Enter some lines. After the final one, type Ctrl-Z,
or some other key combination, to indicate 'end of file':
John
William
Jim
^Z
Length of the longest line: 7.
```

The opposite of **gets** is **puts**. It can be used to print a line (that is, to display a line on the screen) and to go to the beginning of the next line. So the two calls

```
puts("ABC"); puts("DEF");
```

lead to the following output:

```
ABC
DEF
```

Since **gets** does not store the newline character at the end, it is reasonable that **puts** supplies one of its own. By doing this these two functions can work together very well, as the following program demonstrates. It reads three lines and then prints them:

```
#include <stdio.h>
main()
{ char s[100], t[100], u[100];
  gets(s); gets(t); gets(u);
  puts(s); puts(t); puts(u);
}
```

Instead of **gets**, we can use **scanf**, with the conversion specification %s. However, this works quite differently: with **scanf**, any white-space character signals the end of the string. (The term *white-space character* is used for a blank, a tab, or a newline character.) Another point is that **scanf** skips any white-space characters at the beginning of the string. For example, if we use

```
char str[100];
scanf("%s", str);
```

and we enter the text

```
      Charles Dickens
```

(with some blanks at the beginning), only **Charles** is read and placed into **str**, without any leading blanks. The blank between **Charles** and **Dickens** is regarded as being not yet read. Note that we must not write **&str** in the above call to **scanf**, because **str** is the name of an array and therefore denotes an address, as is required. The conversion specification %s can also be used in calls to **printf**; then it must correspond to an address as well. This means that the two statements

```
printf("%s", str);
printf(str);
```

are equivalent; with our example, executing them both gives **CharlesCharles** as output. Here is another pair of equivalent statements; they also print the name **Charles** twice, but this time on two lines:

```
printf("%s\n", str);
puts(str);
```

6.8 STRINGS AS ARGUMENTS AND RETURN VALUES

In Section 6.5 we have discussed how to use the important string functions **strlen,
strcpy, strncpy, strcmp, strncmp, strcat,** and **strncat.** If we like, we can write
such functions ourselves. Although we need not do this for these seven functions,
writing them down is a very good exercise. The C language enables us to give
several solutions. For example, consider the following versions of **strlen:**

```
/* Version 1 */
int strlen(const char *s)
{ int n=0;
  while (s[n] != '\0') n++;
  return n;
}

/* Version 2 */
int strlen(const char *s)
{ int n=0;
  while (*s++ != '\0') n++;
  return n;
}

/* Version 3 */
int strlen(const char *s)
{ char *p=s;
  while (*p != '\0') p++;
  return p - s;
}
```

In all three versions

```
const char *s
```

indicates that an address is expected as an argument, and that the contents of the
memory area given by this address will not be altered. (Recall our discussion of
const at the end of Section 6.5.) In version 1 the array notation **s[n]** is used,
which, incidentally, may be replaced with ***(s+n)**. Version 2 shows that we can
use **s** as a real variable: the pointer **s** is altered, which does not affect the
corresponding argument. Version 3 shows the initialization of a pointer. Here the
initial value of **p** is **s**. After execution of the while-statement, **p** points to the null
character and **s** to the given start point, which means that the desired string
length is equal to the difference **p** − **s**.

Note that we can write all three versions slightly shorter and more efficiently by simply omitting

```
!= '\0'
```

This will be clear if we replace ´\0´ with the equivalent notation 0 and recall Example 6 at the end of Section 3.4.

We will now compare two versions of **strcpy**. The first is no doubt the more readable one, but the second is shorter and faster:

```
/* This function copies from source 'src' to destination 'dest'.
   (Well-readable version)
*/
char *strcpy(char *dest, const char *src)
{ int i=0;
  while (dest[i] = src[i], dest[i] != '\0') i++;
  return dest;
}

/* This function copies from source 'src' to destination 'dest'.
   (Fast version)
*/
char *strcpy(char *dest, const char *src)
{ char *start=dest;
  while (*dest++ = *src++)  ;
  return start;
}
```

In the last version the unary operators * and + + are used. According to Section 4.5, these associate from right to left, which means that

```
*dest++ = *src++
```

is to be read as

```
*(dest++) = *(src++)
```

We see that the *contents of* operator ***** is to be applied to **src** before this variable is incremented. This yields a character that is placed into the location whose address is given by **dest** before this variable is incremented. The while-loop terminates when the null character has been copied, since then the value of the whole assignment is zero.

Like **strlen** and **strcpy**, the other functions mentioned can be written in very compact C code. Here is a version for each of the functions **strcmp** and **strcat**.

You are strongly recommended to write **strncpy**, **strncmp** and **strncat** yourself
as an exercise.

```
int strcmp(const char *s, const char *t)
{ int i=0;
  while (s[i] == t[i])
    if (s[i++] == '\0') return 0;
  return s[i] - t[i];
}

char *strcat(char *dest, const char *src)
{ strcpy(dest+strlen(dest), src);
  return dest;
}
```

Each of the functions **strcpy** and **strcat** alters the area the address of which is
given through its first parameter, hence we must not use **const** for this parameter.
That address is also used as the return value of these functions. When we do
the same in functions of our own, a warning may not be superfluous. We must
always remember that the memory area used by local variables are released when
the function is left. The following function will therefore lead to problems:

```
char *incorrect(void)
{ char str[100];
  str[0] = 'A';
  str[1] = 'B';
  str[2] = 'C';
  str[3] = '\0';
  return str;
}
```

Suppose we use this function as follows:

```
char *p;
...
p = incorrect();
```

Although **p** is assigned the address of a memory area, you cannot sensibly use it,
because the contents of that area, that is, the character sequence **ABC\0**, may
already have been destroyed or will at any rate be used for other purposes. Still
we can allocate a memory area, place some data in it, and return its star
address, as the following corrected version shows:

```
#include <stdlib.h>
...
char *correct()
{ char *str;
  str = malloc(100);
  if (str == NULL) {printf("Not enough memory."); exit(1);}
  str[0] = 'A';
  str[1] = 'B';
  str[2] = 'C';
  str[3] = '\0';
  return str;
}
```

6.9 MULTI-DIMENSIONAL ARRAYS

We can regard a *table* or *matrix* as an array the elements of which are again arrays. The notation for an element of such a table is in accordance with this; we can write

```
table[i][j]
```

to denote the element in the ith row and the jth column of the two-dimensional array **table** (where, as usual, we count from 0). If we want **table** to have 20 rows and 5 columns, and elements of type **float**, for example, we declare:

```
float table[20][5];
```

If you are familiar with Pascal, you must be on your guard not to make the mistake of writing **table[i, j]** instead of **table[i][j]**. Since

```
i, j
```

is a comma expression whose value is the same as that of **j**, the erroneous expression **table[i, j]** is equivalent to **table[j]**.

Function parameters

If **table** is to be a *parameter* of a function, we can write the first line of that function as is done in

```
int f(float table[][5])
```

Only its first dimension (20) may be omitted; the second (5), and any further dimensions, must be present. Remember that inside the function the computer must be able to compute the address of the element **table[i] [j]**. If **table** is regarded as a one-dimensional array, the kth element of which is identical with the element just mentioned, we have $k = 5i + j$, so the value 5 must be available. (Recall that the principle of separate compilation allows us to define function **f** in a module other than that in which array **table** is defined, so the compiler, when dealing with **f**, may not have access to the definition of **table**.)

Pointer notation

As we have seen at the end of Section 6.2, we can use both notations

```
int g(float a[])
int g(float *a)
```

as the first line of a function **g** with an array parameter. Similarly, the first of the following two lines can be replaced with the second:

```
int f(float table[] [5])
int f(float *table[5])
```

Note that in either case the first bracket pair [ ] is omitted in exchange for an asterisk inserted before the name of the parameter.

When we are using array elements, it is worth remembering that, analogous to the equivalence

```
    a[i]              ≡              *(a + i)
```

we also have

```
    table[i] [j]      ≡              *(table[i] + j)
                      ≡              *(*(table + i) + j)
```

Finally, taking the addresses of all these expressions, we find

```
    &a[i]             ≡              a + i

    &table[i] [j]     ≡              table[i] + j
                      ≡              *(table + i) + j
```

Initialization

In Section 5.5 we have seen how to initialize a one-dimensional array. We can easily extend this to two-dimensional ones. Suppose that we want the **int** array **a** to have two rows and three columns with the following initial values:

```
60  30  50
20  80  40
```

We can write either of the following two lines to achieve this:

```
int a[2][3] = {{60, 30, 50}, {20, 80, 40}};
int a[2][3] = {60, 30, 50, 20, 80, 40};
```

The first of these two clearly shows that there are two rows and three columns. This is not the case with the second, which is also allowed.

Arrays of strings can be initialized very conveniently. The following example shows both an initialization of an array of strings and the way these strings can be used:

```
char namelist[3][30] = {"Johnson", "Peterson", "Jacobson"};
for (i=0; i<3; i++) printf("%s\n", namelist[i]);
```

Arrays of pointers

In the example at the beginning of this section, the values of **table[0]**, ···, **table[19]** are start addresses of one-dimensional arrays. It is, of course, possible to store these addresses in an array of pointers. This leads to a more dynamic data structure, because the sequences pointed to can have any length (instead of only 5). Because of this dynamic aspect, we will use the name **dtable** to distinguish it from **table**. We begin by replacing

```
float table[20][5];
```

with

```
float *dtabel[20];
```

It is very important to realize that with this new version the memory space for the actual floating-point numbers still has to be allocated. For example, if we want a table of five columns again, we can write:

```
#include <stdlib.h>
...
for (i=0; i<20; i++)
{ dtable[i] = malloc(5 * sizeof(float));
  if (dtable[i] == NULL) {printf("Not enough memory"); exit(1);}
}
```

After this, we can use the elements **dtable[i] [j]** in exactly the same way as we could use the elements **table[i] [j]** before. However, it is by no means necessary for all 'rows' **dtable[i]** to have the same length. Instead of the constant 5 in the above loop, we can use any expression, the value of which may different for different values of **i**.

Although arrays of pointers are normally used in combination with **malloc**, as was done in our last example, this is not absolutely necessary. For example, suppose that we want to use the **float** 'array elements' **a[i] [j]**, with **i** = 0, 1, 2, and with

length 20 for row **a[0]**,
length 1000 for row **a[1]**, and
length 100 for row **a[2]**.

Instead of using **malloc**, we can also accomplish this as follows:

```
float *a[3], a0[20], a1[1000], a2[100];
a[0] = a0;
a[1] = a1;
a[2] = a2;
```

6.10 PROGRAM PARAMETERS

The **main** function of a program can have parameters, which we call *program parameters*. However, the way of parameter passing is essentially different from what we are used to. Program PROGPARM will make this clear:

```
/* PROGPARM: Demonstration of using program parameters.
*/
#include <stdio.h>

main(int argc, char *argv[])
{ int i;
  printf("argc     = %d\n", argc);
  for (i=1; i<argc; i++) printf("argv[%d] = %s\n", i, argv[i]);
}
```

To run this program, we enter a command line consisting of the program name
followed by number of *program arguments*, written as character sequences and
separated by blanks, as, for example, in

```
PROGPARM ABC DEFG HIJKL
```

With this command line, the output of the program is

```
argc    = 4
argv[1] = ABC
argv[2] = DEFG
argv[3] = HIJKL
```

The parameter **argc** is equal to the number of program arguments if we regard
the program name also as a program argument. This name, possibly together
with some additional information related to the operating system, such as, for
example, C:\PR\PROGPARM.EXE, will be available through **argv[0]**. The
array elements **argv[1]**, ···, **argv[argc − 1]** are used for the program arguments
proper. The elements of array **argv** are pointers, each of them pointing to a
character sequence, that is, to the first character of that sequence. As usual, each
of these character sequences is terminated by a null character. Here we have, for
example,

```
argv[1][0] = 'A'
argv[1][1] = 'B'
argv[1][2] = 'C'
argv[1][3] = '\0'
```

As illustrated by this example, the number of *arguments* is arbitrary, but there are
exactly two program *parameters* (if there are any). The names of these are
normally **argc** and **argv**, short for *argument count* and *argument vector*, although
different names may be used instead. Their types must be as they are here.

The concept of program parameters enables us to write programs that are similar
to conventional operating-system commands. For example, using a copy
command, written as

```
copy a:aaa.txt b:bbb.txt
```

with the MS-DOS operating system, can now be regarded as executing a C
program named **copy** with **a:aaa.txt** and **b:bbb.txt** as program arguments.

6.11 THE FUNCTIONS SSCANF AND SPRINTF

If a character string is stored in an array, we can 'read' data from that array in a way similar to reading data from the keyboard, by using the function **sscanf** instead of **scanf**. The first argument of **sscanf** is the name of the array, or, in general, an expression whose value is an address. This new function is useful when numbers are given in their usual external format, that is, as character sequences, and we want them to be converted into their internal, binary format. We therefore say that we use **sscanf** (and **sprintf**, discussed below) for *in-memory format conversion*. For example, the call to **sscanf** in

```
#include <stdio.h>
...
char s[30]="123    456\n98.765";
int i, j;
double x;
sscanf(s, "%d %d %lf", &i, &j, &x);
```

causes the variables **i**, **j** and **x** to take the values 123, 456, and 98.765, respectively. Like **scanf**, the function **sscanf** returns the number of values that have been successfully read and assigned to variables, so in this example that return value is 3.

It should be noted that, unlike **scanf**, the function **sscanf** has no side effect, that is, it does not keep track of what has been read already. Therefore we cannot replace the above call to **sscanf** with the three calls

```
sscanf(s, "%d", &i);
sscanf(s, "%d", &j);
sscanf(s, "%lf", &x);
```

for if we did, not only the first but also the second and the third statement would start reading at the beginning of **s**, so that **j** and **x** would also be given the value 123.

We use **sprintf** for conversion in the opposite direction, that is, from the internal, binary to the external, character-string format. This means that we can use **sprintf** to fill an array with the same characters as otherwise, with **printf**, would have been 'printed'. As usual, the null character is written at the end. For example, with **s** declared as above, the statement

```
sprintf(s, "Sum: %6.3f  Difference: %6.3f\n, 45 + 2.89, 45 - 2.89);
```

writes the following character sequence, followed by ´\0´, into s:

```
Sum: 47.890  Difference: 42.110
```

Unlike **printf**, we must not split this **sprintf** call into two separate calls for the sum and the difference, for then the difference would again be written at the beginning of **s**, overwriting the sum just placed there.

Like **scanf** and **printf**, the new functions **sscanf** and **sprintf** are declared in **stdio.h**.

6.12 POINTERS TO FUNCTIONS

Like data, functions are stored in memory and have start addresses. In most languages we perform operations on data only, not on functions, but in C we can assign the start addresses of functions to pointers. Later, such a function can be called in an indirect way, namely by means a pointer whose value is equal to the start address of the function in question. For example, if we declare

```
float (*p)(int i, int j);
```

then we can assign the start address of the function

```
float example(int i, int j)
{ return 3.14159 * i + j;
}
```

to the pointer **p** by writing

```
p = example;
```

After this assignment, we can write the following function call:

```
(*p)(12, 34)
```

Its effect is the same as that of

```
example(12, 34)
```

Incidentally, the ANSI standard allows us to omit the asterisk (as well as the parentheses) in the call **(*p)(12, 34)**, which gives

```
p(12, 34)
```

On the one hand, this is an advantage because of its simplicity, but, on the other, we can no longer tell from this call alone whether **p** is a function or a pointer.

The usefulness of pointers to functions becomes clear if we imagine a large program in the beginning of which we want to choose one out of several functions; the chosen function is then to be called a great many times. By using a pointer, the choice has to be made only once: after assigning (the address of) the selected function to a pointer, we can later call it through that pointer.

Pointers to functions also enable us to pass a function as an argument to another function. We will use a very simple example: once you understand the principle, you will be able to write more interesting applications of it yourself. Suppose that we want to write a general function to compute the sum of some values, say,

$$f(1) + f(2) + \cdots + f(n) \tag{1}$$

for *any* function f with return type **double** and with one **int** argument. Our general summation function, say, **funsum**, takes two arguments: n, the number of terms in the sum (1), and f, the function to be used. To show that **funsum** is really a general function, we will call it twice, and compute the sum of

$$reciprocal(k) = 1.0/k \qquad (k = 1, 2, 3, 4, 5)$$
$$square(k) = k^2 \qquad\qquad (k = 1, 2, 3)$$

The following program shows how this can be done:

```
/* PFUN: A function with a function as its argument.
*/
#include <stdio.h>

main()
{ double reciprocal(int k), square(int k),
        funsum(int n, double (*f)(int k));
  printf("Sum of five reciprocals: %10.6f\n", funsum(5, reciprocal));
  printf("Sum of three squares:    %10.6f\n", funsum(3, square));
}

double funsum(int n, double (*f)(int k))
{ double s=0;
  int i;
  for (i=1; i<=n; i++) s += f(i);          /* or: (*f)(i)     */
  return s;
}
```

```
double reciprocal(int k)
{ return 1.0/k;
}

double square(int k)
{ return (double)k * k;
}
```

This program computes the two sums $1 + 1.0/2 + 1.0/3 + 1.0/4 + 1.0/5$ and $1.0 + 4.0 + 9.0$, so its output is

```
Sum of five reciprocals:   2.283333
Sum of three squares:     14.000000
```

Exercises

6.1   Write a program which reads a line of text and prints this line in the reverse order. Write a version that uses an array and no pointer notation, and compare it with another version that uses pointers and no array notation.

6.2   Write the function **reverse(s, t)** which examines the strings **s** and **t** to see if either of these is the reverse of the other. The value to be returned is 1 if this is the case and 0 if it is not.

6.3   Write a program which reads a sequence of integers, followed by a nonnumeric character, and, for each of the integers 0, ···, 99, counts how often that integer occurs in the sequence. You need not, and, for reasons of efficiency, must not, use nested loops. The output is a table with two columns: the first column lists the integers 0, ···, 99, as far as they have occurred at least once in the input data; the second column shows how often these integers have occurred.

6.4   Write a program that reads a sequence of 20 integers and, for each element of this sequence, counts how many smaller elements follow in the sequence.

6.5   Write a program that merges two sequences of integers. First, the sequence $a_1, ···, a_{10}$ is read. This sequence is monotonic non-decreasing, which means that $i < j$ implies $a_i \leq a_j$. Then the sequence $b_1, ···, b_{10}$ is read, which is also monotonic non-decreasing. Finally, the 20 integers read are printed as one monotonic non-decreasing sequence.

6.6 Write the program PARSORT, which takes three program arguments and prints them in alphabetic order. For example, the command line

```
PARSORT John Albert Jack
```

leads to the following output:

```
Albert
Jack
John
```

6.7 Write a program that reads lines of text from the keyboard and prints only the longest of these lines.

6.8 Write a program to solve the *Josephus* problem. The program reads two positive integers, n and k. Suppose that n persons form a circle. In clockwise order, we assign the numbers 1, 2, $\cdots$, n to them. Starting at person 1 and counting clockwise, we remove the kth person from the circle. In the reduced circle, we continue with the person that follows the one just removed and, resuming counting from 1 to k, again eliminate the kth person. This process is repeated until only one person remains: we want to know the number of this person.

6.9 Read a positive integer n from the keyboard and print the first $n + 1$ lines of *Pascal's triangle*. This triangle consists of lines of integers. Starting at the top, these lines are numbered 0, 1, $\cdots$, n, and there are $i + 1$ integers on line i. Each line starts and ends with integer 1. Except for all these integers 1, each integer in the triangle is computed as the sum of the two nearest integers on the line immediately above it. For example, with $n = 5$, Pascal's triangle is as shown below:

```
                1
              1   1
            1   2   1
          1   3   3   1
        1   4   6   4   1
      1   5  10  10   5   1
```

As you may know, the integers on line n, in the given order, are the coefficients a_n, a_{n-1}, $\cdots$, a_1, a_0 that occur in the right-hand side of:

$$(x + 1)^n = a_n x^n + a_{n-1} x^{n-1} + \cdots + a_1 x + a_0$$

6.10   Predict the output produced by the following statements. Use your computer to see if your predictions are correct.

    a. `printf("ABCDEFG\n" + 2);`
    b. `printf("%s\n", "ABCDEFG" + 3);`
    c. `printf("%c\n", "ABCDEFG"[3]);`
    d. `printf("%c\n", ("GFEDCBA" + 1)[3]);`
    e. `printf("%c\n", "GFEDCBA"[1] + 3);`
    f. `printf("%s\n", &("ABCDEFG"[2]));`
    g. `printf("%c\n", *"ABCDEFG");`

6.11   Which serious error is there in the following program?

```
#include <stdio.h>

main()
{ int *pinteger;
  printf("Enter an integer: ");
  scanf("%d", pinteger);
  printf("After squaring: %d\n", *pinteger * *pinteger);
}
```

CHAPTER 7

Structures

7.1 DECLARATIONS AND ASSIGNMENTS

Instead of using only individual variables of the types discussed so far, we can group some variables together into a *structure*, which in some other languages is called a *record*. Structures are somewhat similar to arrays, but their elements, normally called *members*, are not identified by subscripts but by *member names*. Suppose we have objects for each of which we want to store its code number, its name, its weight, and its length. We can define a type for these objects as follows:

```
struct object
{ int code;
  char name[20];
  float weight, length;
};
```

Here only **struct** is a keyword: the names **object**, **code**, **name**, **weight**, and **length** are words chosen by ourselves. This *structure declaration*, as we call it, does not declare any variables. Yet it is useful, because it enables us to use the type **struct object**, in the same way as standard types, such as **int**, **float**, and so on. For example, we can now declare (and, at the same time, 'define') the two structure variables **s** and **t**:

```
struct object s, t;
```

Note that this declaration has the same form as, for example,

```
float x, y;
```

which uses type **float** instead of type **struct object**. We could have combined the declaration of this structure type and that of the variables **s** and **t** by writing

```
struct object
{ int code;
  char name[20];
  float weight, length;
} s, t;
```

In this case we should regard the whole part of the form

```
struct object { ... }
```

as the type, comparable with the keyword **float,** for example. If we use this combined declaration, we can omit the name **object,** although that would deprive us of a short-hand notation for this new type. Remember that in large programs we often need to use the same type several times; in particular, **struct object** may occur in several functions while the variables **s** and **t** are local to one of these functions. It is then very convenient to separate the (global) definition of this type from the (local) variable declarations. If the program consists of several modules and some structure type is to be used in more than one, it is highly recommended to define that type in a header file and to use a **#include** line for this file in all modules in which that type is used.

After declaring the structure variables **s** and **t** in one of the above ways, we can use it as follows:

```
s.code = 123;
strcpy(s.name, "Pencil");
s.weight = 12.3;
s.length = 150.7;
t = s;
```

This program fragment assigns values to all members of **s;** then these are all copied to **t.** The latter is remarkable: recall that we cannot copy an array in a single assignment. With a structure we can, even if it has an array among its members, as is the case here. (This was not possible in the original version of C, but this possibility has been created later.) The situation is now as follows:

s.code	s.name	s.weight	s.length
123	"Pencil"	12.3	150.7

t.code	t.name	t.weight	t.length
123	"Pencil"	12.3	150.7

The above fragment shows that structure members are written with a dot between the structure-variable name and the member name. These members are in fact normal variables. We can use them in the same way as other variables. For example, reading the **code** and **name** members can be done by writing

```
scanf("%d %s", &s.code, s.name);
```

Since **s.name** is an array, it is not preceded by **&**. Because of the similarity of structures and arrays, they are collectively called *aggregates*. (Structures can also have other structures as their members). If an aggregate is part of another aggregate, as is the case with **s.name**, we call it a *subaggregate*.

Like arrays, structures can be initialized by means of constant expressions separated by commas and enclosed in braces. Also, they are implicitly initialized with zeros if they have permanent memory space. In our example, we can write

```
main()
{ struct object
  { int code;
    char name[20];
    float weight, length;
  };
  static struct
  object s = {246, "Pen", 20.6, 147.0}, t;
  ...
}
```

Since **t** is **static**, it is implicitly initialized with zeros (with 20 null characters in array **name**). If we had omitted **static** in this example, **t** would have undefined initial values. The initialization of **s**, however, would in that case be valid as well. (This is new in ANSI C: originally, initialization of structures and arrays was allowed only if these variables were permanent.) The list of constant expressions between braces must not contain more elements than there are members in the structure. If it contains fewer, the remaining members are initialized with zeros (even for 'automatic' variables).

There is another way of initializing structures. Instead of a list of expressions enclosed by braces, we may use any expression without braces, provided it has exactly the right type. For example, in function **f**, we can initialize structure **t** by using structure **s** defined globally:

```
...
static struct object s = {246, "Pen", 20.6, 147.0};
...

void f(void)
{ static struct object t=s;
  ...
}
```

Another aspect that structures have in common with arrays is that we cannot use them as a whole in comparisons, as is attempted in

```
if (s == t) ...   /* Error */
```

Typedef declarations

Although **struct object** is already an abbreviated form, it is often more convenient to write a type as only one word, say **OBJECT**. There is a special means, the *typedef declaration*, to associate types with a new type name. In our case, we can write

```
typedef struct object OBJECT;
```

After this type declaration, we can write **OBJECT** instead of **struct object**, as in

```
OBJECT u, v;
```

If it had only been for cases like this, the typedef declaration would have been a superfluous language facility. After all, instead of the way we have defined type **OBJECT**, we could have written the following line for the same purpose:

```
#define OBJECT struct object
```

But the typedef declaration offers other possibilities as well, as shown by

```
typedef int *ptr;
```

This line says that **ptr** is a pointer type: variables of this type are pointers to integers. Thus instead of

```
int *p;
```

we can now write

```
ptr p;
```

In our example of a structure type, we could also have written

```
typedef
struct
{ int code;
  char name[20];
  float weight, length;
} OBJECT;
...
OBJECT s, t;
```

Note that in this typedef declaration the name **object** has been omitted: instead of **struct object** we can now immediately write **OBJECT**.

A **typedef** declaration does not really introduce a new type, but it only provides a new way of writing down an already existing type. For example, after

```
typedef struct s {int a, b; float c;} S1, S2;
```

following lines show three notations for the same type:

```
struct s
S1
S2
```

Subaggregates

Structure members can have any type, so they can again be structures. We have already seen that structure members can be arrays. In our example, the characters stored in the **name** member are also available as individual array elements. For example, we can write

```
s.name[3]
```

Both the dot and the brackets have the highest precedence, but since they associate from left to right the above means the same as

```
(s.name)[3]
```

It is also possible to use arrays of structures. On the basis of our example, we can declare

```
OBJECT table[2];
```

after which we can write, for example,

```
table[i].length
```

and even

```
table[i].name[j]
```

If we want to initialize array **table**, we can write, for example,

```
OBJECT table[2] = {{123, "Pencil", 12.3, 150.7},
                   {246, "Pen", 20.6, 147.0}};
```

As with arrays, we can omit the innermost braces and write

```
OBJECT table[2] = {123, "Pencil", 12.3, 150.7,
                   246, "Pen", 20.6, 147.0};
```

The former way of initializing is more logical and should therefore be preferred to the latter. It also enables us to omit trailing values for some array elements; for example, the **weight** and the **length** members of both **table[0]** and **table[1]** are given the initial value 0 if we write

```
OBJECT table[2] = {{123, "Pencil"},
                   {246, "Pen"}};
```

7.2 STRUCTURES AND FUNCTIONS

In ANSI C, entire structures can be used as function arguments. Alternatively, we can use only their start addresses as arguments, which may be more efficient, because it is to be expected that copying a whole structure takes more time than copying only its address. In the original version of C, only the latter method was available. We will discuss this first, and use the newer method (which also has some advantages) later. Throughout this section, we will again use the type **OBJECT**, defined as

```
typedef
struct
{ int code;
  char name[20];
  float weight, length;
} OBJECT;
```

Addresses as arguments and return values

To keep our discussion as simple as possible, we will use a very unrealistic function, **increaselength,** which increases the **length** member of our structure variables, in such a way that the call **increaselength(&s, increment)**, shown below, has the effect of **s.length + = increment:**

```
void increaselength(OBJECT *p, float d)
{ (*p).length += d;
}
...
increaselength(&s, increment);
```

In the function **increaselength** the parameter **p** is a local pointer variable, which is given the address of **s** as its initial value when the call shown above is executed. As usual, we write ***p** for the object pointed to by **p**. In our case, this is structure **s**, so that we need a dot and a member name (**.length**) after ***p**. Since the dot is an operator with higher precedence than the unary operator *****, we must enclose ***p** in parentheses. As this situation occurs very frequently, a more convenient and clearer notation is available: we can replace

```
(*p).length
```

with

```
p -> length
```

As we have seen, the use of a structure address (**&s**) as an argument, which acts as the initial value of the corresponding pointer parameter (**p**), is very efficient. It also has the advantage that we can modify the structure (**s**) the address of which is given as an argument. Incidentally, we can also apply the 'address of' operator to a *member* of a structure, so increasing the **length** member could also be done by means of

```
void increase1(float *pf, float d)
{ *pf += d;
}
...
increase1(&s.length, increment);
```

Since the dot has higher precedence than **&**, we should read **&s.length** as **&(s.length)**.

We can also use addresses of structures as *return values*. Again, this works with any C compiler (whereas the possibility of returning whole structures, to be discussed shortly, is new in ANSI C). Suppose that we want to write (and use) a function, **newcopy,** to create a new structure of type OBJECT and to fill it with the content of a structure the address of which is given as an argument. The address of the created structure is the value to be returned by **newcopy**. We can do this as follows:

```
#include <stdlib.h>

OBJECT *newcopy(OBJECT *p)
{ OBJECT *pobj;
  pobj = malloc(sizeof(OBJECT));
  if (pobj == NULL) {printf("Not enough memory"); exit(1);}
  *pobj = *p;
  return pobj;
}

OBJECT *pobject, s, ...;
...
pobject = newcopy(&s);
```

This example offers a good opportunity to discuss a serious programming error, which occurs in the following, incorrect version:

```
OBJECT *newcopy(OBJECT *p)
{ OBJECT obj;
  obj = *p;
  return &obj;  /* Error */
}
```

This error is serious because it is not reported by the compiler but leads to problems only when the program is executed. As we know, an automatic variable exists only as long as the function in which it is defined is being executed. In this example, memory for **obj** is automatically allocated when **newcopy** is entered and released when it is left. This means that in the function in which **newcopy** is called, after that call, the memory occupied by **obj** a short while ago may already be in use for other purposes, although its start address is still available! (This is similar to entering a house the key of which was given to us some time ago by the previous owner who no longer lives there.) One way of avoiding any possibility of making such mistakes is by copying the entire structure instead of only its address, as we will discuss now.

Entire structures as arguments and return values

In ANSI C, it is also possible to use structures themselves as arguments and return values. Remember, this involves copying these structures, which may take more time than copying only their addresses. Yet this method may sometimes be useful and is not always inefficient. Let us again begin with a very simple example. Using the variables **s** and **t** of our structure type **OBJECT**, we replace the two statements

```
t = s;
t.length *= 2;
```

with one call to the function **longerobj**:

```
OBJECT s, t;
...
OBJECT longerobj(OBJECT obj)
{ obj.length *= 2;
  return obj;
}
...
t = longerobj(s);
```

Here a copy of **s** is assigned to **obj**, which in the function **longerobj** is used as a local variable: modifying **obj.length** does not alter the argument **s**. Then the modified structure **obj** is returned and again copied when assigned to **t**. The method used here is convenient because it deals with new types, such as **OBJECT**, in the same way as it would with standard types.

We will now use a more interesting example, which will appeal to you if you are familiar with complex numbers.

We can regard complex numbers as number pairs (a, b), on which the four algebraic operations addition, subtraction, multiplication, and division are defined. We write (a, b) as $a + bi$, and define the sum and product of two complex numbers as follows:

$$(a + bi) + (c + di) \quad = \quad (a + c) + (b + d)i$$
$$(a + bi)(c + di) \quad = \quad ac - bd + (ad + bc)i$$

It follows from this product definition that it makes sense to write $i = \sqrt{-1}$, since we have

$$i^2 = (0 + 1i)(0 + 1i) = 0 - 1 + (0 + 0)i = -1$$

It is very usual and convenient to use single symbols (often z) for complex numbers and to regard them as single objects rather than as pairs of real numbers. The C language offers excellent facilities to do this. After defining type **complex** by means of

```
typedef struct {float Re, Im;} complex;
```

we can write

```
complex z1, z2, zs, zp;
```

By far the most convenient way, available in ANSI C, to write statements for computing the sum **zs** and the product **zp** of the complex numbers **z1** and **z3** is

```
zs = sum(z1, z2);
zp = prod(z1, z2);
```

This is possible only by means of functions that have (entire) structures as arguments and return values:

```
complex sum(complex z, complex w)
{ complex s;
  s.Re = z.Re + w.Re;
  s.Im = z.Im + w.Im;
  return s;
}

complex prod(complex z, complex w)
{ complex p;
  p.Re = z.Re * w.Re - z.Im * w.Im;
  p.Im = z.Im * w.Re + z.Re * w.Im;
  return p;
}
```

It will now be clear that using entire structures as arguments and return values can be much more convenient than using addresses and pointers, as was necessary in the original version of C.

Dynamic data structures

Since structure members can have any type, they can be pointers to other
structures that are of the same type as those they are members of. This is the
case, for example, with structures of the following type:

```
struct element {int num; struct element *p;};
```

Such structures, combined with dynamic memory allocation, offer very interesting
new possibilities. They enable us to create objects dynamically, each containing
one or more pointers to similar objects, also created dynamically, and so on. The
new aspect of such *dynamic data structures* is that the objects in question are
variables that have no names by which we can have access to them. Instead, they
are accessed by following chains of pointers. Examples of dynamic data structures
are *linear lists* and *binary trees*. We will discuss these in Sections 9.4 and 9.5,
respectively.

7.3 UNIONS

With structures, all members are in memory at the same time, so the amount of
memory used by a structure is at least equal to the sum of the amounts of
memory used by its members. In contrast to this, there are also *unions*, the
notation of which in our programs is very similar to that of structures. However,
union members overlay each other. The amount of memory a union takes is only
as large as that of its largest member, which implies that there is only one
member actually present at a time. For example, after writing

```
union intflo {int i; float x;} u;
```

we can use **u.i** and **u.x**, in the same way as if the above keyword **union** were
replaced with **struct**. However, the members **i** and **x** share memory space, so by
executing

```
u.i = 123;
u.x = 98.7;
```

the second statement destroys the value just assigned to **u.i**. Unions can be useful
if we want to store only one of their members. In that case, they are more

economical with memory space, especially if they are elements of an array. However, it is the programmer's responsibility to remember which of the members have been used. One way of realizing this is to use a structure of two members: a 'flag' and a union, the flag being a code for the current member choice in the union. For example, we can write

```
struct {char flag; union {int i; float x;} num;} a[1000];
...
a[i].flag = 'I'; a[i].num.i = 123;
a[j].flag = 'F'; a[j].num.x = 98.7;
...
if (a[k].flag == 'I') printf("Integer value: %d", a[k].num.i); else
if (a[k].flag == 'F') printf("Float value:   %f", a[k].num.x); else
                      printf("Unknown flag");
```

7.4 BIT FIELDS

Normally, the smallest unit of memory used for variables is one byte. However, it is possible for structures to have members that are smaller than one byte. As their sizes are expressed in bits, they are called *bit fields*. In the following example we have a structure **s**, with bit fields **b4**, **b1**, **b2**, consisting of 4, 1, and 2 bits, respectively. Besides, there is a **char** member **ch**:

```
struct example
{ unsigned b4:4, b1:1, b2:2;
  char ch;
} s;
```

Bit fields are similar to other structure members, with one exception: since several of them may be located in the same byte, we cannot uniquely identify them by their addresses, and we must therefore not apply the 'address of' operator & to them. We can write

```
s.b4 = 7;
```

which implies that **s.b4** is an *lvalue* (discussed in Section 6.5), but, unlike other lvalues, it must not be preceded by the unary operator **&**.

Exercises

7.1   Write a program that reads in the names and the ages of ten people. Store these data in structures, which are array elements. Compute the average of the given ages. Also, produce a table of ten lines, with on each line the given age of a person along with the (positive or negative) deviation of that person's age from the average age. Use a character array of 31 bytes for each name. Because of the null character at the end, this means that at most the first 30 characters of names are stored; any remaining characters are ignored.

7.2   The same as Exercise 7.1, but this time the names may be longer than 30 positions. In each structure, not the name itself but rather a pointer to a character sequence is to be stored. Use **malloc** each time a name is to be stored. In spite of the fact that names may be very long, this method is efficient with memory space. You may, however, assume all name lengths to be less than 100 and use one character array of length 100 as a 'buffer'. Each name is first placed into this buffer and then copied to the area allocated by **malloc**.

7.3   Use structures to store rational numbers. Each rational number p/q is represented by a structure, the members of which are the integers p and q. Write a program that reads two rational numbers p_1/q_1 and p_2/q_2 and computes their sum, difference, product and quotient. The two rational numbers are entered on the keyboard as four integers. Check q_1 and q_2 for being nonzero. The quotient is to be computed only if $p_2 \neq 0$. Consult Exercise 5.4 for the computation of the greatest common divisor of two integers. Use this before the addition and subtraction to find a common denominator and after it to simplify the computed sum and difference. Use a function for each of the four arithmetic operations.

CHAPTER 8

Input and Output

8.1 INTRODUCTION

There are no special statements in the C language for input and output (I/O). Instead, we use standard library functions, such as **scanf** and **printf**. Although we have already used these two functions very often, they still present some possibilities worth discussing, so we will look at them in more detail in this chapter. Then we will extend the subject of this chapter in various directions:

- Input from and output to files (on disk)
- Unformatted I/O
- Random access.

At the top of any program module that uses the *standard I/O* facilities discussed in this chapter, we write the line

```
#include <stdio.h>
```

Not only does the header file **stdio.h** declare functions, but it also contains other useful information, such as the definitions of macros. Before dealing with **scanf** and **printf**, we will first have a look at the two macros **getchar** and **putchar**, defined in **stdio.h**. The macro call

```
putchar(ch);
```

writes the character (stored in the variable) **ch** to the video screen. Analogously, we can read a character from the keyboard by writing

```
ch = getchar();
```

Many operating systems, such as UNIX and MS-DOS, enable us to use **getchar** also for reading a character from a file (on disk) by means of a facility called *redirection*. For example, if our program is called COMPUTE and we want to

147

read something from the file MYDATA1 by means of **getchar** (or **scanf**) when using an operating system with the redirection facility, we can start that program as follows:

```
COMPUTE <MYDATA1
```

Analogous to < for input, we can use the character > for redirection with output. For example, **putchar** in program COMPUTE writes characters to the file MYDATA2 instead of to the video screen if we start this program as follows:

```
COMPUTE >MYDATA2
```

We can also redirect both input and output, which in our example can by done by typing

```
COMPUTE <MYDATA1 >MYDATA2
```

Because of this possibility of redirection, it is customary to say that **getchar** and **scanf** read data from the *standard input stream*, named **stdin**, rather than 'from the keyboard' as we have said so far. Analogously, **putchar** and **printf** write data to the *standard output stream* **stdout**, rather than 'to the video display'. The names **stdin** and **stdout** do not often occur in our program text. However, in Section 8.4 we will see that we can use these names explicitly.

We have not yet discussed how, when using **getchar** with redirection, we can detect the end of the input file, nor have we mentioned the type of the variable **ch** in our example. We will now deal with these two points at the same time because they are related to each other. If the type returned by **getchar** were **char**, the only way of signalling 'end of file' would be to reserve one of the 256 possible values of **char** for this purpose. It would then not be possible to read arbitrary files, in which all possible bytes might occur as real data. Therefore a different approach has been taken. The value returned by **getchar** has type **int**, and in case of 'end of file' this return value is equal to a symbolic constant **EOF** (in **stdio.h** normally defined as −1); in all other cases **getchar** returns the value of the byte that has been read. The latter value is nonnegative and less than 256. In most cases, these values are even less than 128, as the ASCII table in Appendix B shows. Do not confuse these character values with numbers to be read. For example, the number 13 is represented externally by the two characters, 1 and 3. You should not expect **getchar** to read these in one call and return the value 13. Instead, two calls to **getchar** could be used, the first returning ´1´ = 49, the second ´3´ = 51 (see Appendix B). Of course, if we want to read some digits such as 1 and 3 and to store the value (13) of the number they represent into the **int** variable **i**, this should be done as follows:

```
scanf("%d", &i)
```

As for **getchar**, it will now be clear that it makes sense to use type **int** for the variable **ch**, although at first sight type **char** might seem more logical:

```
#include <stdio.h>
...
int ch;
...
while (ch = getchar(), ch != EOF)
{ ...   /* Use ch as if it had been of type 'char' */
}
```

Recall that conversion from type **int** to type **char** does not cause any problems. For example, it would be correct to write **str[i] = ch** in the above loop with **ch** of type **int** and **str[i]** of type **char**.

Although **putchar** differs from **getchar** in that we often use it as if it were a 'void' function, it actually returns a value of type **int**, which is equal to the argument **ch** or to **EOF** in case of an output error. Thanks to the close relationship between the types **char** and **int**, the argument of **putchar** can be of type **char**, if we like, in which case it is converted to type **int**.

The fact that **getchar** and **putchar** are macros makes it essential for the header file **stdio.h** to be included: if we omit the **#include** line for this file, the compiler will assume **getchar** and **putchar** to be functions, defined in another module. Later, the linker will search the standard library for these functions and fail to find them. Consequently, there will be an error message about the missing 'functions' **getchar** and **putchar** from the linker, not from the compiler. In contrast to this, the linker would not complain about **scanf** and **printf**, because these are real functions and can be found. Still, it is good practice to include **stdio.h** even in programs that use only the latter two I/O functions. (Note that including or omitting header files does not affect the way the linker searches for functions in the library.)

8.2 THE FUNCTION PRINTF

We use **printf** for formatted output to the stream **stdout**. As we have seen in the last section, **stdout** normally corresponds to the video screen. We often speak about 'printing' rather than 'writing to **stdout**'. A call to **printf** has the form

```
printf(format-string, arg1, arg2, ...)
```

in which the format string can be followed by any number of arguments. (Variable-length argument lists, as used here, will be discussed in Section 9.1.) Although **printf** is often used as a 'void' function, it returns a value, which is normally equal to the number of characters that are written. In case of an error, the return value is negative.

As discussed in Section 6.4, the format string is passed to **printf** in the form of an address. For example, in

```
printf("Temperature: %4.1f degrees centigrade.", temp);
```

the address of the first character, **T**, is passed to **printf**, and this function itself can determine the length of the string because of the null character, internally stored at its end. The fact that an address is passed as an argument explains that the first argument of **printf** can have other forms that also result in addresses. Examples are the name of an array in which a format string is stored, and a conditional expression, as in:

```
char fstr[80] = "If x = %f and y = %f, then z is ";
float x, y, z;
...
printf(fstr, x, y);
printf(z < 0 ? "negative." : z > 0 ? "positive." : "zero.");
```

The format-string can contain two kinds of objects:

- Characters to be printed literally
- Conversion specifications.

There must be a conversion specification for each of the arguments *arg*1, *arg*2, and so on. Each conversion specification begins with % and ends with a *conversion character*. There may be something, such as a 'precision', between these two characters. Let us start with the conversion characters themselves:

d   The (**int**) argument is converted to decimal representation. (Instead of **d**, we may use **i** with the same meaning.)

o   The (**int**) argument is converted to octal representation, without a leading zero.

x   The (**int**) argument is converted to hexadecimal representation, without a prefix **0x**. In addition to the digits **0**, ..., **9**, the lower case letters **a**, ..., **f** are used. We can also write **X** instead of **x**, with the effect that capital letters **A**, ..., **F** are used instead of lower case letters.

u   The (**int** or **unsigned**) argument is converted to 'unsigned' decimal representation. This implies that the leftmost bit of the argument is used as a value bit, not as a sign bit.

c   The (**char** or **int**) argument is (or is interpreted as) a single character.

s   The argument is a string, or, technically, the address of the first element of a character array. The characters starting at this address are printed until a null character is reached or until as many characters have been printed as indicated by the precision (between % and s).

f   The (**float** or **double**) argument is converted to decimal representation of the form $[-]mmm.dddddd$, in which the default precision (that is, the number of digits d in the form just mentioned) is 6. The result is neatly rounded. If we use **0** as a precision, the decimal point is suppressed.

e   The (**float** or **double**) argument is converted to decimal representation of the form $[-]m.dddddd\mathrm{e}\pm xx$, in which the number of digits d is given by the precision (between % and e). The default precision is 6. If we write **0** as a precision, the decimal point is suppressed. If we write **E** instead of **e**, then **E** instead of **e** appears in the output.

g   The (**float** or **double**) argument is converted by means of %f or %e (or %E if we write **G** instead of **g**). In most cases, %f will be used; %e (or %E) is used if the exponent is either less than −4 or greater than the given precision. Neither a point at the end nor any trailing zeros are printed.

p   The argument must have a pointer type, that is, it must be an address. This address is printed in a system-dependent way.

n   The argument must be the address of an integer variable. The number of characters printed so far by the current call to **printf** is placed into that variable. (Nothing is printed.)

%   This is not really a conversion character, and there is no corresponding argument. We simply write %% if we want to include the character % in the output.

Between % and the conversion character, we can insert:

1. 'Flags' (in any order):

    −   The converted argument is left aligned in the positions that are available. (Normally, we do not want this for numerical output, but we do for strings.)

    +   The number being printed is preceded by a plus sign if it is positive and by a minus sign it is negative. (Without this flag, a negative number is preceded by a minus sign but a positive one is not by a plus sign.)

    Blank If a plus or minus sign is omitted, there is a blank instead. (We use the term *blank* for a *space character*.)

    0   Numbers are padded with zeros (not with blanks) on the left.

    #   An alternative form is used. This form depends on the conversion character as follows. With o, the first digit is 0. With x or X, there is a prefix 0x or 0X if the value is unequal to zero. With e, E, f, g, and G, a decimal point always appears in the output; with g and G trailing zeros are printed.

2. A number (written as a sequence of decimal digits), indicating the *field width*. The converted argument is printed in a field of that width or more if more positions are needed. Any room not needed is padded on the left, or, in case of the '− flag', on the right. The padding character is a blank, or, in case of the '0 flag', it is 0. See also the remark below.

3. A period, which separates the field width (see 2.) from the precision (see 4.).

4. A number (written as a sequence of decimal digits), indicating the *precision*. In the case of a string, this is the maximum number of characters to be printed. With f, e, E, it is the number of digits printed after the decimal point; with g and G, it is the number of significant digits. In case of an integer, it is the minimum number of digits to be printed, with leading zeros, if needed. See also the remark below.

5. A 'length modifier' h, l or L. We use h if the argument is **short** or **unsigned short**, l if it is **long** or **unsigned long**, and L if it is **long double**.

Remark:

We can write an asterisk (*****) for the field width (see 2.) and/or for the precision (see 4.). If we do, the argument in question must be preceded by one or two special arguments (depending on whether one or two asterisks are being used). These additional arguments must be of type **int**, and their numerical values are taken as the field width and the precision, respectively.

In the following program, the value of **x** is printed with both the field width and the precision given by special arguments, while **k** has only one special argument, used for its width:

```
#include <stdio.h>

main()
{ int width=5, precision=2, k=1234;
  double x=9.87654321;
  printf("x =%*.*f   k =%*d\n", width, precision, x, width, k);
}
```

The output of this program is:

```
x = 9.88   k = 1234
```

8.3 THE FUNCTION SCANF

We use **scanf** for input from **stdin**, which, as discussed in Section 8.1, usually corresponds to the keyboard. A call to this function has the following form:

scanf(*format-string*, *arg*1, *arg*2, ...)

Actually, **scanf** expects an address as its first argument, in the same way as **printf** does. The arguments that follow, *arg*1, *arg*2, ... are also addresses: they tell where the data items that are read are to be placed.

The return value of **scanf** is equal to the number of data items that have been read and assigned to variables, or to **EOF** if nothing could be read because we were reading from a file the end of which was encountered. (In Section 8.1 we have seen that **stdin** can be redirected to read data from a file.)

The format string contains conversion specifications, each of which starts with **%** and ends with a conversion character. The following conversion characters can be used with **scanf**:

d   The input is a decimal integer and the corresponding argument has type **int ***. (The latter notation means 'pointer to int'.)

i   The input is an integer in decimal, octal, or hexadecimal representation. For example, 19 is decimal, 023 octal, and 0x13 hexadecimal. The argument has type **int ***.

o   The input is an octal integer, with or without leading 0. The argument
            is **int ***.

u   The input is an unsigned integer: it cannot be negative, but, on the
            other hand, its value can be about twice as large as that of type **int**.
            The argument has type **unsigned int ***.

x   The input is a hexadecimal integer, with or without a prefix 0x or 0X.
            The argument has type **int ***.

c   The input consists of a character sequence, the length of which is given
            by the precision (between % and **c**); if no precision is given, only one
            character is read. In contrast to the other conversion specifications, the
            character being read can be a white-space character (unless %c is
            preceded by a blank). No null character is added at the end. The
            argument has type **char ***.

s   As with numeric input data, any leading white-space characters are
            skipped. Then all characters are read, either until as many have been
            read as indicated by the precision or until a white-space character
            follows. A null character is added at the end. The argument has type
            char * and must be the start address of an area large enough to store
            all characters read, including the null character.

f   The input consists of a number, represented as a floating-point or an
            integer constant, and possibly preceded by a sign. The argument has
            type **float ***. Instead of **f**, we may write **e** or **g**.

p   The input is an address, as printed by **printf("%p",...)**. The argument
            is the address of a pointer (to any type).

n   The number of characters read so far in the current call to **scanf** is
            stored in the variable the address of which is given by the argument.
            The argument has type **int ***. Nothing is read.

[···]   Characters are read only as far as they occur between these brackets.
            The first character not belonging to this set terminates reading and is
            considered not to be read. A null character is added at the end. The
            argument has type **char ***. (The set of characters between the brackets
            must not be empty; this convention makes it possible to recognize the
            first] in []···] as a character that belongs to the set.)

[^···] As [···], except that now characters are read that do *not* occur
            between the brackets.

The following example illustrates how %n and %[···] work. First, all characters different from the five characters . , ; ? ! are read and stored in array **str**. Then one more character is read (which can only be one of the five characters just mentioned) and stored in the variable **ch**. The total number of characters read is stored in the variable **n**:

```
#include <stdio.h>

main()
{ int n;
  char str[80], ch;
  scanf("%[^.,;?!]%c%n", str, &ch, &n);
  printf("str=%s  ch=%c  n=%d\n", str, ch, n);
}
```

Executing this program and typing

```
ANSI C!
```

as input data gives the following output:

```
str=ANSI C  ch=!  n=7
```

Between % and the conversion character there can be

- An asterisk (*); a data item is skipped in the input stream, that is, it is read but not assigned to a variable. There must be no argument corresponding to the conversion specification in question.

- A number (written as a sequence of decimal digits) indicating the maximum field width. This is particularly useful when we are reading strings, because it enables us to prevent 'array overflow' in case more characters are read than the data area in which they are stored permits. For example, in

```
  char str[10];
  scanf("%9s", str);
```

not more than nine characters will be read; with the null character at the end, at most ten array elements of **str** will be used, as is permitted.

One of the letters **l** (to be used for the types **double *** and **long ***), **L** (for type **long double ***), and **h** (for type **short ***). For example, the letter **l** must precede the conversion characters **f**, **e**, and **g**, if the argument has type 'pointer to double', as is the case in

```
double xx;
scanf("%lf", &xx);
```

Writing **"%f"** here would be a very serious error: the compiler would not detect this, but things would go wrong during program execution. With an argument of type **long double ***, we would need **%Lf**. Similarly, the letter **l** must precede the conversion characters **d, i, n, o, u,** and **x,** if the argument is **long ***, and the letter **h** must precede them if it is **short ***.

With **printf**, it is quite usual to include text other than conversion specifications in format strings. This is done far less often with **scanf**, because such text is not printed but expected in the input! For example, in

```
scanf("%d/%d/%d", &day, &month, &year);
```

the slashes in the format string force the user to separate the numerical values for **day, month,** and **year** by slashes, as in

```
31/12/1989
```

Since **%d** permits the data items to be preceded by white-space characters, the input can also have other forms, such as

```
31/     12/
1989
```

However, in the input data, white-space characters must not precede the slashes. If we want them to be permitted, we must write at least one blank immediately before the slashes in the format string. (We may as well write blanks following the slashes to make the format string more readable, although this has no effect.) The following call to **scanf** is therefore more practical:

```
scanf("%d / %d / %d", &day, &month, &year);
```

For example, it accepts the following input:

```
31    /   12/1990
```

Note that the presence of blanks in the format-string does not oblige us to enter corresponding blanks in the input, as the final part, **12/1990**, in this example illustrates.

Blanks in the format string are particularly important in combination with **%c**. If the input data

```
123    A
```

is read by

```
scanf("%d %c", &n, &ch);
```

then the character **A** is stored in the variable **ch**. However, if it is read by

```
scanf("%d%c", &n, &ch);
```

(in which there is no blank between **%d** and **%c**), then, after reading 123, the first character that follows is read and stored in **ch**. In our example, this is a blank.

When we are using **scanf** (or **getchar**) to read data from the keyboard, program execution resumes only after we have pressed the Enter key, or, in other words, after we have entered a newline character. Although obviously the computer has 'seen' this newline character, it is considered not to have been read yet. In most cases this will not cause any trouble in any call to **scanf** that follows because the latter will skip over leading white-space characters. However, that will not be the case if **%c** is used, unless this conversion specification is preceded by a white-space character. Therefore the blank in the format string on the fourth line of the following program fragment is by no means superfluous:

```
printf("Enter an integer: ");
scanf("%d", &n);
printf("Enter a character: ");
scanf(" %c", &ch);
```

Note that you cannot skip over the newline character following the integer by replacing the second of these program lines with

```
scanf("%d\n", &n); /* Error */
```

If you try this, you will notice that **\n** (or, in general, a white-space character) at the end of the format string has a very undesirable effect. This white-space character in the format string is interpreted as a command to skip over any white-space characters in the input, until a different character is entered. This means that after entering an integer and pressing the Enter key, the machine will wait until a different character is entered and the Enter key is pressed again. (Recall that the latter is usual: only when the Enter key is pressed is the input, as far as needed by the program, actually processed.) Although all this is already very unpleasant, things may even be worse if there are subsequent calls to **scanf** (or to **getchar**), for then all these additional characters entered are still available in the input stream and will therefore turn up when we may not want them.

8.4 FILES

As we have seen in Section 8.1, some operating systems offer the facility of *redirection*, by which we can read from and write to files on disk, using functions (and macros) that are normally associated with the keyboard and the video display. We will now discuss other means for using files, because:

1. We often want to use more than one file for input or output and to use the keyboard or the video display as well.
2. It may be undesirable for the user to start programs in the somewhat complicated way as discussed in Section 8.1.
3. Not all operating systems support redirection.

The header file **stdio.h** contains a program fragment of the following form:

```
typedef struct { ... } FILE;
```

The type **FILE**, defined in this way, is used in **stdio.h** for some function declarations, such as:

```
FILE *fopen(const char *filename, const char *mode);
int fclose(FILE *fp);
```

Although we need not write these declarations ourselves, seeing them makes it easier for us to understand programs that deal with files. We begin with a very simple one. It writes the integers 1, 2, ···, 10, each in two positions and followed by a newline character, in the file **num.txt**. If a file with this name already exists, its old contents are erased; if not, a new file with that name is created:

```
/* OUTNUM: This program writes the integers 1, 2, ..., 10
           in the file num.txt.
*/
#include <stdio.h>

main()
{ FILE *fp;
  int i;
  fp = fopen("num.txt", "w");
  for (i=1; i<=10; i++) fprintf(fp, "%2d\n", i);
  fclose(fp);
}
```

As mentioned above, the identifier **FILE** is defined in **stdio.h** as the name of a certain structure type. In our program, we declare a pointer to an object of this type by means of

```
FILE *fp;
```

With standard I/O all input and output operations are performed by means of a special kind of pointers, called *file pointers*, or *streams*. The variable **fp** is an example of such a file pointer. Initially, its value is undefined, and we assign a value to it by means of

```
fp = fopen("num.txt", "w");
```

The function **fopen** creates a structure of type **FILE** (in the same way as **malloc** would do this) and stores appropriate initial values in it. It also returns its start address, so that we can assign this to **fp**. We say that the function **fopen** *opens* a file (or a 'stream'). Its first argument, **"num.txt"** is the name of the file on disk. There are several possibilities for its second argument; they are all based on those which, together with their meanings, are given below:

"r"	'Read'.	The file must already exist and will be used for input.
"w"	'Write'.	If the file already exists, its old contents are erased; if not, the file is created. The file will be used for output.
"a"	'Append'.	If the file already exists, new data will be added at its end. Otherwise, **"a"** works like **"w"**.

After calling **fopen** and assigning its return value to **fp** in our example, we use the latter variable as the first argument of **fprintf**. This function is similar to the well-known function **printf**, except for this first argument, which indicates the output stream to be used.

Note that, although we say that we are writing integers, actually *characters* are written. For example, in our first call to **fprintf**, a blank, the character ´1´, and a newline character are written to the file **num.txt**. We can format data written to this file in the same way as with files written to the video screen, and we therefore speak about *formatted* output and about *text files*.

The function **fclose** does the opposite of **fopen**: the file is *closed*, which means that the structure of type **FILE** is released (in the same way as **free** releases memory), and, in the case of output, the 'buffer is flushed'. To understand what the latter means, we should know that for reasons of efficiency output is normally buffered so that the drive of the disk we are writing to need not be activated each time we perform output operations in our program. We often omit calls to **fclose**, since files are automatically closed when a program terminates in the normal way. For the sake of completeness, it should be mentioned that **fclose** returns a value of type **int**, namely 0 if it succeeds and EOF (see Section 8.1) if it fails.

We will now discuss a program that reads the file **num.txt**, written by our last program, OUTNUM, to compute the sum of the integers in this file. This program would not be very interesting if we made it suitable only for files with exactly ten integers. Instead, we will make the program more general and more realistic: it will work for any text file which contains integers separated by white-space characters. If it encounters an invalid character, such as a letter, it will print an error message and the sum computed so far. If this happens, the rest of the input file will be ignored:

```
/* INNUM: This program reads integers from the file num.txt
          and computes their sum. It terminates as soon as
          an invalid character is encountered or the end of the
          file is reached.
*/
#include <stdio.h>
#include <stdlib.h>

main()
{ FILE *fp;
  int sum=0, x;
  fp = fopen("num.txt", "r");
  if (fp == NULL)
  { printf("File num.txt not available.\n");
    exit(1);
  }
  while (fscanf(fp, "%d", &x) == 1) sum += x;
  printf("The sum is: %d\n", sum);
  if (!feof(fp))
  { printf("Invalid character read.\n");
  }
  fclose(fp);
}
```

Note the second argument, **"r"**, of **fopen**. In this case it is very desirable to verify if the attempt to open the file has been successful. This is done for **fopen** in the same way as for **malloc**, as discussed in Section 6.6: each of these functions returns the value NULL if it fails to perform its task properly. In case of success, the return value is an address, which is different from NULL. In program OUTNUM we have not tested the value returned by **fopen** because for a file to be opened with "w" it may or may not exist. (Opening a file for output may fail only in rather unlikely circumstances, such as with an existing file for which we have no permission to write to; if this can happen, it would, of course, be wise to include the test under discussion.) An attempt to open a file with **"r"** will fail if the file does not exist. As this is by no means a far-fetched possibility, it is wise to include a test on the value returned by **fopen** whenever this function is used for an input file: it would be a very serious error if a call to **fscanf** (or to **fprintf**) took place with NULL as its first argument. The conditional statement (consisting of four lines) immediately after opening the file **num.txt** in program INNUM will now be clear.

The return value of **fscanf** (like that of **scanf**) is equal to the number of data items that have been read and assigned to variables. In our example this value should be 1. If the attempt to read an integer fails, **fscanf** returns either 0 or **EOF** (see Section 8.1). The latter value is returned if we try to read beyond the end of the file. If we had excluded the possibility for the file to contain invalid characters, the line

```
while (fscanf(fp, "%d", &x) == 1) sum += x;
```

would have been sufficient to form the sum of all integers in the file. If there are, for example, ten integers in the file, the call to **fscanf** is executed eleven times, so we deliberately try to read beyond the end of the file. There is no risk of obtaining run-time error messages or similar problems. As soon as a call to **fscanf** is unsuccessful, this function no longer returns 1 and the while loop terminates. In case of a correct input file, the return value of **fscanf** is **EOF**. (Note that it would not be correct to omit the three characters $== 1$ in the above program line, because besides the alternative 0 there is also the possibility for **fscanf** to return EOF, which is normally equal to -1 and would therefore be interpreted as 'true' if used as a logical value.)

If we have to include the possibility of invalid characters, we can use **feof**, as we did in program INNUM. This is normally a macro (not a function) defined in **stdio.h**. If it were a function, it would be declared as follows:

```
int feof(FILE *fp);
```

The value returned by **feof** is 0 if the end of the file has not yet been reached and nonzero if it has. If we apply program INNUM to the file produced by program OUTNUM, the end of the file is reached; this means that **feof** returns a nonzero value and **!feof(fp)** is equal to 0. In this case the output is

```
The sum is: 55
```

It is instructive to apply a program editor (or a text processor) to the file **num.txt**, to verify that this file contains one column with the integers 1 to 10.

Inserting a letter just after the fifth line, for example, and running program
INNUM once again, will cause a failure in the attempt to read the sixth integer.
In that case **feof(fp)** is 0, so **!feof(fp)** is 1, and the output is

```
The sum is: 15
Invalid character read.
```

As you may have noticed, we do not really need **feof** in program INNUM,
because **fscanf**, when failing to read an integer, returns either **EOF** or 0. We
could therefore also have used the following method:

```
int sum=0, x, code;
...
while ((code = fscanf(fp, "%d", &x)) == 1) sum += x;
printf("The sum is: %d\n", sum);
if (code != EOF) {printf("Invalid character read.\n");}
```

Reading and writing single characters

Using **EOF** is perhaps more natural when we are reading one character at a
time. Program COPYTEXT copies a text file: the file names are passed to this
program as program arguments, discussed in Section 6.9. For example, if we
want to copy file AAA to file BBB, we can write

```
COPYTEXT AAA BBB
```

Note the difference with redirection: we do not write **<AAA** and **>BBB** here.
Although we could use the functions **fscanf** and **fprintf** with format string "%c",
we prefer the elementary macros **getc** and **putc** in this case for reasons of
efficiency. These macros are similar to **getchar** and **putchar**, but they take a file
pointer as an (additional) argument. Note that with **putc** this argument is the
second. For example, we can write

```
ch = getc(fp); putc(ch, fp);
```

Program COPYTEXT shows clearly how to test for the end of the file. We will
discuss this subject in more detail after having a look at the complete program:

```
/* COPYTEXT: This program copies a text file.
             Usage: COPYTEXT source destination
*/
#include <stdio.h>
#include <stdlib.h>

main(int argc, char *argv[])
{ int ch;
  FILE *fpin, *fpout;
  if (argc != 3)
  { printf("Type COPYTEXT, followed by a source and a destination.\n");
    exit(1);
  }
  fpin = fopen(argv[1], "r");
  fpout = fopen(argv[2], "w");
  if (fpin == NULL || fpout == NULL)
  { printf("Can't read from %s or write to %s.\n", argv[1], argv[2]);
    exit(1);
  }
  while ((ch = getc(fpin)) != EOF) putc(ch, fpout);
  fclose(fpin); fclose(fpout);
}
```

The core of this program is the while statement on the third line from the bottom. Repeatedly, a character **ch** is read by **getc** and written by **putc**. When the end of the input file is encountered, the call **getc(fpin)** fails and the value it returns is **EOF**. We have discussed in Section 8.1 why **ch** must have type **int** instead of type **char**.

Note that **getc**, like **getchar**, reads only one character, not an integer that may consist of several characters as type **int** might suggest. Another common misconception is the idea of **EOF** being a character actually read from the file. This is not the case. When **getc** returns **EOF**, this simply means that nothing could be read.

After using **getc** to read a character **ch** from the stream **fp**, we can undo this by writing

```
ungetc(ch, fp);
```

This statement puts **ch** back in the input buffer so it is read next time. We can do this for only one character, as with a buffer of length 1. For the sake of completeness it should be mentioned that both **putc** and **ungetc** return an **int** value, equal to the character **ch** in question or to **EOF** in case of an error.

Reading and writing a whole line

It is important to realize that after declaring, for example,

```
char str[100];
```

we cannot read a whole line by means of

```
code = fscanf(fp, "%s", str);
```

because, first, this statement would skip all leading white-space characters, and, second, it would stop reading as soon as it encounters a blank. Instead of **fscanf**, we can use the function **fgets**, which, together with a similar function for output, is declared in **stdio.h** as follows:

```
char *fgets(char *s, int n, FILE *fp);
int fputs(const char *s, FILE *fp);
```

The function **fgets** stops reading when $n-1$ characters have been read or when a newline character has been read, whichever happens first. In the latter case, the newline character is also stored in the array **s**; in both cases a null character is stored at the end. The function **fputs** does not write a newline character other than the one that may occur at the end of the array **s** (which is likely if this array has been filled by **fgets**.) The value returned by **fgets** is the address given as its first argument, unless the end of the file has been reached; in that case **fgets** returns **NULL**. The function **fputs** returns a nonnegative value in case of success or **EOF** if an error occurs.

In our example, we can now write, for example,

```
code = fgets(str, 80, fp);
```

The streams stdin, stdout and stderr

Three file pointers, also called *streams*, are immediately available, so we can use them without declaring them and without using **fopen** to assign values to them. They are

stdin	('standard input')	for the keyboard;
stdout	('standard output')	for the video display;
stderr	('standard error output')	for the video display.

We can now understand how the macros **getchar** and **putchar** are defined in **stdio.h**:

```
#define getchar() getc(stdin)
#define putchar(c) putc((c), stdout)
```

For example, the macro call

```
putchar(ch);
```

is expanded by the preprocessor with the following result:

```
putc((ch), stdout);
```

You may have noticed that we have not discussed a function (or macro) **ungetchar**, which would relate to **getchar** as **ungetc** relates to **getc**. Curiously enough, it is not available. However, this is not a serious problem, because we can write

```
ungetc(ch, stdin);
```

Another possibility is to define a macro **ungetchar** of our own:

```
#define ungetchar(c) ungetc((c), stdin)
```

Now that we are familiar with the standard streams **stdin** and **stdout**, we revert to the functions **fgets** and **fputs**, discussed a short while ago. Although at first sight these may seem to be generalized versions of the functions **gets** and **puts**, discussed in Section 6.7, there are some essential differences, not only because of their numbers of parameters but, less apparent and therefore more dangerous, in the way they deal with newline characters. You may find this confusing when using both kinds of functions at the same time. Fortunately, the latter is not necessary. Suppose you want to read a line from the keyboard and you prefer **fgets** to **gets**. Then you can simply write, for example,

```
fgets(str, 80, stdin);
```

In contrast to **gets**, this call to **fgets** stores a newline character, if read, in the array **str**. Analogously, you can use the following call to write the line stored in **str** (with a newline character stored at the end) to the video display by means of

```
fputs(str, stdout);
```

Rewinding a file

So far we have used *sequential access*: reading and writing was done in the way a magnetic tape is used; after opening a file we have used it either only for input or only for output. We will see in Section 8.6 that there is another way of using files, called *random access*. Here we mention two simple but useful ways of reading and writing, which, although still belonging to sequential I/O, offer some interesting new possibilities. First, we can close a file and open it again in the same program. This enables us, after having written data to a file, to go back to its beginning and read the data we have written ourselves. This method has the effect of 'rewinding' combined with switching from output to input mode. If this mode is to remain the same, we can rewind the stream **fp** more quickly as follows:

```
rewind(fp);
```

The append mode

Another extension to normal sequential access is the *append mode*, with **"a"** as second argument of **fopen**. Suppose we want a program to implement a simple bulletin board: from time to time we want to add short messages to those that are already in the file **bulboard.txt**. If this file does not yet exist, it must be created. The following program can be used for this purpose:

```
/* BULBOARD: This program adds a line, entered on the keyboard to
             the file bulboard.txt. This file is created if it does
             not yet exist.
*/
#include <stdio.h>

main()
{ FILE *fp;
  char str[100];
  fp = fopen("bulboard.txt", "a");
  printf("Enter a one-line message:\n");
  fgets(str, 100, stdin);
  fputs(str, fp);
  fclose(fp);
}
```

8.5 'BINARY FILES'

The files discussed so far are so-called *text files*. They consist of variable-length lines of text and contain only characters. Examples of text files are C programs, as typed in by means of a program editor, and files with lines of numbers, such as, for example:

19 23
8

Not all files are used to store data in this way. For example, an object module, produced by a compiler, is a file which does not consist of characters and has no line structure. We call such files *binary* or *unformatted* files. Numbers, too, can be written to a file in the same (binary) format as they are stored in the computer's memory. For example, if we write the integer 19 in binary format to a file, it will not be represented by the two decimal digits 1 and 9 (possibly preceded by some blanks), but, if integers are two bytes long and each byte consists of eight bits, it is stored as the bit sequence

00000000 00010011

Note that a binary file consists of a sequence of bytes, as does a text file. Operating systems therefore normally do not distinguish between these two file types; we as users must make this distinction and remember which kind of type we are dealing with. We cannot simply print a binary file or load it with an editor as we do with text files.

To write data to binary files or to read data from them, some operating systems, such as MS-DOS, require the C programmer to add a **b** (short for binary) at the end of the second argument of **fopen**. Thus instead of **"r"**, **"w"**, **"a"**, or **"r+"**, **"w+"**, **"a+"**, to be discussed in the next section, we then write **"rb"**, **"wb"**, **"ab"**, **"r+b"**, **"w+b"**, and **"a+b"** as the second argument of **fopen**. Although not required by all operating systems, and therefore, in a sense, system dependent, adding this **b** is defined by the ANSI standard and therefore allowed by all C compilers that conform to this standard.

The rest of this discussion is not essential for you if you use the UNIX operating system. It is, however, if you use MS-DOS; when using **fopen** for binary files, you must use this letter **b** with this system, and it is worthwhile to know why.

As said before, every file consists of a sequence of bytes. Assuming that, as usually, a byte consists of eight bits, we can store 256 distinct bit sequences in a byte. Now the essential difference between a binary file and a text file is the fact that in the former all these 256 bit configurations can occur, while with text files some of them may be reserved for special purposes. For example, with MS-DOS the value 0x1A (or Ctrl-Z) in a text file will cause reading this file to terminate because it is interpreted as 'end of data'. In normal text files this value does not occur but in binary files it may occur because the bytes in such files can be part of purely binary coded integers of floating-point numbers, which in principle can have all kinds of bit configurations. If we try to read a binary file as a text file, as, for example, program COPYTEXT in the last section would do, the occurrence of byte value 0x1A would be used as an 'end of data' signal, which is clearly undesirable. This problem will not occur if we use the letter **b** in the second argument of **fopen**, as in

```
fp = fopen("binfile", "rb");
```

There is another problem, associated with going to the beginning of a new line. With MS-DOS, for example, there are in fact two characters to achieve this:

Carriage Return = 0x0D = 13
Line Feed   = 0x0A = 10

However, in the C language we use only one character, ´\n´ (= 0x0A = 10), to go to the beginning of a new line. Therefore, when our C program is writing this 'newline character', as it is called in C, actually the two byte values just mentioned are placed in the file, which is an exception to the rule that each character written by our program corresponds to one byte. Normally we do not have to bother about this phenomenon, because exactly its opposite occurs when we are reading from a text file: the two byte values 13 and 10 are read by, for example, a single call to **getc**, and the return value is ´\n´. All this is the case if **"w"** and **"r"** are used as the second argument of **fopen**. On the other hand, if we use **"wb"** instead of **"w"**, every call to **putc** writes only one byte, and, analogously, after using **"rb"** every call to **getc** reads only one byte. In Section 8.6, when discussing random access, we will read and write data items by specifying their exact positions in files. It will be clear that this can reasonably be done only if we can determine these positions in a transparent and reliable way, so with random access we will consistently use binary files.

Now that we know the effect **"rb"** and **"wb"**, we can use these modes not only for binary files, but also for text files, provided that we use two calls to **getc** and to **putc**, respectively, for each transition to a new line. We can now see that it makes sense to distinguish between text and binary *modes*, rather than between text and binary *files*: we can open *any* file in text mode with **"r"** and **"w"**, and in binary mode with **"rb"** and **"wb"**. Recall that it is not safe to use program COPYTEXT of Section 8.4 for binary files because of possible occurrences of byte values 0x1A (= Ctrl-Z), which might be seen as 'end of data'. However, there is a very simple remedy: we only have to replace **"r"** with **"rb"** and **"w"** with **"wb"**. These corrections are really advantageous, for although they make the program suitable for binary files, they do not affect its usefulness for text files! If the program counted how many bytes are copied, this count might be higher in the corrected program than in the original one, because of the different ways of dealing with newline characters.

This concludes our discussion about using the letter **b** in the second argument of **fopen**. As mentioned before, this subject may not be relevant to you if you work with UNIX, but it is if you want to use standard I/O with MS-DOS.

The functions fread and fwrite

Now that we know how to read (and copy) a given binary file, we will see how we can generate such files ourselves. Remember that data have the same format in binary files as in memory. For example, assuming that integers take two bytes, we know that after

```
int i=257;    /* or:  int i=0x0101; */
```

the two bytes that represent **i** contain the following bit sequence:

```
0000 0001 0000 0001
```

If we now use, for example,

```
fprintf(fp, "%5d", i);
```

then five bytes (two blanks and the digits 2, 5, and 7) are written to the file with file pointer **fp**. For some applications, the conversion from the given two bytes to those five bytes is by no means necessary: it would then be simpler and more efficient to write the two bytes that represent **i** without any alterations. This can be done as follows:

```
fwrite(&i, sizeof(int), 1, fp);
```

When we want to read these two bytes later, we use the analogous statement

```
fread(&i, sizeof(int), 1, fp);
```

The four arguments of **fwrite** and **fread** are, in this order:

1. The start address of the memory area that contains the data to be written by **fwrite** or of the area that is to contain the data read by **fread**.
2. The number of bytes needed for each of the data elements that are written or read (see also the next point).
3. The number of data elements (such as integers, float-values, and so on) to be written or read.
4. The file pointer that identifies the file.

In the above examples, only one integer is written or read, and its size can best be given by means of the operator **sizeof**, discussed in Section 3.2. Instead of only one integer, we can write or read quite large amounts of data, as, for example, in

```
typedef struct complicated { ... } COMPLICATED;
COMPLICATED table[1000];
...
fwrite(table, sizeof(COMPLICATED), 1000, fp);
```

The value returned by **fwrite** and **fread** is equal to the number of data elements that are written or read. If nothing can be written or read, these functions return the value 0.

We must realize that **fwrite** and **fread**, though efficient, deprive us of the possibility of using a normal editor or a printer to see what data the files in question contain. If we want this possibility very much, we may decide to use **fprintf** and **fscanf** (and text files) rather than **fwrite** and **fread** (and binary files) for this reason, especially if the consequent loss of efficiency is not serious. However, there is an important class of applications that require using **fwrite** and **fread** for a reason other than efficiency, as the next section shows.

8.6 RANDOM ACCESS

We use the term *random access*, also known as *direct access*, if we are reading or writing data somewhere in the middle of a file, at a given position, without the restriction that this position follows the one that was used the last time. With the opposite, sequential access, we always begin by reading or writing at the beginning of the file, then read or write the next data element, and so on. Besides using random access, we can also open a file in such a way that we can both read and write, which gives us the possibility of updating a file. For the latter, we must insert a **+** in the second argument of **fopen**. It is highly recommended to use random access only in connection with binary files, so that, in that argument, we also use the letter **b**, which must be placed at the end. The following new strings, used as the second argument of **fopen**, open a file for update in binary mode:

"**r+b**" Open an *existing* file for update: both reading and writing will be possible.

"**w+b**" Create a *new* file for update: after writing data to it we can read these data from the file. If the file already exists, its old contents are lost.

"**a+b**" Open a file for *append* and update: additional data can be written at the end of the file and then read and updated.

(If your operating system regards text mode and binary mode as identical, as is the case with UNIX, you can omit the letter **b** in these strings.)

The bytes of a file are numbered 0, 1, 2, ⋯ (so the third byte has number 2). We identify a byte position by means of the function **fseek**, which together with **ftell**, is declared in **stdio.h** as follows:

```
int fseek (FILE *fp, long offset, int fromwhere);
long ftell(FILE *fp);
```

The argument **fromwhere** is a code with 0, 1, and 2 as possible values. We may write them as symbolic constants, defined in **stdio.h** as shown below:

Name	Value	Meaning
SEEK_SET	0	Count from the beginning of the file
SEEK_CUR	1	Count from the current position
SEEK_END	2	Count from the end

In most cases we use **SEEK_SET** (or 0); in that case, **offset** is the absolute byte number (0L for the first byte, 1L for the second, and so on). When using **SEEK_END**, only negative **offset** values can identify existing bytes in the file.

The value returned by **fseek** is zero, unless something is wrong: it is nonzero in case of an error. We can therefore write

```
if (fseek(fp, position, SEEK_SET))
{ printf("Error in call to fseek");
  exit(1);
}
```

The function **ftell** returns the *current position*. Program LENGTH shows that we can use this function to determine the length of a file:

```
/* LENGTH: This program determines the length of a file.
*/
#include <stdio.h>

main()
{ FILE *fp;
  char filename[51];
  printf("File name: "); scanf("%50s", filename);
  fp = fopen(filename, "r+b");
  if (fp != NULL)
  { fseek(fp, 0L, SEEK_END);
    printf("Length: %ld bytes.\n", ftell(fp));
    fclose(fp);
  } else printf("File does not exist.\n");
}
```

This program illustrates that **0L** as second argument of **fseek** (with **SEEK_END** as its third argument) corresponds to the position immediately after the final byte of the file. For example, with a file of five bytes the situation is as follows:

Position when **0L** is used
in combination with **SEEK_END**

Since we count from 0, the number 5 denotes both the first position after the end of the file and the number of bytes in the file.

Note that program LENGTH does not read from or write to the file in question. Therefore the characters **+** and **b** in the second argument of **fopen** are not essential: with "rb", "r+", or "r" instead of "r+b" the program works equally well. If we use the letter **a** instead of **r**, the program still behaves in the same way for *existing* files. However, if no file with the given name exists, the letter **a** causes a new file (with length 0) to be created, while in that case the letter **r** leads to the message:

```
File does not exist.
```

Using the letter **w** instead of **r** or **a** is much worse, because in this case the program, when applied to an existing file, will destroy this.

A file-update example

Using **fseek** is more interesting if we really want to read and write. Let us use a very simple example. A club has members each of whom has a member number. These numbers are relatively small, so we can use them as record numbers in a file. Remember that *structures*, as used in C, are often called *records*. A member's record will only contain his or her name and year of birth. (In a real situation it is most likely that there will be other data as well, such as the member's address. Adding such additional items here would not make the example more interesting for our purpose.) Each name will be stored in an array of 40 elements. When a member leaves the club, his or her number becomes available for a new member who may join the club. Program MEMBERS can be used to create and maintain a file with member records. The member numbers are used to locate the records and need therefore not be stored: we use the (binary) file **club.bin** like an array, with member numbers corresponding to subscript values. Some more explanation follows after the program, which can be used both to create and to update the file **club.bin**:

```
/* MEMBERS: With a given member number, the member's name and year of
            birth can be entered to create or update the file 'club.bin'.
*/

#include <stdio.h>
#include <stdlib.h>
#include <string.h>
#include <ctype.h>

void file_error(void)
{ printf("There is a problem with the file 'club.bin'.\n");
  exit(1);
}

main()
{ FILE *fp;
  int nr, code;
  long pos, filelength, i;
  char answer;
  struct rec {char name[40]; int year;} r;
  fp = fopen("club.bin", "r+b");
  if (fp == NULL) fp = fopen("club.bin", "w+b");
  if (fp == NULL) file_error();

  for ( ; ; )
  { printf("\nMember number (or STOP): ");
```

```
      if (scanf("%d", &nr) < 1 || nr < 0) break;
      pos = (long)nr * sizeof(struct rec);
      if (fseek(fp, OL, SEEK_END)) file_error();
      filelength = ftell(fp);
      for (i=filelength; i<pos+sizeof(struct rec); i++) code = putc('\0', fp);
      if (code == EOF) file_error();
      if (fseek(fp, pos, SEEK_SET)) file_error();
      if (fread(&r, sizeof(struct rec), 1, fp) != 1) file_error();
      if (r.name[0] == '\0') answer = 'Y'; else
      { printf("Name: %s   Year of birth: %d\n", r.name, r.year);
        printf("Update? Y/N): ");
        scanf(" %c", &answer);
        answer = toupper(answer);   /* To upper case, see Section 10.2 */
      }
      if (answer == 'Y')
      { printf("Name and year of birth (or 0 0 to clear the record): ");
        scanf("%s %d", r.name, &r.year);
        if (r.name[0] == '0') r.name[0] = '\0';
        if (fseek(fp, pos, SEEK_SET)) file_error();
        if (fwrite(&r, sizeof(struct rec), 1, fp) != 1) file_error();
      }
    }
  fclose(fp);
}
```

Program MEMBERS is not *robust*, that is, there are not enough checks in it to make it react satisfactorily to incorrect input data. In practice, such checks are highly desirable, but improving the program in this respect is more difficult than you may expect. It would also make the program more difficult to understand and therefore obscure the subject we are discussing. It is more comprehensible in its present form, especially in connection with the following demonstration, in which bold characters have been used for the data entered by the user:

```
Member number (or STOP): 123
Name and year of birth (or 0 0 to clear the record): Smith 1961


Member number (or STOP): 419
Name and year of birth (or 0 0 to clear the record): Johnson 1965


Member number (or STOP): 87
Name and year of birth (or 0 0 to clear the record): Williams 1963


Member number (or STOP): 419
Name: Johnson   Year of birth: 1965
Update? Y/N): y
Name and year of birth (or 0 0 to clear the record): Shaw 1959
```

```
Member number (or STOP): 419
Name: Shaw    Year of birth: 1959
Update? Y/N): n

Member number (or STOP): stop
```

As mentioned before, random file access is similar to using arrays. Instead of writing an expression between square brackets, we use **fseek**. The second argument of this function is a byte number derived from the record number. Program MEMBERS first tries to open the file **club.bin** for input. If this file does not yet exist, this attempt fails. In many other programs, we would in that case print an error message and terminate program execution, but here we once again try to open the file, but this time for output. Although it is very unlikely for this attempt to fail as well, a test has again been included. When the user, as requested, enters a member number, this is examined to see if it is small enough to be used as the number of an existing record. For example, if the maximum record number used so far is 10, a given new member number 20 cannot immediately be used as a basis for the second argument of **fseek**, but we must first extend the file. The latter is done here by means of a for-statement, in which **putc** adds a sufficient number of null characters at the end of the file. On the other hand, if the given record number is small enough to correspond to a record inside the file, **putc** is not called. Note that such an extension is only possible with a file, not with an array. (As discussed in Section 6.6, we can use a pointer instead of an array and extend the 'array length' by means of **realloc**, but this may involve much copying work, which is not the case when we are extending a file!).

Perhaps the most important point that should be noted in program MEMBERS is that a file is updated by calling **fseek** twice, namely just before calling each of the functions **fread** and **fwrite**. Omitting many details, we can write the simplified program structure as follows:

```
for (...)
{ ...                                   /* Compute position.         */
  fseek(fp, pos, SEEK_SET);             /* Set file position.        */
  fread(&r, sizeof(struct rec), 1, fp); /* Read record.              */
  ...                                   /* Update record in memory.  */
  fseek(fp, pos, SEEK_SET);             /* Set file position again.  */
  fwrite(&r, sizeof(struct rec), 1, fp); /* Write record.            */
}
```

Even if program MEMBERS were extended with appropriate tests for the correctness of its input data, it is not likely to be a practical program, because it is more convenient for a club administration to use member names than member numbers as 'keys'. One way of doing this, with names as a basis for computing the positions where records are to be stored, is by using a method called *hashing*. This method is explained by means of C program text in *Programs and Data Structures in C*, listed in the Bibliography.

Exercises

In each of the following exercises, the names of the files involved are to be read from the keyboard after an appropriate request from your program. The exercises are formulated in slightly abbreviated form. For example, *Print xxx* should actually be read as *Write a program that prints xxx*.

8.1   Print the longest line of a given text file.

8.2   A given text file contains only words, separated by white-space characters. Read a positive integer *n* from the keyboard. Count how many distinct words there are in the file, unless there are more than *n*. In the latter case, just print the text *Limit exceeded*. (Do not confuse the number of distinct words with the total number of words in the file; the latter number may be greater than *n*.)

8.3   The text of a given file has been typed by someone with little typing experience: comma characters in the file may not be followed by a blank. Copy the file to a corrected version in which each comma is followed by a blank. (If there is already a blank after a comma, you must not insert another one.)

8.4   Two text files are given, each of which contains a sequence of integers in increasing order. Merge these files to obtain an output file in which all numbers read from the original files occur in increasing order.

8.5   As 8.4, but with words in alphabetic order instead of integers in increasing order.

8.6   Examine if there is a file with a name read from the keyboard. If not, create such a file and write *n* zeros to it, where *n* is also read from the keyboard. If the file already exists, repeatedly read an integer *k* (less than *n*) from the keyboard to update the integer in position *k* in the file, according to directions given by the user. After reading the integer in the *k*th position, print it, and give the user the opportunity to replace it with another integer. The positions are numbered from 0. Use binary I/O and random access.

CHAPTER 9

Advanced Subjects

9.1 VARIABLE-LENGTH ARGUMENT LISTS

You may have noticed that the functions **scanf** and **printf** have the very remarkable characteristic that their argument lists have variable length. They always have at least one argument, a format string, which specifies (by means of some conversion specifications in this string) how many arguments follow. The language concepts discussed so far do not enable us to write such functions ourselves. Since the two functions mentioned are very complicated, we will use a much simpler example to demonstrate how to write functions with variable-length argument lists. Let us write a function **sum**, the first argument of which tells how many arguments follow to compute their sum. For example, we have

```
sum(3, 10.0, 20.0, 30.0)       =       60.0,
sum(2, 100.0, 200.0)           =       300.0,
sum(0)                         =       0.
```

As you can see, the first argument has type **int**, and any following arguments have type **double**. (Recall that floating-point constants as those used here have type **double**.) In general, functions with variable-length argument lists have a fixed number *named* parameters, followed by a variable number of *unnamed* ones. The terms named and unnamed parameters (with corresponding 'named' and 'unnamed' arguments) are immediately clear if we look at the beginning of a function such as **sum**:

```
double sum(int n, ...)
```

Note that this line, including the three dots ..., should be taken literally! In this book we have often used three dots meaning 'Something else to be inserted here', but that is not intended here.

To write the function **sum**, we must use the header file **stdarg.h**. For our purpose, the following is defined in this file:

- The type **va_list**, to be used in the declaration of a special kind of pointer which we will call **argp**. This pointer will give us access to the arguments. It is declared as follows:

  ```
  va_list argp;
  ```

- The macro **va_start**, which assigns an initial value to the pointer **argp** just mentioned. This macro has two arguments: the variable **argp** and the final named parameter, **n**, in our example. To gain access to the first unnamed argument, which follows the final named argument, **n**, we write

  ```
  va_start(argp, n);
  ```

- The macro **va_arg**, which returns the value of the argument that is to be used next. This macro also makes **argp** point to the next argument. It can do this only if it is given the type of the argument to be returned; after all, the unnamed arguments can take more than one byte, so that the difference between two successive values of **argp** can be greater than one. The unnamed arguments need not all have the same type (as is the case in our example). Remember, the second argument in a call to **va_arg** must be the type of the value returned by this call. In our example, we want to use this returned value to update the current sum **s**, so we write

  ```
  s += va_arg(argp, double);
  ```

- The macro **va_end**, to be used at the end: after the final call to **va_arg**, the following macro call must be executed before the function (**sum**) is left:

  ```
  va_end(argp);
  ```

Putting all this in practice, we write the complete function **sum** as shown in the program VARARG:

```
/* VARARG: A program that demonstrates variable-length argument lists.
*/
#include <stdarg.h>
#include <stdio.h>

main()
{ double sum(int n, ...);   /* Literal program text! */
  printf("%f\n", sum(2, 1.2, 3.4));
  printf("%f\n", sum(5, 10.0, 20.0, 30.0, 40.0, 50.0));
}
```

```
double sum(int n, ...)      /* Literal program text! */
{ va_list argp;
  float s=0;
  va_start(argp, n);
  while (n--) s += va_arg(argp, double);
  va_end(argp);
  return s;
}
```

Note that it must be possible for a function to determine how many arguments there are. Here we have done this in a very straightforward way, namely by giving the first argument **n** this required value. As mentioned already, we can instead derive the required information by analyzing a format string. Yet another way would be to use a final argument with a special value, different from the other arguments. In that case, the loop in which **va_arg** is called terminates when this special value is detected. (This is similar to using the null character at the end of a string, and to using a special value at the end of a number sequence to be read, as in Exercise 2.1.)

In our example, the function **sum** follows the function **main**, so that we need an explicit declaration of **sum**. As you can see, this declaration has its usual form: it is identical to the beginning of the function definition and ends with a semicolon.

Remember, automatic type conversion does not apply to the unnamed arguments: the three dots in the function declaration does not provide the compiler with parameter types to which the arguments should be converted. The following call to **sum** would therefore be incorrect:

```
sum(5, 10, 20, 30, 40, 50)
```

As the compiler cannot detect this error, it is a very serious one: this call will be executed with undefined result.

The functions vprintf, vfprintf, and vsprintf

We sometimes want to write a function, say **myprintf**, the arguments of which consist of a format string followed by a variable-length argument list, in the same way as with **printf**. Instead of analyzing the format string ourselves, we want to use it in a call to one of the standard functions **printf**, **fprintf**, and **sprintf**. However, this is not possible with the means discussed so far: supplying the format string to these standard functions is no problem at all, but what about any subsequent arguments? Remember, in the call to **myprintf** these are unnamed and only the format string contains information about how many there are.

To solve this problem, we use three new standard functions, which have been derived from **printf** (see Section 8.2), **fprintf** (see Section 8.4), and **sprintf** (see Section 6.11). In **stdio.h** they are declared as follows:

```
int vprintf(const char *formatstring, va_list argp);
int vfprintf(FILE *fp, const char *formatstring, va_list argp);
int vsprintf(char *s, const char *formatstring, va_list argp);
```

As you can see, the final argument of each of these functions has type **va_list**. The following demonstration program shows how **vprintf** can be called in a function, **myprintf**, of our own. It is used in the same way as **printf**, and it prints the same text, preceded and followed by some additional text:

```
/* VPRDEMO: A program to demonstrate vprintf.
*/
#include <stdio.h>
#include <math.h>
#include <stdarg.h>

void myprintf(char *formatstring, ...) /* To be taken literally! */
{ va_list argp;
  printf("\nHere is output text:\n");
  va_start(argp, formatstring);
  vprintf(formatstring, argp);
  va_end(argp);
  printf("\nThis concludes the output text.\n");
}

main()
{ myprintf("The square root of 2 is approximately %7.5f.", sqrt(2.0));
}
```

Thanks to **vprintf**, the function **myprintf** need not analyze the format string to see how often **va_arg** is to be called. All this, including the calls to **va_arg** themselves, is taken care of by **vprintf**. Note the use of **va_start** and **va_end**. Between these calls, we write a single call to **vprintf** instead of several calls to **va_arg**.

It will be clear that this program produces the following output:

```
Here is output text:
The square root of 2 is approximately 1.41421.
This concludes the output text.
```

9.2 BINARY SEARCH

In many applications a table with items in increasing order is to be searched for one of these items, and this is to be done efficiently. Usually, these items are structures, and one particular member of each structure is called a *key*. Then the items are in increasing order of their keys, and we are actually to search the table for an item with a given key. Since the way of searching is independent of the complexity of the items, we might as well use an array of very simple items as an example. As it is pointless to define structures of only one member, we will rather use integers, which are used both as keys and as complete items. Suppose that array **a** has the following ten elements:

. 3 5 8 10 11 20 25 27 28 30

When searching this array for some integer, we first compare this with an integer in the middle of the array; in our example, it would be compared with 11 or 20. If the integer we are looking for is less than the element in the middle, we repeat the process with the left half of the table; if it is greater, we continue with the right half, and so on. The following program reads an integer from the keyboard and searches the array **a** with the above contents for it. If it does not occur in the array, it says where it logically belongs in the array:

```
/* BINSEARCH: A function of our own for binary search applied to
              an array of integers.
*/
#include <stdio.h>

int binsearch(int x, int *a, int n)
/* The sequence a[0], a[1], ..., a[n-1] is searched for x.
   Return value:
      0 if x <= a[0], or
      i if a[i-1] < x <= a[i], or
      n if x > a[n-1].
*/
{ int middle, left=0, right=n-1;
  if (x <= a[left]) return 0;
  if (x > a[right]) return n;
  while (right - left > 1)
  { middle = (left + right)/2;
    if (x <= a[middle]) right = middle; else left = middle;
  }
  return right;
}
```

```
main()
{ int table[10]={3, 5, 8, 10, 11, 20, 25, 27, 28, 30},
    num, N=10, i;
  printf("The sequence 3 5 8 10 11 20 25 27 28 30 will be searched.\n");
  printf("Enter an integer: ");
  scanf("%d", &num);
  i = binsearch(num, table, N);
  if (i < N && num == table[i])
  { printf("Found in position %d.\n", i);
    printf("(The positions count from 0.)\n");
  }
  else
  { printf("This integer does not occur in the array.\n");
    if (i == 0) printf("It is less than the smallest.\n"); else
    if (i == N) printf("It is greater than the greatest array element.\n");
         else printf("It lies between %d en %d.\n", table[i-1], table[i]);
  }
}
```

Here is a demonstration of this program:

```
The sequence 3 5 8 10 11 20 25 27 28 30 will be searched.
Enter an integer: 10
Found in position 3.
(The positions count from 0.)
```

The correctness of the function **binsearch** can easily be verified by means of the following condition, which holds inside the while-loop at the moment that a value is assigned to **middle**:

$$a[left] < x \le a[right]$$

Because of the two if-statements that precede the while-loop, this condition holds when the loop is entered; the if-statement in the loop updates either **right** or **left**, in such a way that the condition remains valid.

Very often, we find binary-search functions that only return some special value, such as − 1, if the value searched for cannot be found. Our version has the advantage of indicating where the item searched for belongs, which is very useful if it has to be inserted in the table.

The standard function bsearch

Binary search can also be done by means of a standard function, called **bsearch**. As follows from the beginning of this section, this function would be no good if we could use it only for sequences of integers. Instead, we can use it for all kinds of items. Due to its generality, using **bsearch** is more complicated than using a special-purpose function, such as the one we have just been discussing. Fortunately, it is not as difficult as its declaration in the header file **stdlib.h** might suggest:

```
void *bsearch(const void *key, const void *base,
            size_t n, size_t width,
            int (*fcmp)(const void *, const void *));
```

Although we need not write this declaration ourselves, it is useful for us to see what the order and types of the parameters are. The meaning of these is as follows:

key	The address of a variable whose value is the key to be searched for.
base	The address of the first element of the array to be searched.
n	Length of the array. (We will discuss the type **size_t** in Section 10.10; for the time being you may consider it identical with **unsigned int**.)
width	Size of one array element, in bytes.
fcmp	A function for the comparison of keys.

It follows from this that the sequence **base[0]**, ⋯, **base[n−1]** is searched for the item with key value ***key**. As **bsearch** can be used not only for numbers but also for strings, it cannot always compare keys by means of the normal 'less than' operator (<). We therefore have to supply a function for this comparison; recall that in Section 6.12 we have seen how to use addresses of functions as arguments in calls to other functions. In **bsearch**, the comparison function will be called as **(*fcmp)(key, ⋯)** where the second argument is the address of some element **base[i]**. The value returned by the comparison function is similar to that returned by **strcmp** (see Section 6.5): 0 means 'equal', negative 'less than', and positive 'greater than'. We need to know all this, because we have to write this comparison function ourselves. As for **bsearch**, this function returns the address of the element with the given key, if this is found. If not, it returns **NULL**.

Our first application of **bsearch** is the same problem as the one we have solved with our own binary-search function. However, if the integer searched for cannot be found, we do not give an indication where it belongs (because **bsearch** does not supply us with such information):

```
/* BSEARCH: Binary search by means of the standard function bsearch,
            applied to a sequence of integers.
*/
#include <stdio.h>
#include <stdlib.h>

int compare(const void *pkey, const void *pelement)
{ int key = *(int *)pkey, element = *(int *)pelement;
  return (key < element ? -1 : key > element ? +1 : 0);
}


main()
{ int table[10]={3, 5, 8, 10, 11, 20, 25, 27, 28, 30}, num, N=10, *p;
  printf("The sequence 3 5 8 10 11 20 25 27 28 30 will be searched.\n");
  printf("Enter an integer: "); scanf("%d", &num);
  p = bsearch(&num, table, N, sizeof(int), compare);
  if (p != NULL)
  { printf("Found in position %d.\n", p - table);
    printf("(The positions count from 0.)\n");
  }
  else printf("Not found.\n");
}
```

Structures with strings as keys

Our next application of **bsearch** has two interesting new aspects: first, the items will be structures, and, second, the keys will be strings. We will search a telephone directory for a given name. As usual, we do this to obtain the corresponding telephone number, which is stored in the same structure as the name. Instead of looking in a conventional telephone directory, the user enters the name on the keyboard, and the desired number will appear on the screen. For reasons of generality and efficiency, we will actually store the names in separately allocated memory rather than in the structures themselves. The latter will instead contain pointers to the first characters of the names. Our program will begin by reading a telephone directory of the following form from the file **phone.dat**:

adams	3491
brooks	7263
goldberg	4217
grey	1964
hughes	8536
jackson	4866
johnson	7271
smith	1132

Then, in an endless loop, the program will repeatedly ask for a name to be entered and, if possible, find the corresponding number. To stop the program, a period can be entered.

```
/* PHONEDIR: Searching a telephone directory.
*/

#include <stdio.h>
#include <stdlib.h>
#include <string.h>
#define N 5000

struct phone {char *persname; int telnr;} table[N], *p;

int compare(const void *p1, const void *p2)
{ return strcmp((char *)p1, ((struct phone *)p2)->persname);
}

main()
{ FILE *fp;
  char buf[81], *p0;
  int n=0, number;
  fp = fopen("phone.dat", "r");
  if (fp == NULL) exit(1);
  while (fscanf(fp, "%80s %d", buf, &number) == 2)
  { if (n == N) {printf("Telephone directory too long.\n"); exit(1);}
    p0 = malloc(strlen(buf)+1);
    if (p0 == NULL) {printf("Not enough memory.\n"); exit(1);}
    table[n].persname = p0;
    strcpy(table[n].persname, buf);
    table[n].telnr = number;
    n++;
  }
  for ( ; ; )
  { printf("Enter a name (or a period to stop): ");
    scanf("%80s", buf);
    if (buf[0] == '.') break;
    p = bsearch(buf, table, n, sizeof(struct phone), compare);
    if (p == NULL) printf("Not found.\n");
    else printf("Telephone number: %d\n", p->telnr);
  }
}
```

As you can see, we have limited the number of entries to 5000. To change this limit, only the line **#define N 5000** has to be modified. Another point to note is

that the names must not contain blanks. With the input file already shown, we
can use this program as follows:

```
Enter a name (or a period to stop): hughes
Telephone number: 8536
Enter a name (or a period to stop): adams
Telephone number: 3419
Enter a name (or a period to stop): smith
Telephone number: 1132
Enter a name (or a period to stop): chapman
Telephone number: Not found.
Enter a name (or a period to stop): .
```

9.3 QUICKSORT

We frequently have to re-arrange arrays so that their elements are placed in
increasing order. There are many well-known algorithms for this operation, which
is called *sorting*. We restrict ourselves to one that, even for large arrays, is very
fast. The computing time for this algorithm is proportional to $n \cdot \log n$, where n
is the array length. With more primitive sorting methods, computing time is
normally proportional to n^2, which is considerably worse. The fast algorithm
mentioned was published in the form of an ALGOL60 procedure named
quicksort by C. A. R. Hoare in 1962. This name, quicksort, is also used for the
algorithm in general and for various implementations of it, published later.

Like binary search, quicksort has been considered important enough to include
a function for it in the standard library, but again we will begin with having a
look at the method itself, so that we can see how it works. Let us, for example,
use an array of **float** elements. Suppose that both its first address **a** (which may
be the array name) and **n**, the number of array elements, are given. Thus we are
given the sequence

$$a_0, a_1, \cdots, a_{n-1}$$

We now select one of these n numbers, and call it x; we will take the one that
is (about) in the middle of the sequence, so in C we could write

```
x = a[(n-1)/2];
```

We now start at the left, looking for an element **a[i]** greater than x. We also search the sequence from right to left for an element **a[j]** less than **x**. These two elements are then interchanged, and we repeat this process; each time **i** is incremented and **j** is decremented, until we have **j** < **i** and there is a set on the left with elements not greater than **x** and a set on the right with elements not less than **x**, as shown in Fig. 9.1. The same method is then applied to each of these two sets, which can be done very easily by means of two recursive calls, as the following implementation of the quicksort algorithm shows:

```
void qsort1(float *a, int n)
{ int i=0, j=n-1;
  float x=a[j/2], w;
  do
  { while (a[i] < x) i++;
    while (a[j] > x) j--;
    if (i < j) {w = a[i]; a[i] = a[j]; a[j] = w;} else
    if (i > j) break;
  } while (++i <= --j);
  if (j > 0) qsort1(a, j+1);     /* a[0], ..., a[j]   <= x */
  if (i < n-1) qsort1(a+i, n-i); /* a[i], ..., a[n-1] >= x  */
}
```

(With this version, the do-while-loop can end either with **i** = **j** + 1, as suggested in Fig. 9.1, or with **i** = **j** + 2. In the latter case, the element **a[i+1]** is equal to **x** and is already in its correct position; this situation occurs, for example, with {5, 4, 3, 2, 1} as the sequence to be sorted. In most cases, however, the situation after partitioning is exactly as shown in Fig. 9.1.)

In almost all cases quicksort is very fast. However, it is possible to construct sequences for which it is very slow. Take, for example, the case that in each subsequence the selected value of x happens to be the smallest element of that subsequence. Then each time the left subsequence will be very short and the right one very long. Not only would that lead to a very time-consuming process, but, worse, it might also result in a very high recursion depth with the danger of stack overflow. Fortunately, we can use **qsort1** to derive a new version, **qsort2**, from it, which limits the recursion depth considerably so that the danger of stack overflow is eliminated. This new version deals recursively only with the shorter of the two subsequences: the longer is dealt with iteratively. Consequently, applying **qsort2** to n elements can only lead to a recursive call to this function sorting at most ½n elements. The recursion depth will therefore be not greater than $\log_2 n$:

```
void qsort2(float *a, int n)
{ int i, j;
  float x, w;
  do
  { i=0; j=n-1;
    x = a[j/2];
    do
    { while (a[i] < x) i++;
      while (a[j] > x) j--;
      if (i < j) {w = a[i]; a[i] = a[j]; a[j] = w;} else
      if (i > j) break;
    } while (++i <= --j);

    if (j+1 < n-i)
    { if (j > 0) qsort2(a, j+1);
      a += i; n -= i;
    } else
    { if (i < n-1) qsort2(a+i, n-i);
      n = j + 1;
    }
  } while (n > 1);
}
```

The test **if (j+1 < n-i)**..., which follows the innermost do-while-loop, examines which of the two subsequences is the shorter one. Figure 9.1 shows the situation we are dealing with.

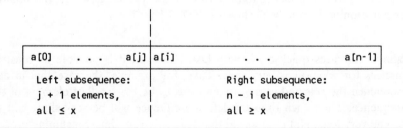

Fig. 9.1. Left and right subsequences

If the left subsequence is the shorter one, **qsort2** is applied recursively to it, and the do-while loop is continued for the right subsequence. To this end, we increase the pointer **a** by **i**, which makes it point to the element that previously was denoted by **a[i]**, but from now on is written **a[0]**. At the same time, **n** is assigned the value **n−i**, that is, the length of the right subsequence. On the other hand, if the right subsequence is the shorter one, the statements after **else** are executed, which means that the right subsequence is dealt with recursively and the left one iteratively. To do this, we need not alter the pointer **a**: it is sufficient to make **n** equal to **j + 1**, that is, the length of the left subsequence.

The standard function qsort

Like the general standard function **bsearch**, discussed in Section 9.2, there is an equally general standard function, **qsort**. With this function, we can apply the quicksort algorithm to any sequences. Again, a consequence of the generality of this function is that we have to supply a separate function for comparisons. In the header file **stdlib**, the function **qsort** is declared as follows:

```
void qsort(void *base, size_t n, size_t width,
           int (*fcmp)(const void *, const void *));
```

where the parameters have the following meaning:

base   The address of the first element of the given array.
n   Number of elements of the array.
width Number of bytes taken by each element.
fcmp   Comparison function.

We can use **qsort** to sort the array elements **table[0]**, ···, **table[N−1]**, of type **float**, as follows:

```
#include <stdlib.h>
#define N ...        /* Length of array 'table' to be inserted */

int compare(const void *p, const void *q)
{ float a = *(float *)p, b = *(float *)q;
  return a < b ? -1 : a > b ? +1 : 0;
}
...
float table[N];
...
qsort(table, N, sizeof(float), compare);
```

If you want to compare the speed of our own function **qsort2** with that of the standard function **qsort**, you should bear in mind that the special comparison function needed by **qsort** is rather time consuming, especially because, if ***p** is not less than ***q**, another comparison, ***p** > ***q**, will take place. In a test with Turbo C on a low-speed PC and with **n** = 8000, our own function **qsort2** took 153 seconds, compared with 218 seconds taken by the standard function **qsort**.

Sorting structures with strings

After our previous, rather academic example, we will now turn to a more practical application. The objects to be sorted will be structures (or 'records') each of which contains a string to be used as a key. After sorting, the records are to be in increasing order of their keys. The example is in fact the same as the one in Section 9.2. Our objects are entries in a telephone directory. Initially, they are in the file **unsorted.dat**, which, for example, can have the following contents:

```
johnson      7271
smith        1132
adams        3491
grey         1964
brooks       7263
hughes       8536
jackson      4866
goldberg     4217
```

On each line the name and the telephone number may be separated by any number of blanks and tabs. Program TELSORT reads this file, sorts it as required, and writes the result in the file **phone.dat** (which can then be used by program PHONEDIR of Section 9.2). In its current form the program accepts at most 5000 elements; as this number occurs only once in the program, it can easily be replaced.

```c
/* TELSORT: This program can be used to produce a telephone directory.
           Unsorted input file:      unsorted.dat.
           Sorted output file:       phone.dat.
*/
#include <stdio.h>
#include <stdlib.h>
#include <string.h>

#define N 5000

struct phone {char *persname; int telnr;} table[N];

int compare(const void *p1, const void *p2)
{ return strcmp(((struct phone *)p1)->persname,
            ((struct phone *)p2)->persname);
}

main()
{ FILE *fpin, *fpout;
  char buf[81], *p0;
```

```
    int n=0, number, i;
    fpin = fopen("unsorted.dat", "r");
    fpout = fopen("phone.dat", "w");
    if (fpin == NULL || fpout == NULL)
    { printf("Does file unsorted.dat exist?\n");
      exit(1);
    }
    while (fscanf(fpin, "%80s %d", buf, &number) == 2)
    { if (n == N) {printf("Too many entries in input file.\n"); exit(1);}
      p0 = malloc(strlen(buf)+1);
      if (p0 == NULL) {printf("Not enough memory.\n"); exit(1);}
      table[n].persname = p0;
      strcpy(table[n].persname, buf);
      table[n++].telnr = number;
    }
    printf("%d entries read from file unsorted.dat.\n", n);
    qsort(table, n, sizeof(struct phone), compare);
    printf("Sorting complete.\n");
    for (i=0; i<n; i++)
      fprintf(fpout, "%-15s %6d\n", table[i].persname, table[i].telnr);
    printf("Telephone directory phone.dat is ready.\n");
}
```

After the execution of this program, with the input file **unsorted.dat** as shown, the output file **phone.dat** has the following contents:

```
adams         3491
brooks        7263
goldberg      4217
grey          1964
hughes        8536
jackson       4866
johnson       7271
smith         1132
```

9.4 LINEAR LISTS

We will now deal with structures (or 'records') each of which contains a pointer member. This member contains either the address of another structure or the value **NULL**. An example of such a set of connected records is a *linear list*, as shown in Fig. 9.2 and built by program LIST1:

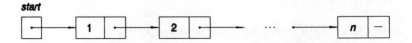

Fig. 9.2. Linear list

```
/* LIST1: This program builds a linear list containing the
          integers 1, ..., n.
          Then the list is traversed and the integers stored
          in it are printed.
*/
#include <stdio.h>
#include <stdlib.h>

main()
{ int i, n;
  struct list {int num; struct list *ref;} *start, *p;
  printf("Enter n: ");
  scanf("%d", &n);
  start = NULL;
  for (i=n; i>0; i--)
  { p = start;
    start = malloc(sizeof(struct list));
    if (start == NULL) {printf("Not enough memory.\n"); exit(1);}
    start->num = i; start->ref = p;
  }
  p = start;
  printf("Output:\n");
  while (p != NULL) {printf("%8d\n", p->num); p = p->ref;}
}
```

Here is a demonstration of this program:

```
Enter n: 5
Output:
        1
        2
        3
        4
        5
```

A linear list is a special case of a *dynamic data structure*. This term is used for certain collections of records, which have no variable names of their own, but are instead accessible through chains of pointers.

In our example, each record contains only an **int** member, **num**, and a pointer member, **ref**. An advantage of a linear list over an array is that we can insert and delete elements very efficiently. If you are interested in such operations and how they are implemented in C, you are referred to *Programs and Data Structures in C*, listed in the Bibliography. The same applies to the subject of the next section.

9.5 BINARY TREES

Another well-known dynamic data structure is a *binary tree*. This too has one start pointer, called the *root* of the tree. In illustrations, the root of a binary tree is usually placed at the top, as shown in Fig. 9.3. The records of which a binary tree consists are called *nodes*. In our example, we simply use integers as the objects to be stored in the nodes. Besides, each node has two pointer members, which can point to other nodes, called a left and a right *child node*. The binary tree of Fig. 9.3 is a *binary search tree*, because it can be searched very efficiently, as we did in Section 9.2. The integers stored in the tree are used as *keys*; in general, nodes may contain any number of data members, only one of which is used as a key. If, in a binary search tree, a node has k as its key and has a left child with key l, then $l < k$. If it has a right child with key r, then $r > k$.

The smallest possible binary tree consists only of a root, which is a normal pointer variable. Bearing this in mind, we can say that each node of a binary tree contains the roots of a left and a right subtree. This recursive formulation suggests the use of recursive functions.

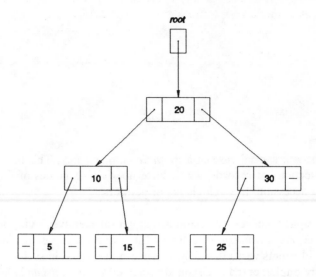

Fig. 9.3. Binary tree

Program BSTREE builds the binary tree shown in Fig. 9.3 if the integers to be stored in it are entered on the keyboard as follows:

20   30   10   15   25 5

Initially, the tree is empty, that is, the variable **root** has the value **NULL**. Each time an integer is read, the tree is searched for it. If it is found, it is ignored, for we do not want it to be inserted once again. If the integer is not found in the tree, the value **NULL** (representing an empty subtree) encountered at the end of the search process is replaced with a pointer to a new node, allocated by means of **malloc**, into which this integer is stored. Because of the call-by-value parameter mechanism in C, we must supply the *address* of the root as an argument to the **insert** function to give this function the opportunity to assign a new value to this root. Since the root is a pointer, a variable that contains its address can be called a 'pointer to a pointer'. This explains the two asterisks in **struct node **pp**. This is not really confusing. Remember, this notation only means that we can store the address of a pointer in **pp**. Initially, the address of **root** is stored in **pp**. If **root** is not equal to **NULL**, we assign the address of either **root->left** or **root->right** to **pp**. Instead of, for example, **pp = & root->left**, we use the more general form **pp = & (*pp)->left** in the loop, so that the loop works properly all the way down to the bottom of the tree, where a new node is to be inserted.

After the integers have been inserted in the tree, we can print them in increasing order in a very simple way. Given the root of a binary search tree, we can visit all nodes in the required order by means of the following, recursively defined method:

0. Do nothing if the root has the value **NULL**.

If the root points to a node, which we call a *root node*, perform the following three actions:

1. Visit all nodes in the left subtree of the root node.
2. Visit the root node itself.
3. Visit all nodes in the right subtree of the root node.

The function **printtree** shows how simple it is to implement this. Although it is recursive, you may find it easier to understand than the function **insert**. (We could write a recursive version for the latter function as well, but then each call to it would result in the execution of at most one recursive call. In such cases recursion is normally not advantageous.)

```
/* BSTREE: This program builds a binary search tree in which
           integers read from the keyboard are stored.
           These integers are then printed in increasing order.
*/

#include <stdio.h>
#include <stdlib.h>

struct node
{ int num;
  struct node *left, *right;
};

main()
{ int i;
  struct node *root;
  void insert(struct node **pp, int i);
  void printtree(struct node *p);
  root = NULL;
  printf("Enter integers, followed by a nonnumeric character:\n");
  while (scanf("%d", &i) == 1) insert(&root, i);
  printf(
  "The integers stored in the tree are printed in increasing order:\n");
  printtree(root);
}
```

```
void insert(struct node **pp, int i)
/* This function inserts i in a tree given by its root.
   The address of this root is given as pp.
*/
{ while (*pp != NULL)
  { if (i < (*pp)->num) pp = & (*pp)->left; else
    if (i > (*pp)->num) pp = & (*pp)->right; else return;
  }
  *pp = malloc(sizeof(struct node));
  (*pp)->left = NULL;
  (*pp)->num = i;
  (*pp)->right = NULL;
}
```

```
void printtree(struct node *p)
{ if (p != NULL)
  { printtree(p->left);
    printf("%d\n", p->num);
    printtree(p->right);
  }
}
```

9.6 SYSTEMS OF LINEAR EQUATIONS

In many areas of science and engineering, systems of linear equations are to be solved. Although a thorough discussion of this subject falls outside the scope of this book, there are two reasons for presenting a function that solves this problem. First, this function illustrates an important aspect of C programming, namely how to use a square matrix of arbitrary dimension as a function argument, and, second, the function may be useful to C programmers who are not familiar with numerical analysis and who simply want to use it, without spending much time on the underlying mathematics. For the initiated, it might be mentioned that the function to be presented is based on Gauss elimination with scaled partial pivoting.

A system of linear equations may have a unique solution if there are as many equations as there are unknowns. In the following example, we have three equations and three unknowns (x, y, z):

$$
\begin{aligned}
2x - y + 4z &= 15 \\
10x - 2y + 21z &= 88 \\
2x + 5y + 8z &= 49
\end{aligned}
\tag{1}
$$

According to Gauss elimination, we can solve this system by replacing it with an equivalent one, such as:

$$x - 0.5y + 2z = 7.5$$
$$y + (1/3)z = 13/3 \qquad\qquad (2)$$
$$z = 4$$

We say that this system is in *triangular form*, which makes it easy to solve for z, y, and x, in that order:

$$z = 4$$
$$y = 13/3 - (1/3)z = 3$$
$$x = 7.5 + 0.5y - 2z = 1$$

The latter operation, called *back substitution*, is very straightforward. We will therefore focus on the former process, that is, replacing the original system (1) with an equivalent system (2) in triangular form.

In our example, we can proceed as follows. We divide the first equation of (1) by the coefficient of x, that is, by 2, which gives:

$$x - 0.5y + 2z = 7.5$$
$$10x - 2y + 21z = 88 \qquad\qquad (3)$$
$$2x + 5y + 8z = 49$$

We will now subtract multiples of the first equation from those that follow, in such a way that in the latter all coefficients of x become zero. In other words, we use the first equation to subtract its 10-fold from the second and its 2-fold from the third. The result is:

$$x - 0.5y + 2z = 7.5$$
$$3y + z = 13 \qquad\qquad (4)$$
$$6y + 4z = 34$$

We can now use the same principle to the second equation; we first divide it by 3 and then and subtract its 6-fold from the third equation. Finally, we only have to divide the third equation by the coefficient of z to obtain the desired system (2).

Unfortunately, this method does not always work: applying it literally may lead to division by a zero coefficient. To prevent this, it is sometimes necessary to exchange two equations. If that is not possible because all remaining equations also have zeros in the column in question, then the system has no unique solution. Our C function will return the value 0 in such abnormal cases and 1 in case of a unique solution.

Besides the problem of division by zero, there is also the danger of obtaining bad results due to round-off errors. Such results will occur if the *pivot*, that is, the coefficient by which we divide, is very small in absolute value compared with the other coefficients of the same equation. Both problems are solved at the same time by a technique known as *pivoting*, that is, by selecting the pivot very carefully. In our example (1) this is done as follows. As you can see, the first column contains the numbers 2, 10, and 2, in that order, as coefficients of x. We relate each of these numbers to the (absolutely) greatest coefficient of the equation in which it occurs. Thus, we look for the greatest of the three quotients 2/4, 10/21, and 2/8. Since 2/4 is the greatest, we select the coefficient 2 of the first equation as a pivot. If, for example, 10/21 had been the greatest of the three, we would have exchanged the first and the second equations.

We can write a system of linear equations as a matrix product

$$Ax = b \tag{5}$$

where A is an $n \times n$ matrix and x and b are matrices of one column and n rows. Matrices of only one column are called *column vectors*. In our example, we have

$$A = \begin{bmatrix} 2 & -1 & 4 \\ 10 & -2 & 21 \\ 2 & 5 & 8 \end{bmatrix} \qquad b = \begin{bmatrix} 15 \\ 88 \\ 49 \end{bmatrix}$$

It is our task to compute the following column vector from these:

$$x = \begin{bmatrix} 1 \\ 3 \\ 4 \end{bmatrix}$$

So much for the mathematical part of our work. It is now time to see how all this can be realized in C. As we want our C function to be general and economical with memory space, we must neither limit n to a fixed maximum nor use a considerable amount of work space if this can be avoided. We will therefore use the matrix A and the vectors b and x as work space, which implies that matrix A and vector b will be altered. The programmer who uses our function must be aware of this and, before calling the function, save the contents of A and b if these are required later for other purposes.

A very interesting problem is associated with passing matrix A as a function argument. If, in the function, we want to use this matrix in the normal way as a two-dimensional array, with elements A[i][j], then we have a problem in declaring it as a parameter. As we have seen in Section 6.9, we can use a two-dimensional array as a parameter only if we specify its second dimension, and as this must be a constant, we cannot use n for this purpose. We solve this problem by performing the two-dimensional address calculation ourselves. Since the elements of a matrix are stored row by row and count from 0, we can use a one-dimensional array in the function, writing

    A[n * i + j]   instead of   A[i][j]

in which row number i and column number j assume the values $0, 1, \cdots, n-1$. For example, with $n = 3$, as in our example, we use

    A[0]   A[1]   A[2]
    A[3]   A[4]   A[5]
    A[6]   A[7]   A[8]

instead of

    A[0][0]   A[0][1]   A[0][2]
    A[1][0]   A[1][1]   A[1][2]
    A[2][0]   A[2][1]   A[2][2]

There are two reasons why this hardly reduces program readability. First, we can define a macro A with two parameters in such a way that instead of using the rather unreadable form A[n*i+j], we can write A(i, j), with exactly the same meaning. Second, it is still possible to use a two-dimensional array outside our function, as we will do in our demonstration program. In the function call, we then write either &A[0][0] or A[0] to denote the address of the first element of matrix A.

Due to the pivoting process, as we have been discussing, function **lineareq** is rather complicated, but, fortunately, it is easy to use, efficient, and suitable to many applications.

The text of this function (which, if desired, can also be compiled separately) is followed by a simple demonstration program for the example discussed in this section. As we already know, this example has x[0] = 1, x[1] = 3, x[2] = 4 as its solution. Writing a more general main program, also based on function **lineareq**, is left as an exercise for the reader; see also Exercise 9.10.

```
/* Function lineareq solves the linear system Ax = b, that is, the
   following system of n linear equations in x[0], ..., x[m]
   (where m = n-1):

   A(0,0) * x[0] + A(0,1) * x[1] + ... + A(0,m) * x[m] = b[0]
   A(1,0) * x[0] + A(1,1) * x[1] + ... + A(1,m) * x[m] = b[1]
                               . . .
   A(m,0) * x[0] + A(m,1) * x[1] + ... + A(m,m) * x[m] = b[m]


   Return value:
      1 if a unique solution has been found;
      0 if there are many solutions or none at all.


   Note that the arrays A and b are altered: after calling lineareq,
   these arrays correspond to an equivalent system in triangular form.

   Method used: Gauss elimination with scaled partial pivoting.
   See also:
   Kreyszig, E. (1988) Advanced Engineering Mathematics (6th Edition),
      New York: John Wiley.
*/
#include <math.h>
#define A(i, j) A[n*(i) + (j)]

int lineareq(int n, double *A, double *b, double *x)
{ int i, j, ipivot, ii;
  double max, pivot, factor, temp;
  for (i=0; i<n; i++)
  { for (ii=i; ii<n; ii++)
    { max = 0;
      for (j=i; j<n; j++)
      { temp = fabs(A(ii, j));
        if (temp > max) max = temp;
      }
      if (max == 0.0) return 0;
      x[ii] = max;
    }
    ipivot = i; max = fabs(A(i, i)/x[i]);
    for (ii=i+1; ii<n; ii++)
    { temp = fabs(A(ii, i))/x[ii];
      if (temp > max) {max = temp; ipivot = ii;}
    }
    /* Exchange the rows with row numbers ipivot and i:
    */
    if (ipivot != i)
    { for (j=i; j<n; j++)
```

```
           { temp = A(ipivot, j);
             A(ipivot, j) = A(i, j);
             A(i, j) = temp;
           }
           temp = b[ipivot]; b[ipivot] = b[i]; b[i] = temp;
        }
        /* Divide row i by A(i, i):
        */
        pivot = A(i, i);
        if (pivot == 0.0) return 0;
        A(i, i) = 1; b[i] /= pivot;
        for (j=i+1; j<n; j++) A(i, j) /= pivot;
        /* Clear the rest of column i:
        */
        for (ii=i+1; ii<n; ii++)
        { factor = A(ii, i); A(ii, i) = 0;
          for (j=i+1; j<n; j++) A(ii, j) -= factor * A(i, j);
          b[ii] -= factor * b[i];
        }
     }
     /* Back substitution:
     */
     for (i=n-1; i>=0; i--)
     { x[i] = b[i];
       for (j=i+1; j<n; j++) x[i] -= A(i, j) * x[j];
     }
     return 1;
  }
  #undef A


  /* So much for function lineareq.
     Here is a simple demonstration program, which, if desired,
     can be compiled separately from function lineareq.
  */
  #include <stdio.h>

  main()
  { int i;
    double A[3][3] =
    {{2, -1, 4},
     {10, -2, 21},
     {2, 5, 8}
    },
    b[3] = {15, 88, 49}, x[3];
    if (lineareq(3, &A[0][0], b, x) == 0) printf("No unique solution.\n");
    else for (i=0; i<3; i++) printf("%15.10f\n", x[i]);
  }
```

Exercises

9.1   Write the function **readint** to read any number of integers from the keyboard. Its first argument says how many numbers are to be read and to be stored at the addresses given as the arguments that follow. The value returned by **readint** must be the same as that returned by **scanf** if the latter function were used for the same purpose. For example, the following two function calls must be equivalent:

```
readint(3, &i, &j, &k)
scanf("%d %d %d", &i, &j, &k)
```

9.2   Write the (**void**) function **assignchar**, which assigns the characters of a (null-terminated) string to **char** variables. For example, after the call

```
assignchar("ABC", &ch1, &ch2, &ch3);
```

the variables **ch1**, **ch2**, and **ch3** contain ´A´, ´B´, and ´C´, respectively. The function assumes that there are as many arguments that follow the string argument as there are characters in the string that precede the null character.

9.3   Write a program based on *insertion sort*. Integers are read from the keyboard and inserted in their correct positions in an array in which the integers read so far have been stored in increasing order. Each time an integer is read, use the binary-search method to find the position where it is to be inserted. The integers that will follow the new one are to be shifted one position to make room for it.

9.4   Use the function **qsort2** of Section 9.3 to write a new version that can sort strings instead of numbers.

9.5   Use the standard function **qsort** in a program that reads a sequence of integers from the keyboard and sorts them in a very special way: instead of applying the 'less than' relation to the integers themselves, it is to be applied to the sum of their decimal digits. For example, sorting the numbers sequence

    51 20 17 111 9 23

in increasing order of the sum of their digits will result in the following sequence:

    20 111 23 51 17 9

9.6 Write a sort program which reads the file **unsorted.dat** to sort it in increasing order either of the names or of the numbers, depending on the user's request (entered on the keyboard). You may limit the length of the file to, say, 1000 lines. Use an array of structures, each of which contains both a pointer to a memory area (allocated with **malloc**) in which a name is stored and a telephone number. The sorted table is to be written in a new file, **sorted.dat**.

9.7 Use the function **gets**, discussed in Section 6.7, to read lines of text; store each line in a memory area allocated with **malloc**. Also, for each line that is read, insert a new element in a linear list, and store the start address obtained with **malloc** in this element. Use an empty line as a signal for the end of the input data. When this signal is given, print all lines read previously.

9.8 Extend program BSTREE of Section 9.5, in such a way that, after building a binary tree, it repeatedly reads an integer from the keyboard and searches the tree for it. The program then reports whether or not this integer could be found in the tree.

9.9 Write a program that behaves like program PHONEDIR of Section 9.2, except that it reads its data from the file **unsorted.dat,** as used in Section 9.3. However, the entries of the telephone directory are to be stored in a binary search tree instead of in array **table**. Each node of the tree is to contain a pointer to a name and a number, besides the usual pointers to other nodes. Use the names as keys, so that we can quickly search the tree for a name to find the corresponding telephone number.

9.10 Use the function **lineareq** of Section 9.6 in a general program that solves any system of n linear equations in n unknowns (provided that it has a unique solution). The order n of the system, followed by the coefficients given row by row, are to be read from a file, the name of which is to be read from the keyboard. For example, in the system used in Section 9.6, this file has the following contents:

```
3
 2   -1    4    15
10   -2   21    88
 2    5    8    49
```

Do not use an array with a fixed size, but allocate memory space by means of **malloc** and use the expression $ni + j$ to locate the matrix element in row i and column j, in the same way as is done in function **lineareq**.

CHAPTER 10

Standard Library

Object modules, obtained by compiling source modules, can be grouped together in libraries, and we can instruct the *linker* to search these libraries. Most C programmers do not *make* libraries but simply *use* them. We should distinguish the standard library, as defined by ANSI, and non-standard libraries, which are not everywhere available and are possibly related to the hardware that is used. It is wise to use non-standard libraries only if we really need them, that is, if we want something that is not available in the standard library.

The functions in the standard library are called *standard functions*. They are divided into groups; all functions that belong to the same group are declared in one header file. Many standard functions have already been discussed in this book. They are also included in this chapter, often with references to previous sections. This chapter also includes many new standard functions. Besides function declarations (or *function prototypes*), there is other useful information in the standard header files, such as macro definitions. Different C implementations need not have identical standard header files, but although the contents of these files may differ, they can be used in the same way. We will therefore focus on their use, not on their contents. The names of the standard header files, enclosed in angular brackets as we write them in our programs, are

<assert.h>   <ctype.h>   <errno.h>   <float.h> <limits.h>
  <math.h>   <setjmp.h>   <signal.h>   <stdarg.h>   <stddef.h>
 <stdio.h>   <stdlib.h>   <string.h>   <time.h>

In our program modules, we may use **#include** lines for these header files in any order, and they may occur more than once.

This chapter will often be used as a reference. The header files just mentioned are therefore discussed in alphabetic order. To use a function or a macro, we want to know its number of arguments, their types, and the type of its return value. This information will be given in the form of function declarations, and this will be done even in case of macros.

204

10.1 DIAGNOSTICS: <assert.h>

```
void assert(int expression);
```

This is a macro. If *expression* is zero, an error message, such as

```
Assertion failed: expression, file filename, line nnn
```

appears, after which the program terminates execution. If we write the line **#define NDEBUG 1** prior to **#include** < assert.h >, the call to **assert** is ignored.

10.2 CHARACTER CLASSIFICATION: <ctype.h>

In the following list, the declaration of each function is followed by a description of its return value:

```
int isalnum(int ch);
```
$\ne 0$ (true) if **ch** is a letter or a digit (and 0 otherwise).

```
int isalpha(int ch);
```
$\ne 0$ if **ch** is a letter.

```
int iscntrl(int ch);
```
$\ne 0$ if **ch** is a control character.

```
int isdigit(int ch);
```
$\ne 0$ if **ch** is a decimal digit.

```
int isgraph(int ch);
```
$\ne 0$ if **ch** is a printable character, other than white space.

```
int islower(int ch);
```
$\ne 0$ if **ch** is a lower-case letter.

```
int isprint(int ch);
```
$\ne 0$ if **ch** is a printable character, including a blank.

```
int ispunct(int ch);
```
$\ne 0$ if **ch** is a printable character other than a letter, a digit, or a white-space character.

```
int isspace(int ch);
```
$\ne 0$ if **ch** is a space, a form feed, a newline, a carriage return, a tab, or a vertical tab.

```
int isupper(int ch);
```
$\ne 0$ if **ch** is an upper-case letter.

```
int isxdigit(int ch);
```
$\ne 0$ if **ch** is a hexadecimal digit.

There are also two functions to convert the case of letters:

```
int tolower(int ch);
```
The lower-case letter whose upper-case counterpart is **ch**. If **ch** is not an upper-case letter, the return value is **ch**.

```
int toupper(int ch);
```
The upper-case letter whose lower-case counterpart is **ch**. If **ch** is not a lower-case letter, the return value is **ch**.

For example, suppose that we want to convert **ch** if it denotes a lower-case letter; in that case we want its new value to be the corresponding upper-case letter. If **ch** does not denote a lower-case letter, it is not to be altered. We then write

```
ch = toupper(ch);
```

10.3 ERROR NUMBERS: <errno.h>

If we write

```
#include <errno.h>
```

in our program, then after an error occurs we can consult the value of the system variable **errno** to obtain more information about that error. Two symbolic constants defined in **errno.h** are

EDOM   is assigned to **errno** in case of a domain error, as occurs, for example, if we try to compute **sqrt(−1)**.

ERANGE   is assigned to **errno** in case of a range error, as occurs, for example, if we try to compute **exp(1e8)**.

10.4 FLOATING-POINT PRECISION: <float.h>

Even when using standard C, we must be aware that the results of our computations may depend on our hardware. The header file **float.h** supplies us with detailed information about the floating-point arithmetic that is used. In this section the names that we use for this purpose are listed, together with their meaning, and, between parentheses, the minimum or maximum values considered acceptable by ANSI. To explain some new notions, we will first briefly discuss some fundamentals of the floating-point representation of numbers. Note that our discussion is only about principles: the floating-point format used on your machine may be slightly different from what is discussed below.

A real number x can be approximated by

$$x \approx m \times 2^n$$

where n is integer, and m satisfies the following condition to *normalize* the representation:

$0.5 \leq |m| < 1$ or $m = 0$ (in the latter case, we also have $n = 0$)

We call m the *mantissa* and n the *exponent* of the floating-point representation (m, n). Instead of 2, a different base, say, b, may be raised to the power n (in which case the number 0.5 in the normalization condition is replaced with $1/b$). This base is also known as the *radix* of the floating-point representation. The normalization condition makes the representation of x by the pair (m, n) unique (except for round-off errors). For example, with $x = 9/4$, we have

$$m = 9/16, \; n = 2$$

Instead of x, both its (approximated) mantissa m and its exponent n are stored. Although x may have very large and very small (absolute) values, the numbers m and n that represent it can very well be stored in fixed numbers of bits. These numbers of bits determine both the precision and the maximum magnitude of x.

The above background information may be helpful in understanding the meaning of the following symbolic constants, defined in **float.h**:

FLT_RADIX   Radix of the floating-point representation; for example, 2 or 16.
FLT_ROUNDS   Floating-point rounding mode for addition.

Special information about type **float**:

FLT_DIG   Precision: number of decimal digits (at least 6).
FLT_EPSILON   Smallest number x such that $1.0 + x \neq 1.0$ (at most 10^{-5}).
FLT_MANT_DIG Number of digits of the mantissa when this is written in the number system with radix **FLT_RADIX**.
FLT_MAX   Maximum **float** value (at least 10^{37}).
FLT_MAX_EXP   Greatest n such that $\text{FLT\_RADIX}^n - 1$ can be represented.
FLT_MIN   Smallest positive normalized value of type **float** (at most 10^{-37}).
FLT_MIN_EXP   Smallest n such that 10^n can be normalized.

Special information about type **double**:

DBL_DIG   Precision: number of decimal digits (at least 10).
DBL_EPSILON   Smallest number x such that $1.0 + x \neq 1.0$ (at most 10^{-9}).
DBL_MANT_DIG Number of digits of the mantissa when this is written in the number system with radix **FLT_RADIX**.
DBL_MAX   Maximum **double** value (at least 10^{37}).
DBL_MAX_EXP   Greatest n such that $\text{FLT\_RADIX}^n - 1$ can be represented.
DBL_MIN   Smallest positive normalized value of type **double** (at most 10^{-37}).
DBL_MIN_EXP   Smallest n such that 10^n can be normalized.

10.5 MAXIMUM INTEGER ETC.: <limits.h>

All elementary types for which no floating-point representation is used are sometimes called *integral* types. The header file **limits.h** supplies us with very useful information about these types:

CHAR_BIT	Number of bits in a **char** (at least 8).
CHAR_MAX	Maximum **char** value.
CHAR_MIN	Minimum **char** value.
INT_MAX	Maximum **int** value (+32767 or greater).
INT_MIN	Minimum **int** value (−32767 or less).
LONG_MAX	Maximum **long** value (+2147483647 or greater).
LONG_MIN	Minimum **long** value (−2147483647 or less).
SCHAR_MAX	Maximum **signed char** value (+127 or greater).
SCHAR_MIN	Minimum **signed char** value (−127 or less).
SHRT_MAX	Maximum **short** value (+32767 or greater).
SHRT_MIN	Minimum **short** value (−32767 or less).
UCHAR_MAX	Maximum **unsigned char** value (255 or greater).
UINT_MAX	Maximum **unsigned int** value (65535 or greater).
ULONG_MAX	Maximum **unsigned long** value (4294967295 or greater).
USHRT_MAX	Maximum **unsigned short** value (65535 or greater).

10.6 MATHEMATICAL FUNCTIONS: <math.h>

In Section 5.7, we discussed a number of mathematical standard functions. Here are their declarations once again:

```
double cos(double x);
double sin(double x);
double tan(double x);
double exp(double x);
double log(double x);
double log10(double x);
double pow(double x, double y);
double sqrt(double x);
double floor(double x);
double ceil(double x);
double fabs(double x);
double acos(double x);
double asin(double x);
double atan(double x);
double atan2(double y, double x);
```

```
double cosh(double x);
double sinh(double x);
double tanh(double x);
```

The header file **math.h** also declares four functions that are associated with floating-point representation, discussed in Section 10.4:

```
double ldexp(double x, int n);          Returns x · 2ⁿ.
double frexp(double x, int *exponent);  See below.
double modf(double x, double *ip);      See below.
double fmod(double x, double y);        See below.
```

As you can see, **ldexp** computes a floating-point number from its mantissa and its exponent. The opposite of this is done by **frexp**. For example, after the execution of

```
int n;
double x, mantissa;
x = ...;
mantissa = frexp(x, &n);
```

we have

$$x = mantissa \times 2^n$$

where

$$0.5 \leq |mantissa| < 1 \quad \text{if } x \neq 0$$
$$mantissa = n = 0 \quad \text{if } x = 0$$

We can use **modf** to split a real number x into its integral part n and its fraction f. After calling **modf** in

```
int n;
double x, f;
x = ...;
f = modf(x, &n);
```

the sum of n and f is equal to x, the signs of n and f are the same as that of x, and $|f| < 1$. We can use **modf**, for example, to split 123.456 into 123 and 0.456.

Our last function should not be confused with **fmod**, which computes the remainder when one floating-point number is divided by another. After

```
double a, b, r;
a = ...; b = ...; /* b unequal to 0 */
r = fmod(a, b);
```

the value of r is such that $a - r$ is a whole multiple of b, the sign of r is the same as that of a, and

$$0 \leq |r| < |b|$$

For example, **fmod(2.8, 1.1)** is equal to 0.6 (= 2.8 − 2 × 1.1).

Besides the function declarations mentioned above, we also find the definition of the following symbolic constant in **math.h**:

HUGE_VAL   A very large positive value of type **double**.

10.7 NON-LOCAL JUMPS: <setjmp.h>

Suppose that function **main** calls function **f**, which in turn calls function **g**. If we leave **g** in the normal way, the jump back will not be directly to **main** (but, instead, to **f**). However, there is a language facility to realize such a jump from **g** back directly to **main**. In general, this facility enables us to jump back from a low-level function (such as **g**) back directly to a higher-level function (such as **main**), from which, possibly through other functions (such as **f**) a call to that low-level function was activated. The tools to be used for this purpose are a standard type, **jmp_buf**, defined in the header file **setjmp.h**, and two functions (possibly implemented as *macros*):

```
int setjmp(jmp_buf env);
```
Save state information, including the current position, in **env**, for use by **longjmp**.

```
void longjmp(jmp_buf env, int val);
```
Restore the state as stored in **env**; use the position stored there to perform a jump back to the **setjmp** call.

If **setjmp** is executed in the normal, sequential way, it returns 0; if it is executed as a result of executing **longjmp** (which, after all, jumps back to **setjmp**) it returns the (nonzero) value **val**, the second argument of **longjmp**. This enables us to tell which case applies. The following complete program illustrates all this. In accordance with the beginning of this section, **main** calls **f**, which in turn calls **g**. It depends on the input data whether or not **longjmp** is executed:

```
/* SETJMP: Demonstration of setjmp and longjmp.
*/
#include <stdio.h>
#include <setjmp.h>
jmp_buf position;
void f(void), g(void);

main()
{ if (setjmp(position) == 0) f(); else printf(
  "Jumped back directly from the middle of g.\n");
  printf("Ready.\n");
}

void f(void)
{ g();
  printf("Function f completed.\n");
}

void g(void)
{ char ch;
  printf("Do you want to jump back directly to main? (Y/N): ");
  scanf(" %c", &ch);
  if (ch == 'Y' || ch == 'y') longjmp(position, 1);
  printf("Function g completed.\n");
}
```

Note how the value returned by **setjmp** is used. The first time this value is 0. If and when **longjmp** is executed, **setjmp** returns 1, because this was the second argument in the call to **longjmp**.

10.8 SPECIAL SITUATIONS: <signal.h>

The header file **signal.h** contains the following function prototypes:

```
int raise(int sig);
```
   'Send signal **sig**'; the return value is 0 if this call is successful and nonzero otherwise. See also **signal**.

```
void (*signal(int sig, void (*handler)(int)))(int);
```
   Specify the action that is to be performed immediately if and when 'signal **sig** is sent' by **raise**.

A call to **signal** looks considerably simpler than the above declaration of this function. The first argument, **sig**, can take the following values, defined in **signal.h**:

SIGABRT   The program has been terminated abnormally, as, for example, by means of a call to the function **abort,** mentioned in Section 10.12.
SIGFPE   An arithmetic error, such as, for example, division by zero, has occurred.
SIGILL   An illegal instruction has been executed.
SIGINT   An interrupt has occurred.
SIGSEGV   An attempt has been made to access memory that is not available.
SIGTERM   There has been a request to terminate the program..

So much for the first argument of **signal**. The second argument, **handler,** can be the name of a function of our own. Instead, we can also write:

SIG_IGN   Ignore the signal.
SIG_DFL   Perform the default action, as defined by the implementation.

The value returned by **signal** is the second argument, **handler,** unless an error has occurred. In that case the return value is **SIG_ERR**, also defined in **signal.h**.

10.9 VARIABLE-LENGTH ARGUMENT LISTS: <stdarg.h>

As we have discussed variable-length arguments lists in Section 9.1, we will deal with this subject more briefly here.

We will consider the beginning of a function, **fun**, the first three parameters, **c,** **x,** and **k** of which have the types **char, float,** and **int**, respectively. In total, there are $3 + n$ arguments ($n \geq 0$). The first three arguments supply **fun** with information to determine how many arguments follow and what the type of each of these is. Then we write the first line of function **fun** as follows:

```
int fun(char c, float x, int k, ...)
```

Note that this should be taken literally, including the three dots. If we want a separate declaration of **fun**, this takes the same form as this line followed by a semicolon.

We then introduce a variable, traditionally called **argp**, of type **va_list** (defined in **stdarg.h**). Thus, at the beginning of **fun** we declare:

```
va_list argp;
```

This variable **argp** will act as a pointer to the next argument to be used. This process is initialized by executing the following macro call:

```
va_start(argp, k);
```

This expresses that **argp** is to point to the argument that follows the one that corresponds to parameter **k**. In order to obtain the value of the argument pointed to by **argp**, we must not use the normal notation ***argp**, but, instead, we write:

```
va_arg(argp, type)
```

where *type* is the type of the argument pointed to by **argp** (which means that *type* is also the type of this whole macro call). Thus, we can call **va_arg**, for example, as follows:

```
y = va_arg(argp, double);
```

As an important side effect, **va_arg** also alters **argp**, so that it points to the next argument, and so on. Therefore **va_arg** will in practice be called in a loop. After the termination of this loop, the following macro call is to be executed:

```
va_end(argp);
```

For a complete program that uses variable-length argument lists you are referred to Section 9.1.

10.10 SPECIAL TYPES: <stddef.h>

The following two special types are defined in the header file **stddef.h**:

size_t   The type of the value returned by the operator **sizeof**.
ptrdiff_t   The type which can always safely be used for the difference of
                two pointer values (that is, of two addresses).

In Sections 3.2 and 6.1, it was suggested that both **sizeof** and pointer differences have type **int**. Although in many cases we can use type **int** to store such values, more bits may be needed than are provided by this type. For example, if 32767 is the largest **int** value, this may be too small for the difference of two addresses, so that type **long** may be needed. However, there are also machines with an **int** type that is perfectly suitable for that purpose. To prevent us from having to use types that are system dependent, the types **size_t** and **ptrdiff_t** have been defined. Depending on your compiler, **size_t** is identical with either **unsigned int** or **unsigned long int**. Similarly, **ptrdiff_t** is identical with either **int** or **long int**. For example, we can write:

```
#include <stddef.h>
#define LENGTH 30000

main()
{ size_t n;
  ptrdiff_t d;
  double a[LENGTH];
  char *p, *q;
  p = (char *) a;
  q = (char *)(a + LENGTH);
  n = sizeof(a);
  d = q - p;
  ...
}
```

Note that **n** denotes the length of array **a** *expressed in bytes*; if one **double** value takes 8 bytes, we have **n** = 30 000 × 8 = 240 000 bytes, which may be too large for type **unsigned int**. If a machine has integers of only four bytes but nevertheless allows such large arrays as are used here, the value assigned to **n** will still be correct, thanks to the fact that type **size_t** is defined as **unsigned long** for that machine. In this example, the difference **d** of **q** and **p** will be as large as **n** and therefore possibly not representable by type **int** either. If that is the case, type **ptrdiff_t** will be identical with type **long int**, so it will be possible for **d** too to be assigned its correct value.

There are applications in which we are certain that both **sizeof** and computed address differences will only yield values that are not too large for type **int**. (Recall that the ANSI standard guarantees that the maximum **int** value is not less than 32767, as discussed in Section 10.5.) In these cases, type **int** is as good as the above new types. But even if we never use these new types ourselves it is desirable to know what they mean so that we can read programs and header files written by others.

10.11 INPUT AND OUTPUT: <stdio.h>

We have dealt with the most important I/O functions in Chapter 8 and elsewhere. The present section lists their declarations once again, with a reference to the sections that give more information about them. Then we will discuss some more standard I/O functions.

Many I/O functions make use of type **FILE**, defined in **stdio.h**. We have access to files (on disk) by using file pointers of type 'pointer-to-**FILE**', or type **FILE ***, for short. There are three standard file pointers, also called *streams*, namely **stdin, stdout,** and **stderr**. They are normally used for input from the keyboard, output to the video display, and the display of error messages, respectively.

The following lines with function declarations also contain references to the sections that give more information about these functions (and macros); note that type **size_t**, discussed in the previous section, is used for **fread** and **fwrite**:

```
FILE *fopen(const char *filename, const char *mode); /* Section 8.4 */
int fclose(FILE *fp);                               /* Section 8.4 */
int fscanf(FILE *fp, const char *format, ...);      /* Section 8.4 */
int fprintf(FILE *fp, const char *format, ...);     /* Section 8.4 */
int scanf(const char *format, ...);                 /* Section 8.3 */
int printf(const char *format, ...);                /* Section 8.2 */
int getc(FILE *fp);                                 /* Section 8.4 */
int putc(int ch, FILE *fp);                         /* Section 8.4 */
int ungetc(int ch, FILE *fp);                       /* Section 8.4 */
int getchar(void);                          /* Sections 8.1 and 8.4 */
int putchar(int ch);                        /* Sections 8.1 and 8.4 */
char *gets(char *s);                                /* Section 6.7 */
int puts(const char *s);                            /* Section 6.7 */
char *fgets(char *s, int n, FILE *fp);              /* Section 8.4 */
int fputs(const char *s, FILE *fp);                 /* Section 8.4 */
size_t fread(void *bufptr, size_t size, size_t nobj, FILE *fp);
                                                    /* Section 8.5 */
size_t fwrite(const void *bufptr, size_t size, size_t nobj, FILE *fp);
                                                    /* Section 8.5 */
int fseek(FILE *fp, long offset, int fromwhere);    /* Section 8.6 */
long ftell(FILE *fp);                               /* Section 8.6 */
void rewind(FILE *fp);                              /* Section 8.4 */
int feof(FILE *fp);                                 /* Section 8.4 */
int vprintf(const char *format, va_list argp);      /* Section 9.1 */
int vfprintf(FILE *fp, const char *format, va_list argp);
                                                    /* Section 9.1 */
int vsprintf(char *s, const char *format, va_list argp);
                                                    /* Section 9.1 */
int sscanf(char *s, const char *format, ...);       /* Section 6.11 */
int sprintf(char *s, const char *format, ...);      /* Section 6.11 */
```

The following functions have not yet been discussed:

```
int fgetc(FILE *fp);
```
Analogous to **getc**, but implemented as a function, not as a macro.

```
int fputc(int ch, FILE *fp);
```
Analogous to **putc**, but implemented as a function, not as a macro.

```
FILE *freopen(const char *filename, const char *mode, FILE *fp);
```
You can use this function for a stream **fp** that has been opened by means of **fopen,** to alter its physical file name or its mode. You can also use it to associate one of the streams **stdout, stdin,** or **stderr** with a real file. For example:

```
    fp = freopen("result.dat", "w", stdout);
```

After the execution of this statement, **printf** will write output data to the file **result.dat** instead of to the video display. The return value is equal to the third argument, unless an error occurs; in that case it is **NULL.**

```
int fflush(FILE *fp);
```
A call to this function is defined only if **fp** is being used for output. It then flushes the buffer: any output data that still is in the output buffer is actually written to the external device, such as a disk. This is done automatically when a program terminates normally and when **fclose** is called. The return value is normally 0; it is **EOF** if an error occurs.

```
FILE *tmpfile(void);
```
Creates and opens a temporary file in the mode **"w+b"**; this file is automatically deleted when the program terminates normally. The return value is a file pointer, or **NULL** if the file cannot be opened.

```
char *tmpnam(char s[L_tmpnam]);
```
After a call to this function, **s** contains a string different from all existing file names. The start address of **s** is returned. As many as **TMP_MAX** distinct file names can be generated. The symbolic constants **L_tmpnam** and **TMP_MAX** are defined in **stdio.h.**

```
int remove(const char *filename);
```
Deletes a file with the given name. If this is indeed possible, **remove** returns 0; if not, it returns a nonzero value.

```
int rename(const char *oldname, const char *newname);
```
Renames a given file, and returns 0, unless renaming is not possible; in that case **rename** returns nonzero.

```
int setvbuf(FILE *fp, char *buf, int mode, size_t size);
```
Sets the buffering method for the stream **fp**. If **buf** is equal to **NULL**, memory space for a buffer is created automatically; otherwise **buf** is used as a buffer. (If you use a normal local variable for **buf**, do not forget to close the file in question before the function is left!) There are the following possibilities for **mode**:

> `_IOFBF` complete buffering;
> `_IOLBF` line buffering for text files;
> `_IONBF` no buffering.

(These three symbolic constants are defined in **stdio.h**.) The buffer size is given by the fourth parameter, **size**. Normally, 0 is returned; in case of an error, the return value is nonzero.

```
void setbuf(FILE *fp, char *buf);
```
If **buf** is **NULL**, the stream **fp** will be unbuffered. If **buf** is equal to a real address, the call

```
setbuf(fp, buf);
```

has the same effect as

```
setvbuf(fp, buf, _IOFBF, BUFSIZ);
```

(The symbolic constant **BUFSIZ** is defined in stdio.h.

```
int fgetpos(FILE *fp, fpos_t *ptr);
```
The current position in the stream **fp** is written into ***ptr**. Type **fpos_t** is defined in **stdio.h**. (Unlike **ftell**, which uses a byte number, **fgetpos** uses a more technical representation of the position in a file. (See also **fsetpos**.) The return value is 0, unless an error occurs; in that case it is nonzero.

```
int fsetpos(FILE *fp, const fpos_t *ptr);
```
The stream **fp** is positioned at the point given by **ptr**; see also **fgetpos**. The return value is 0, unless an error occurs; in that case it is nonzero.

```
int ferror(FILE *fp);
```
Returns nonzero if an error has occurred in an I/O operation on stream **fp**. (The occurrence of errors is registered in *status indicators*, such as **errno**, mentioned in Section 10.3.)

```
void perror(const char *s);
```
Prints **s**, together with an implementation-dependent error message that corresponds to the value of **errno**; see also Section 10.3.

```
void clearerr(FILE *fp);
```
Clears the error indicator and the end-of-file indicator for the stream **fp**. For example, if **feof(fp)** returns nonzero and the call **clearerr(fp)** is executed, then immediately after the latter call **feof(fp)** will return 0.

10.12 MISCELLANEOUS: <stdlib.h>

The header file **stdlib.h** declares useful functions for various purposes:

```
double atof(const char *s);
```
If the string **s** contains a valid character representation of a number, then this number, converted to type **double**, is returned. If not, **errno** is given a nonzero value; see Section 10.3.

```
int atoi(const char *s);
```
As **atof**, except that **s** is converted to type **int**.

```
long atol(const char *s);
```
As **atof**, except that **s** is converted to type **long**.

```
double strtod(const char *s, char **endp);
```
Converts the beginning of string **s** to type **double**. If **endp** is not **NULL**, the address of the first character that follows the converted substring is assigned to ***endp**. In case of an error, **errno** is given a nonzero value; see Section 10.3.

```
long strtol(const char *s, char **endp, int base);
```
Converts the beginning of string **s** to type **long**. If **endp** is not **NULL**, the address of the first character that follows the converted substring is assigned to ***endp**. If **base** satisfies $2 \leq base \leq 36$, the number in **s** is assumed to be written in the number system with radix **base**. If **base** is greater than 10 (but not greater than 36) the letters **A, B, ···** (or **a, b, ···**) act as the digits 10, 11, ···, **base** − 1. If **base** is 0, the assumed radix is 16 if **s** starts with **0X** or **0x**, 8 if **s** starts with 0 not followed by **X** or **x**, or 10 in all other cases. In case of an error, **errno** is given a nonzero value; see Section 10.3.

```
unsigned long strtoul(const char *s, char **endp, int base);
```
As **strtol**, except that the beginning of string **s** is converted to type **unsigned long**.

```
void abort(void);
```
Causes abnormal program termination, as if by **raise(SIGABRT)**; see Section 10.8.

```
void exit(int status);
```
Causes normal program termination; any open files are closed, as if the program terminates normally without calling **exit**. The use of the argument **status** is system dependent; its normal values are 0 for 'success' and 1 for 'failure'. Instead of 0 and 1, the symbolic constants **EXIT_SUCCESS** and **EXIT_FAILURE**, defined in **stdlib.h**, may be used.

```
int atexit(void (*fcn)(void));
```
Registers the function **fcn**, so that the latter will be called when the program (normally) terminates. The return value is nonzero if the registration cannot be made. If you register more than one function in this way, the most recently registered one is executed first, and so on, as the following example shows:

```
#include <stdio.h>
#include <stdlib.h>

void ready(void)
{ printf("Ready.\n");
}

void almost_ready(void)
{ printf("Almost ready.\n");
}

main()
{ atexit(ready);
  atexit(almost_ready);
  printf("Not ready.\n");
}
```

The output of this program is

```
Not ready.
Almost ready.
Ready.
```

```
int system(const char *s);
```
The string **s** is passed to the command processor of the operating system, so that it will be interpreted and executed as a command. The value returned by **system** is system dependent.

```
char *getenv(const char *name);
```
If there is an 'environment variable' **name** in the operating system, the value of this variable is returned; if not, **NULL** is returned. Details are system dependent.

```
int abs(int n);
```
Returns the absolute value of its argument **n**. Remember, **abs** can be used only for **int** arguments. See also **labs** and **fabs**.

```
long labs(long n);
```
Returns the absolute value of its **long** argument **n**.

```
div_t div(int num, int denom);
```
Performs the integer division **num/denom** and computes both the quotient and the remainder. The return value is a structure of type **div_t**, defined in **stdlib.h** as follows:

```
typedef struct {int quot, rem;} div_t;
```

The quotient and the remainder will be found in the **quot** and **rem** members, respectively. (As with most machines the quotient and the remainder can be obtained in one divide instruction, these two results may be computed more efficiently by this **div** function than by the two C operators **/** and **%**, for which two divide instructions would be required.)

```
ldiv_t div(long num, long denom);
```
As **div**, except that type **long** is used for the numerator **num** and the denominator **denom**. The quotient and the remainder also have type long: type **ldiv_t** is defined in **stdlib.h** as

```
typedef struct {long quot, rem;} ldiv_t;
```

```
int rand(void);
```
Returns a nonnegative pseudo-random integer, not greater than **RAND_MAX**; this symbolic constant is defined in **stdlib.h** and is not less than 32767. See also **srand**.

```
void srand(unsigned int seed);
```
Specifies that **seed** is to be used as the initial value in the process of generating pseudo-random numbers by means of successive calls to **rand**. If we do not call **srand**, that initial value is 1.

We can use **srand** if the same pseudo-random number sequence is to be generated more than once: for each sequence, we call **srand** with the same argument, prior to entering the loop in which calls to **rand** generate the elements of that sequence.

On the other hand, we may want to write a program that generates a sequence of pseudo-random numbers, different from the sequence that is generated when the program is executed once again. In this case we want the seed value to be different each time we run the program. This can be achieved by using the function **time** (discussed in Section 10.14), because this function supplies us with a different value each time the program is executed. For example, the following function, **rand10**, shows how this principle can be applied to generate a pseudo-random integer in the range 1, 2, $\cdots$, 10:

```
#include <time.h>
#include <stdlib.h>

int rand10(void)
{ static int firstcall=1;
  if (firstcall)
  { srand((unsigned int)time(NULL));
    firstcall = 0;
  }
  return rand() % 10 + 1;
}
```

The following functions have been dealt with in Section 6.6. (Note the use of **size_t**, discussed in Section 10.10.)

```
void *malloc(size_t nbytes);
void *calloc(size_t nobj, size_t objectsize);
void *realloc(void *p, size_t nbytes);
void free(void *p);
```

Finally, we repeat the declarations of the following two functions, which can also be found in Sections 9.2 and 9.3:

```
void *bsearch(const void *key, const void *base,
              size_t n, size_t width,
              int (*fcmp)(const void *, const void *));

void qsort(void *base, size_t n, size_t width,
           int (*fcmp)(const void *, const void *));
```

10.13 STRING FUNCTIONS: <string.h>

The following functions have been discussed in Section 6.5:

```
size_t strlen(const char *s);
int strcmp(const char *s1, const char *s2);
```

```
int strncmp(const char *s1, const char *s2, size_t maxlen);
char *strcpy(char *dest, const char *src);
char *strncpy(char *dest, const char *src, size_t maxlen);
char *strcat(char *dest, const char *src);
char *strncat(char *dest, const char *src, size_t maxlen);
```

The header file **string.h** also declares the following string functions:

```
char *strchr(const char *s, int ch);
```
    Returns the address of the first occurrence of character **ch** in string **s**, or **NULL** if **ch** does not occur in **s**.

```
char *strrchr(const char *s, int ch);
```
    Returns the address of the *last* occurrence of character **ch** in string **s**, or **NULL** if **ch** does not occur in **s**.

```
size_t strspn(const char *s1, const char *s2);
```
    Returns the length of the longest possible prefix of **s1** consisting of characters that also occur in **s2**.

```
size_t strcspn(const char *s1, const char *s2);
```
    Returns the length of the longest possible prefix of **s1** consisting of characters that *do not* occur in **s2**.

```
char *strpbrk(const char *s1, const char *s2);
```
    Searches **s1** (starting at **s1[0]**) for a character that also occurs in **s2**. If such a character is found, its address is returned; if not, the return value is **NULL**.

```
char *strstr(const char *s1, const char *s2);
```
    Searches **s1** (starting at **s1[0]**) for a substring identical with **s2**. If this substring is found, its start address is returned; if not, the return value is **NULL**.

```
char *strerror(int errnum);
```
    Returns (the address of) a string that contains an error message belonging to the current value of **errnum**. See also Section 10.3.

```
char *strtok(char *s1, const char *s2);
```
    Consider the call **strtok(s1, s2)**. Then a *token* is a substring of **s1** consisting of characters that do not occur in **s2**; an additional requirement is that a token cannot be a substring of a longer token. For example, if we take the call **strtok("!ABC.;DEF", ";?.!/")**, there are precisely two tokens, namely **ABC** and **DEF**. The value returned by **strtok(s1, s2)** is the address of the first token in **s1**. After this initial call (in which **s1** was not **NULL**), we write a loop in which the call **strtok(NULL, s2)** occurs; each time, **strtok** returns the next

token in the string **s1** of the initial call. If no more tokens are to be found, **strtok** returns **NULL**. Each time a token is found in **s1**, the first character that follows this token is overwritten by the null character, as the following program demonstrates:

```
#include <string.h>
#include <stdio.h>

main()
{ char *p, s[] = "31/12-1990---23.59 h";
  int n=0, len, i;
  len = strlen(s);
  p = strtok(s, " /.,;-");
  while (p != NULL)
  { printf("%s;", p);
    p = strtok(NULL, " /.,;-");
  }
  for (i=0; i<=len; i++) if (s[i] == '\0') n++;
  printf("\nThere are now %d null characters in array s.\n", n);
}
```

This program produces the following output:

```
31;12;1990;23;59;h;
There are now 6 null characters in array s.
```

The following functions manipulate byte sequences that are not necessarily strings. Remember that a string ends with a null character, on which most functions rely. The following do not. They can therefore also deal with byte sequences that may contain null characters in any positions.

`void *memcpy(void *dest, const void *src, size_t n);`
> Copies **n** bytes from **src** to **dest** and returns **dest**. The result is undefined if **src** and **dest** overlap.

`void *memmove(void *dest, const void *src, size_t n);`
> The same as **memcpy**, except that **src** and **dest** may overlap.

`int memcmp(const void *s1, const void *s2, size_t n);`
> The same as the well-known function **strncmp** (discussed in Section 6.5), except that comparing characters does not terminate if a null character is encountered.

`void *memchr(const void *s, int ch, size_t n);`
> Returns the address of the first occurrence of character **ch** in the sequence $s[0], \cdots, s[n-1]$, or **NULL** if **ch** does not occur in this sequence.

```
void *memset(void *s, int ch, size_t n);
```
Assigns **ch** to all elements **s[0]**, ···, **s[n−1]**, and returns **s**.

10.14 TIME AND DATE: <time.h>

The types **time_t** and **clock_t** are defined in the header file **time.h** to represent the time as a number. These types may be defined, for example, as **long**. Bearing this in mind will be helpful in understandig the following function declarations:

```
time_t time(time_t *pt);
```
Returns the current calendar time, expressed in seconds; the return value may be the time elapsed since January 1st 1970, 0.00 h GMT. If the time is not available, −1 is returned. If **pt** is not **NULL**, the return value is also assigned to ***pt**.

```
double difftime(time_t t2, time_t t1);
```
Returns the difference **t2 − t1**, expressed in seconds.

```
clock_t clock(void);
```
Returns the processor time used since the beginning of program execution. This time is expressed in *ticks*. The number of ticks per second is given by the symbolic constant **CLK_TCK**, defined in **time.h**. It follows that a tick is 1/**CLK_TCK** seconds, and that the quotient **clock( )/CLK_TCK** gives the processor time in seconds. If the time is not available, the return value is −1.

To make the time available in other forms, type **struct tm** is defined in **time.h** as follows:

```
struct tm
{ int tm_sec;    /* Seconds (< 60) after the minute               */
  int tm_min;    /* Minutes (< 60) after the hour                 */
  int tm_hour;   /* Hours (< 24) since midnight                   */
  int tm_mday;   /* Day of the month (≤ 31)                       */
  int tm_mon;    /* Month: 0 = Jan., ..., 11 = Dec.               */
  int tm_year;   /* Years since 1900                              */
  int tm_wday;   /* Day of the week: 0 = Sunday, ..., 6 = Saturday */
  int tm_yday;   /* Day of the year; b.v. 0 = Jan. 1st, 31 = Feb. 1st */
  int tm_isdst;  /* Daylight Saving Time:                         */
                 /*    Positive: Daylight Saving Time in effect   */
                 /*    0:        Daylight Saving Time not in effect */
                 /*    Negative: The information is not available  */
};
```

The following functions are based on this type. The functions **localtime**, **gmtime**, **asctime**, **ctime** return the addresses of static objects, which may be overwritten by subsequent call to these functions.

```
struct tm *localtime(const time_t *pt);
```
Converts the time ***pt**, as returned by **time**, into local time.

```
struct tm *gmtime(const time_t *pt);
```
Converts the time ***pt**, as returned by **time**, into Coordinated Universal Time (UTC). It returns **NULL** if UTC is not available.

```
char *asctime(const struct tm *pt);
```
Converts the time available in the structure ***pt** into a string of the form

```
Fri Jul 14 09:06:43 1990\n\0
```

```
char *ctime(const time_t *pt);
```
Returns a string similar to the one returned by **asctime**, but based on the time available in ***pt** (as returned by **time**). Thus, **ctime(pt)** is equivalent to **asctime(localtime(pt))**.

```
time_t mktime(struct tm *pt);
```
Converts the local time given in ***pt** into calendar time in the same representation as used by **time**.

```
size_t strftime(char *s, size_t smax, const char *fmt, const struct tm *pt);
```
Formats the date and time information given in ***pt** into **s**, according to the format string **fmt**, which can contain special conversion specifications listed below. Like **sprintf**, discussed in Section 6.11, **strftime** places the resulting string into memory locations the address of which is given by its first argument, **s**. No more than **smax** characters are transmitted to **s**. If **smax** is too small to place all characters that are generated into **s**, the return value is 0; otherwise it is the number of characters placed into **s**, excluding the null character, which is written at the end. Ordinary characters in **fmt**, not belonging to conversion specifications, are copied into **s**. The following conversion specifications can be used:

%a	Abbreviated weekday name.
%A	Full weekday name.
%b	Abbreviated month name.
%B	Full month name.
%c	Date and time.
%d	Two-digit day of the month (01 to 31).
%H	Two-digit hour (24-hour clock) (00 to 23).
%I	Two-digit hour (12-hour clock) (00 to 12).

%j   Three-digit day of the year (001 to 366).

%m   Two-digit month (01 to 12).

%M   Two-digit minute (00 to 59).

%p   AM or PM.

%S   Two-digit second (00 to 59).

%U   Two-digit week number where Sunday is the first day of the week (00 to 53).

%w   Weekday, where 0 is Sunday (0 to 6).

%W   Two-digit week number where Monday is the first day of the week (00 to 53).

%x   Date.

%X   Time.

%y   Two-digit year without century (00 to 99).

%Y   Year with century.

%Z   Time zone name, or no characters if no time zone.

%%   Character %.

As you can see, these conversion specifications are quite different from those used for **sprintf**. Note also that, unlike **sprintf**, **strftime** has a fixed number of arguments: all conversion specifications refer to the same structure, the address of which is given as the last argument. The order of the conversion specifications in the format string may be different from the order of the members in that structure.

Since most of the functions discussed in this section have addresses as arguments, we will often have to use the operator **&**. Some of these functions are used in the following demonstration program:

```
/* TIMEDEMO: Demonstration of time and date functions.
*/
#include <time.h>
#include <stdio.h>

main()
{ struct tm s;
  time_t t;
  char str[80];
  time(&t);
  s = *localtime(&t);
  printf("\nTime in structure s (of type struct tm):\n");
  printf("sec=%d min=%d hour=%d mday=%d mon=%d year=%d ",
    s.tm_sec, s.tm_min, s.tm_hour, s.tm_mday, s.tm_mon, s.tm_year);
  printf("wday=%d yday=%d isdst=%d\n",
    s.tm_wday, s.tm_yday, s.tm_isdst);
  printf("Time obtained by asctime         : %s", asctime(&s));
```

```
    printf("The same result obtained by ctime: %s", ctime(&t));
    printf("The following line contains data "
           "obtained by means of strftime:\n");
    strftime(str, 80,
    "It is %M minutes after %I o'clock %p  %A, %B %d 19%y", &s);
    printf("%s\n", str);
}
```

At the moment this program was executed, the result was as follows:

```
Time in structure s (of type struct tm):
sec=49 min=38 hour=19 mday=24 mon=4 year=90 wday=4 yday=143 isdst=1
Time obtained by asctime        : Thu May 24 19:38:49 1990
The same result obtained by ctime: Thu May 24 19:38:49 1990
The following line contains data obtained by means of strftime:
It is 38 minutes after 07 o'clock PM  Thursday, May 24 1990
```

APPENDIX A

More Exercises

In addition to the exercises at the end of Chapters 1 to 9, here are some more recommended programming problems. As is usually the case in practice, you will have to choose yourself among several facilities of the C language that can be used to solve a given problem. Be economical with computer time and memory space. In particular, do not use arrays if you can easily do without them.

1   When three numbers are given, it may or may not be possible to use them as the lengths of the sides of a triangle. Write a program to find this out for three real numbers read from the keyboard. If such a triangle exists, examine if it has an obtuse or a right angle.

2   Write a program which reads the three real numbers a, b, and c, to compute the real numbers x_1 and x_2 that satisfy the quadratic equation $ax^2 + bx + c = 0$, if such real numbers exist.

3   A sequence of positive integers is to be read from the keyboard, followed by a nonnumeric character. For each of the factors 2, 3, and 5, count how many of the integers that are read are multiples of that factor.

4   Write a program that reads a sequence of 20 integers to determine the smallest and the largest of them as well as the positions of these two elements in the sequence. In case they occur more than once, find the position of the first occurrence of the smallest number and that of the last occurrence of the largest number.

5   A sequence of real numbers, followed by a nonnumeric character, is to be read from the keyboard. Compute the sum of the 1st, 3rd, 6th, 10th, 15th, 21st, ⋯ elements of this sequence.

6   A sequence of 20 integers is to be read from the keyboard. For each pair of successive integers in this sequence, compute the absolute value of their difference. The largest of these absolute values is to be printed.

7   A sequence of 10 integers is to be read from the keyboard. Search this sequence for the first element that is equal to the tenth, and print the position of that first element. (If all elements are equal, that position is 1; if they are all distinct, it is 10.)

8   Write a program that reads a positive integer n (not greater than 25), to print a table of n lines and n columns, which has the following form:

```
1  1  1   ...   1
1  2  2   ...   2
1  2  3   ...   3
   .  .  .        .
   .  .  .        .
   .  .  .        .
1  2  3   ...   n
```

9   Write a program that reads a sample of n real values x_i, followed by a nonnumeric character. The following numbers, used in statistics to characterize certain properties of the sample, are to be computed:

a. The mean value: $(\Sigma x_i)/n$
b. The variance: $\{(\Sigma x_i^2) - (\Sigma x_i)^2/n\}/(n - 1)$
c. The range ($=$ largest value $-$ smallest value)

(Σx_i is the sum of all x_i; Σx_i^2 is the sum of all x_i^2.)

10   A given input file contains the values $x_1, y_1, x_2, y_2, \cdots, x_n, y_n$, in that order. Each pair (x_i, y_i) represents a point in the xy-plane. We want to compute the coefficients a and b of the equation

$$y = a + bx$$

which represents a *regression line*, that is, a straight line which fits 'best' through the n given points. Use the *method of least squares* by Gauss, according to which a and b are found as the solution of the following system of linear equations:

$$an\ \ \ + b\Sigma x_i\ \ \ = \Sigma y_i$$
$$a\Sigma x_i + b\Sigma x_i^2 = \Sigma xy_i$$

11   A ladder has a given length L. It is placed against a wall, and touches a box, which is a cube with height 1, as shown in Fig. A1. Compute the distance x between the box and the bottom of the ladder.

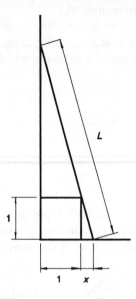

Fig. A1. Ladder and box

12   Both a real number x and an integer n are to be read from the keyboard. Compute the following sum, which is an approximation of the mathematical expression e^x ($e = 2.718281828459\cdots$; $n! = 1 \times 2 \times \cdots \times n$):

$$1 + x + \frac{x^2}{2!} + \frac{x^3}{3!} + \cdots + \frac{x^n}{n!}$$

13   A file contains the positive integers k and n, followed by $k \times n$ real numbers in a table with k rows and n columns. Compute the arithmetic means of each of the n columns. The name of the input file is to be supplied as a program argument.

14   Write a program that reads two dates of the same (non-leap) year to compute how many days the second date falls after the first. The dates are given as four-digit integers *mmdd*. For example, 1231 is the last day of the year. Print the algebraic difference: the result is negative if the first given date falls after the second.

15   A file contains the integer n, followed by two sequences: first, n integers a_i and, second, n integers b_i. Compute $\Sigma \max(a_i, b_i)$, that is, the sum of the n larger values of each pair (a_i, b_i). The name of the input file is to be entered on the keyboard.

16   Count how many decimal integers occur in a given text file, and compute the sum of these integers. The integers may be separated by any nonnumeric characters. The name of the input file is to be supplied as a program argument. For example, the file consisting or the two lines shown below contains five integers, the sum of which is 1034.

     123.111?abc200
     500 100def

17   Write a program which reads a positive integer, doubles it, and prints the decimal digits of its result, separated by a blank. For example, if 3912 is read, the output is 7 8 2 4.

18   Write a program that reads an integer n and prints all possible sequences of n bits in which no successive zeros occur. For example, $n = 3$ leads to

     010
     011
     101
     110
     111

19   Write a program that reads n, followed by the n^2 integers:

$$a_{11}, a_{12}, \cdots, a_{1n}$$
$$a_{21}, a_{22}, \cdots, a_{2n}$$
$$\cdots$$
$$a_{n1}, a_{n2}, \cdots, a_{nn}$$

most of which are zero. Compute the largest absolute value $|i - j|$ for which a_{ij} is nonzero.

20   Write a program that sorts the real numbers $a_0, a_1, \cdots, a_{n-1}$, read from the keyboard, using the *straight selection* sorting method. It is given that n will be no greater than 25, so the n real numbers can be placed in an array. First, search the sequence for its smallest element and exchange this with a_0. Then, deal with the remaining sequence, starting with a_1, in the same way, and so on. When, finally, there is a remaining sequence of length 1, all elements in the array are in increasing order and can be

printed. (Remember, this sorting method should be used only for sequences of moderate length, as in this example. For long sequences, the quicksort method, discussed in Section 9.3, is much faster.)

21   Write a program which reads 25 positive integers a_0, $\cdots$, a_{24}, which are absolute frequencies, and represent them by a *frequency histogram*. The latter is to consist of 25 vertical bars, the jth bar ($0 \leq j < 25$) being a column of a_j letters **I**. The lower endpoints of all bars are to appear on the same horizontal line.

22   Write a program that reads a positive integer and writes it as a product of prime factors. For example, we have $120 = 2 \times 2 \times 2 \times 3 \times 5$.

23   Write a program which reads a sequence of integers, followed by a nonnumeric character, and counts how often each of the integers 0, 1, $\cdots$, 15 occurs in this sequence. Print the result in a table.

24   We are given 25 gears with the following numbers of teeth:

30	35	37	40	45
47	50	52	55	57
60	65	68	70	75
78	80	82	85	86
87	90	95	97	99.

In order to transmit power from one shaft to another, we need to use pairs of gears, as illustrated in Fig. A2. The left and the right gears have *a* and *b* teeth, respectively. In view of the allowed center distances *d*, the sum of the numbers of teeth must satisfy

$$130 \leq a + b \leq 140.$$

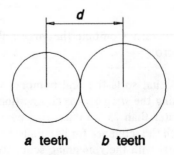

Fig. A2. Gears

Furthermore, we are only interested in pairs (a, b) that give a gear ratio $q = a/b$ satisfying $0.5 \leq q < 1$. Write a program that produces a table of all allowed pairs (a, b), together with their gear ratios q:

a	b	q
.	.	.
.	.	.
.	.	.

(If you think this exercise too elementary, you can make it more interesting by requiring that the above lines be printed in increasing order of q.)

25 Write a program that looks for all occurrences of a given word in a given text file. Both the word (consisting of letters only) and the file name are supplied as program arguments. Print each line of the file in which the given word occurs.

26 We can write $8/35 = 1/(4 + 3/8)$. Applying the same process to $3/8$, we obtain $8/35 = 1/\{4 + 1/(2 + 2/3)\}$. We proceed in this way until the final plus sign is followed by the numerator 1. In our example, this is the case after another step, which gives $8/35 = 1/[4 + 1/\{2 + 1/(1 + 1/2)\}]$. We can represent such an expression, called a *continued fraction*, by listing all integers that occur in it except for all numerators 1. In this example we obtain 4, 2, 1, 2. Write a program which reads two positive integers a and b and computes the sequence representing the continued fraction for a/b.

27 Write a program which reads the positive integers $a_1, a_2, \cdots, a_n$ to find all pairs (i, j) for which the greatest common divisor of a_i and a_j is equal to 1. See also Exercise 5.5.

28 In a factory, there is a machine that examines a great many samples of, say, a liquid product. For each sample, the machine checks whether or not each of the elements $E_0, E_1, \cdots, E_7$ is present in the sample, and the eight answers are coded (as 1 for present and 0 for absent) in the bits b_0, $b_1, \cdots, b_7$ of a byte. All these bytes are written in the file **element.dat**. Write a program that reads this file, and, for each of the eight elements, counts how many times it has been present in the tested samples.

29 Write a program to approximate the value of x (between $\frac{1}{2}\pi$ and π) that satisfies the following equation:

$$\sin x - \tfrac{1}{2} x = 0$$

Use the Newton–Raphson method (also known as the Newton method), which is a well-known numerical method for solving equations of the form $f(x) = 0$. Starting with some value x_0 as an approximation of the solution x, you repeatedly replace the approximation x_n with a better one, x_{n+1}, which is computed as:

$$x_{n+1} = x_n - f(x_n)/f'(x_n)$$

In our case we have $f(x) = \sin x - \frac{1}{2}x$ and $f'(x) = \cos x - \frac{1}{2}$. You can use, for example, $x_0 = 3$ as a start value. Find a termination condition yourself. The Newton–Raphson method can be explained as follows. We begin by drawing the tangent to the graph of f at point $(x_0, f(x_0))$, to find the point where this tangent intersects the x-axis. The x-coordinate of this new point is x_1. Then x_2 is derived from x_1 in the same way as x_1 has been derived from x_0, and so on.

30   Write a program that finds all prime numbers less than 100 000, using the 'sieve of Eratosthenes'. The smallest prime number is 2; furthermore, a positive integer n is a prime number if it is not a multiple of any smaller prime number. You can use an array of 12 500 bytes. As each byte contains 8 bits, we can also regard this array as a sequence of 12 500 × 8 = 100 000 bits. Let us denote this sequence as

$$b_0, b_1, b_2, \cdots, b_{99999}$$

We want each bit b_i to be 0 if i is a prime number, and 1 if it is not. Initially we set $b_0 = b_1 = 1$ and $b_i = 0$ for all i greater than 1. As 2 is a prime number, b_2 remains 0. Obviously, no multiple of 2 is a prime number. We therefore place the value 1 into b_4, b_6, b_8, and so on. Similarly, b_3 remains 0, but we place 1 into b_6, b_9, b_{12}, and so on. Examining b_4, we find that it has already obtained the value 1, which means that 4 is a multiple of a smaller prime number; we then know that all multiples of 4 also have been set to 1; so the fact that b_4 is 1 means that we can immediately proceed to the next element, b_5. As this is 0, we do not alter it, but place the value 1 into b_{10}, b_{15}, b_{20}, and so on. We continue this process until all elements b_i have their correct values. Note that you can stop as soon as you have reached an element b_j such that $j^2 > 100\ 000$. Write all prime numbers found in this way to the file **prime.dat**, and count how many there are. (The correct answer is 9592.) Also, print the greatest prime number that is less than 100 000.

31   With a given integer n, compute the nth element F_n of the Fibonacci sequence, which can be defined as follows:

$$F_0 = 0$$
$$F_1 = 1$$
$$F_n = F_{n-1} + F_{n-2} \quad (n \geq 2)$$

For reasons of efficiency, do not use recursion. For some large values of n, also compare the quotient F_n/F_{n-1} with the following number:

$$\tau = 2 \cos 36° = \tfrac{1}{2}(1 + \sqrt{5}) = 1.6180339887\cdots$$

(Verify the fact that the sequence

$$\cdots, \tau^{-2}, \tau^{-1}, 1, \tau, \tau^2, \cdots$$

is similar to the Fibonacci sequence in that the sum of any two successive elements is equal to the next element in the sequence.)

32   Write a program that can read any text file to check it with regard to parentheses and braces, which are allowed to occur only in pairs and arranged in the usual way. For example, the following is correct:

$$(\{((\cdots)(\cdots))\}())$$

Note that all parentheses ( ) between the two braces { } are paired in the proper way. Incorrect examples are:

$$\{()\}$$
$$\{()\}$$

33   Write a program that can read any text file to print both its longest and its second longest line. If several lines are candidates for being the longest, only the first is to be taken. The same applies to the second longest line.

34   Write a program with two program arguments, which are the names of input and output files. The input file contains text lines; all characters have the same width, say, 0.1 inch. We want to apply a process technically known as *justification* to this file. This means that, except for the final line of the file, all words that are at the end of a line are right aligned, so that the right margin of the page is made even. The modified version is to be written to the output file. The program is to read a line length (that is, the desired number of characters on each line of the output file) from the keyboard. You may regard all character sequences separated by blanks or

newline characters as 'words'. These words are to be copied from the input file to the output file. Each line of the output file is to contain as many words as the given line length permits; the words are to be separated by at least one blank, but zero or more additional blanks are to be distributed as evenly as possible between the words to let the line exactly have its required length.

35   Write a program which reads the name of a text file from the keyboard to produce a *concordance* for all words in this file. All these words are to printed (only once) in alphabetic order, followed by the numbers of the lines on which they occur. Upper-case and lower-case letters are to be regarded as identical. For example, with the input file

```
To be or
not to be,
that is the question.
```

the following concordance is produced:

```
be          1  2
is          3
not         2
or          1
question    3
that        3
the         3
to          1  2
```

36   Write a program that examines if two given text files contain exactly the same words, regardless of their order and frequency. Two files, say, A and B, contain the same words if each word of A also occurs in B and each word of B also occurs in A.

37   Write a program to count how many times a given word, read from the keyboard, occurs in a given text file. Note that the word 'under' occurs only once in the following text:

```
The importance of understanding the
wise lessons presented in the book
under consideration is easily under-
estimated.
```

38   Write a program that reads a file containing a (possibly incorrect) C
      program. The program is to check that

      a. for each start (/*) of comment, its end (*/) is also present;
      b. for each start (") of a string, its end (") is also present.

      A double quote in comment, as in /* "ABC */, does not count as the
      start of the end of a string, nor are the character pairs /* and */ in a
      string (as in "ABC /*") related to comment. The double quote is also to
      be ignored if it occurs in a string, preceded by a backslash (as in "\""), or
      in a character constant (´"´). Neither strings nor comments can be nested.
      The double-quote pairs of a string must be on the same line, unless lines
      are continued by means of the backslash (\).

39   Write a program which multiplies two integers each of which consists of
      at most 30 decimal digits. These integers are to be entered by the user on
      separate lines, and their product is to be printed.

40   Solve Exercise 6.8, the Josephus problem, once again; this time, use a
      circular list, which is a linear list the last element of which contains a
      pointer to the first. (Dynamic data structures, such as linear lists, had not
      yet been dealt with in Chapter 6.) Use an element in the circular list for
      each person in the circle, and implement removing each kth person by
      deleting the corresponding element of the circular list.

41   Write a program that reads the following integers:

      $$m, l_1, u_1, l_2, u_2, \cdots, l_m, u_m$$

      The integers l_i and u_i are the lower and upper bounds of a 'running
      variable' r_i ($i = 1, 2, \cdots, m$). Print all distinct sequences $r_1, r_2, \cdots, r_m$,
      for which $l_i \leq r_i \leq u_i$. For example, with $m = 3, l_1 = 5, u_1 = 7, l_2 = 2, u_2
      = 2, l_3 = 8, u_3 = 9$, the output will be

          5   2   8
          5   2   9
          6   2   8
          6   2   9
          7   2   8
          7   2   9

The following exercises, marked by asterisks, are more difficult than the previous ones. Their answers are therefore included in this book; they can be found after Exercise 47. Remember, however, you will benefit most from these problems if you seriously try to solve them yourself before consulting their answers.

42*   When working with binary trees, as discussed in Section 9.5, we want these to be more or less balanced, like trees in nature. A binary tree is said to be *perfectly balanced* if the number of nodes in its left subtree differs at most by 1 from that in its right subtree, provided that this also holds for every subtree of the given tree. If we are given a monotonic increasing sequence of numbers, and we know in advance the length of this sequence, we can build a perfectly balanced binary search tree to store these numbers. Write a program to realize this. Use an input file, **num.dat**, which contains the sequence length n, followed by n integers in increasing order, and, after storing these in a perfectly balanced binary search tree, print this set of numbers in the form of that tree, rotated counterclockwise through 90°, that is, with the root on the left instead of on the top. For example, if the file **num.dat** contains

        9
        1   2   4   6   8   10 20 25 30

then the following output is required:

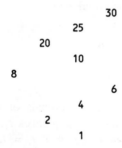

The root of this tree points to a node which contains the number 8, printed here on the left. The left and the right children of this node contain the numbers 2 and 20, respectively, and so on.

43*   Write a program to solve the problem known as the *Towers of Hanoi*. There are three pegs, A, B, C, on which disks with holes in their centers can be placed. These disks have all different diameters. A larger disk must never be placed on top of a smaller one. There are n disks, numbered 1, 2, ···, n from the smallest to the largest. Initially all these disks, in the right order, are on peg A, so that pegs B and C are empty. The problem is to move all disks, one by one, from peg A to peg C, never placing a larger disk on a smaller one; peg B may be used as auxiliary. Write a program that reads n and prints the solution to this problem. If $n = 2$, for example, we want the following output:

```
Disk 1 from peg A to peg B.
Disk 2 from peg A to peg C.
Disk 1 from peg B to peg C.
```

44* Write a program which reads the positive integer n and generates all permutations of the sequence 1, 2, ⋯, n in increasing order. (What this means is explained below.) For example, with $n = 3$, the required output is:

```
1  2  3
1  3  2
2  1  3
2  3  1
3  1  2
3  2  1
```

If we regard each of these lines as a three-digit integer, we obtain 123, 132, 213, 231, 312, 321 in that order. As these numbers form a monotonic increasing sequence, we say that the above permutations are in increasing order.

45* Write a program that reads the integers n and k and generates all combinations of k elements out of the integers 1, 2, ⋯, n. For example, if $n = 4$ and $k = 2$, the following output is required:

```
1  2
1  3
1  4
2  3
2  4
3  4
```

46* The Eight Queens problem is to place eight queens on a chessboard so that no queen is attacking any other queen. It was investigated by C.F. Gauss in 1850, but he did not completely solve it. We generalize this problem to the n queens problem for an $n \times n$ board. Write a program that reads n (not greater than 10) and prints all solutions.

47* Write a program for the Knight's Tour problem. As in the previous exercise, we are given an $n \times n$ board with n^2 squares. A knight, being allowed to move according to the rules of chess, is initially placed on the square in the lower-left corner of the board. In a tour of $n^2 - 1$ moves, the knight is to visit all other squares of the board exactly once. Present your solution in an $n \times n$ table consisting of the numbers 1, 2, $\cdots$, n^2, with 1 in the initial position of the knight, 2 in the square visited as a result of the first move, and so on. As for the integer n, read by your program, start with only the value 5: for higher values, such as 8, the program may be very time consuming.

Answers to Exercises 42 to 47:

42
```
/* PERFBAL: This program builds a perfectly balanced
              binary search tree.
   Input: The file NUM.DAT, containing n, followed
   by n integers in increasing order.
*/

#include <stdio.h>
#include <stdlib.h>
struct node {int num; struct node *left, *right;};
FILE *fp;

main()
{ int n;
  struct node *root, *pbtree(int n);
  void printtree(struct node *p, int blanks);
  fp = fopen("num.dat", "r");
  if (fp == NULL)
  { printf("File num.dat cannot be opened.\n");
    exit(1);
  }
  fscanf(fp, "%d", &n);
  root = pbtree(n);
  printtree(root, 6);
  fclose(fp);
}

struct node *pbtree(int n)
{ int nleft, nright;
  struct node *p;
  if (n == 0) return NULL;
  nleft = (n - 1)/2;
```

```
    nright = n - nleft - 1;
    p = malloc(sizeof(struct node));
    if (p == NULL)
    { printf("Not enough memory.\n");
      exit(1);
    }
    p->left = pbtree(nleft);
    fscanf(fp, "%d", & p->num);
    p->right = pbtree(nright);
    return p;
}

void printtree(struct node *p, int blanks)
{ if (p != NULL)
  { printtree(p->right, blanks+6);
    printf("%*d\n", blanks, p->num);
    printtree(p->left, blanks+6);
  }
}
```

43   ```
     /* HANOI: Solution to the Towers of Hanoi problem.
     */

     #include <stdio.h>

     void Hanoi(char source, char auxiliary, char destination, int n)
     /* A tower of n disks is moved from peg 'source' to
        peg 'destination'; peg 'auxiliary' may be used temporarily.
     */
     { if (n > 0)
       { Hanoi(source, destination, auxiliary, n-1);
         printf("Disk %d from peg %c to peg %c.\n",
                     n, source, destination);
         Hanoi(auxiliary, source, destination, n-1);
       }
     }

     main()
     { int n;
       printf("Enter n, the number of disks: ");
       scanf("%d", &n);
       Hanoi('A', 'B', 'C', n);
     }
     ```
     ```

44
```
/* PERMUT: Generating permutations in their natural order.
*/
#include <stdio.h>
#include <stdlib.h>
#define LEN 11
int n, r[LEN];

void action(void)
{ int i;
  for (i=1; i<=n; i++) printf("%3d", r[i]);
  printf("\n");
}


void permut(int k)
/* Generate all permutations of the n - k + 1 integers
   r[k], r[k+1], •••, r[n].
*/
{ int i, j, aux;
  if (k == n) {action(); return;}
  for (i=k; i<=n; i++)
  { /* For each i, a class of permutations is generated.
       Move r[i] to position k, and shift the (old) elements
       in the positions k, k+1, ..., i-1 one position to the
       right; in other words, rotate the elements in the
       positions k, k+1, ..., i one position to the right:
    */
    aux = r[i];
    for (j=i; j>k; j--) r[j] = r[j-1];
    r[k] = aux;
    permut(k+1); /* Recursive call  */
    /* Restore the old situation:   */
    for (j=k; j<i; j++) r[j] = r[j+1];
    r[i] = aux;
  }
}

main()
{ int i;
  printf("Enter n ( < %d): ", LEN); scanf("%d", &n);
  if (n >= LEN) {printf("Too large.\n"); exit(1);}
  for (i=1; i<=n; i++) r[i] = i;
  printf("\nOutput:\n\n");
  permut(1);
}
```

45
```
/* COMBIN: Generating combinations.
*/
#include <stdio.h>
#include <stdlib.h>

#define LEN 100
int n, k, r[LEN];

void action(void)
{ int i;
  for (i=1; i<=k; i++) printf("%3d", r[i]);
  printf("\n");
}

void combin(int m)
{ int i;
  if (m > k) action(); else
  for (i=r[m-1]+1; i <= n-k+m; i++)
  { r[m]=i; combin(m+1);
  }
}

main()
{ printf("Enter n ( < %d): ", LEN); scanf("%d", &n);
  if (n >= LEN) {printf("Too large.\n"); exit(1);}
  printf("Enter k ( < %d): ", n+1); scanf("%d", &k);
  if (k > n) {printf("Too large.\n"); exit(1);}
  printf("\nOutput:\n\n");
  combin(1);
}
```

46
```
/* QUEENS: Solution to the n queens problem.
*/

#include <stdio.h>
#include <stdlib.h>

#define N 30
int n, a[N], count=0;

void printsolution(void)
{ int k;
  for (k=1; k<=n; k++) printf(" %2d", a[k]);
  printf("\n"); count++;
}
```

```
int permitted(int k, int j)
/* This function examines if a queen in column k and row j
   is permitted with regard to all queens that are already
   in the columns 1, 2, ..., k-1.
*/
{ int kk;
  for (kk=1; kk<k; kk++)
  if (a[kk] == j || abs(j-a[kk]) == k - kk) return 0;
  return 1;
}


void ok(int m)
/* The columns 1, 2, ..., m are already O.K. */
{ int k=m+1, j;
  if (m == n) {printsolution(); return;}
  for (j=1; j<=n; j++)
  if (permitted(k, j)) {a[k] = j; ok(k);}
}


main()
{ printf("\nEnter n, the number of queens on an n x n board: ");
  scanf("%d", &n);
  if (n >= N) {printf("Too large.\n"); exit(1);}
  printf("Each of the following lines is a solution\n");
  printf("in the form of the row numbers for the columns\n");
  printf("1 to %d.\n\n", n);
  ok(0);
  printf("\nThere are %d solutions.\n", count);
}
```

47   /* KNIGHT: A knight's tour on an n x n board.
        */

```
#include <stdio.h>
#include <stdlib.h>

#define N 10

int n, n2, a[N][N]; /* Implicitly initialized with zeros    */
/* Element a[i][k] denotes the square in row i and column k. */

void printsolution(void)
{ int i, k;
  for (i=n; i>0; i--)     /* The top row has number n */
  { for (k=1; k<=n; k++) printf(" %2d", a[i][k]);
    printf("\n");
```

```
    }
  }


void moveknight(int i, int k, int m)
/* Try to place the knight on the square with row number i
   and column number k. If this is possible, that square is
   the mth square visited and we write m in the corresponding
   element of array a.
*/
{ int m1=m+1;
  if (m > n2) {printsolution(); exit(0);}
  if (i > n || k > n || i < 1 || k < 1 || a[i][k] != 0) return;
  a[i][k] = m;
  /* The following recursive calls examine whether this move
     leads to a solution. If it does, that solution will be
     printed and program execution will terminate.
  */
  moveknight(i+1, k+2, m1); moveknight(i+2, k+1, m1);
  moveknight(i+2, k-1, m1); moveknight(i+1, k-2, m1);
  moveknight(i-1, k-2, m1); moveknight(i-2, k-1, m1);
  moveknight(i-2, k+1, m1); moveknight(i-1, k+2, m1);
  a[i][k] = 0; /* Undo the move mentioned above if it did
                  not lead to a solution.
             */
}


main()
{ printf("\nEnter n, for an n x n board (for example, 5): ");
  scanf("%d", &n);
  if (n >= N) {printf("Too large.\n"); exit(1);}
  printf("\nThe following integers, arranged in a square,\n");
  printf("display the order in which the squares are visited:\n\n");
  n2 = n * n;
  moveknight(1, 1, 1); /* Start in the lower-left corner. */
}
```

APPENDIX B

ASCII Table

HEX	DEC	CHAR	HEX	DEC	CHAR	HEX	DEC	CHAR	HEX	DEC	CHAR
00	0	^@ NUL	20	32	SPC	40	64	@	60	96	`
01	1	^A SOH	21	33	!	41	65	A	61	97	a
02	2	^B STX	22	34	"	42	66	B	62	98	b
03	3	^C ETX	23	35	#	43	67	C	63	99	c
04	4	^D EOT	24	36	$	44	68	D	64	100	d
05	5	^E ENQ	25	37	%	45	69	E	65	101	e
06	6	^F ACK	26	38	&	46	70	F	66	102	f
07	7	^G BEL	27	39	'	47	71	G	67	103	g
08	8	^H BS	28	40	(	48	72	H	68	104	h
09	9	^I HT	29	41	)	49	73	I	69	105	i
0A	10	^J LF	2A	42	*	4A	74	J	6A	106	j
0B	11	^K VT	2B	43	+	4B	75	K	6B	107	k
0C	12	^L FF	2C	44	,	4C	76	L	6C	108	l
0D	13	^M CR	2D	45	-	4D	77	M	6D	109	m
0E	14	^N SO	2E	46	.	4E	78	N	6E	110	n
0F	15	^O SI	2F	47	/	4F	79	O	6F	111	o
10	16	^P DLE	30	48	0	50	80	P	70	112	p
11	17	^Q DC1	31	49	1	51	81	Q	71	113	q
12	18	^R DC2	32	50	2	52	82	R	72	114	r
13	19	^S DC3	33	51	3	53	83	S	73	115	s
14	20	^T DC4	34	52	4	54	84	T	74	116	t
15	21	^U NAK	35	53	5	55	85	U	75	117	u
16	22	^V SYN	36	54	6	56	86	V	76	118	v
17	23	^W ETB	37	55	7	57	87	W	77	119	w
18	24	^X CAN	38	56	8	58	88	X	78	120	x
19	25	^Y EM	39	57	9	59	89	Y	79	121	y
1A	26	^Z SUB	3A	58	:	5A	90	Z	7A	122	z
1B	27	^[ESC	3B	59	;	5B	91	[	7B	123	{
1C	28	^\ FS	3C	60	<	5C	92	\	7C	124	|
1D	29	^] GS	3D	61	=	5D	93	]	7D	125	}
1E	30	^^ RS	3E	62	>	5E	94	^	7E	126	~
1F	31	^_ US	3F	63	?	5F	95	_	7F	127	DEL

Note: 20 HEX (or 32 DEC) denotes the space character (or *blank*).

Bibliography

Ammeraal, L. (1987). *Programs and Data Structures in C*, Chichester: John Wiley.

Ammeraal, L. (1989). *Graphics Programming in Turbo C*, Chichester: John Wiley.

Gehani, N. (1988). *C - An Advanced Introduction (ANSI C Edition)*, New York: Computer Science Press.

Kernighan, B. W. and D. M. Ritchie (1988). *The C Programming Language, Second Edition*, Englewood Cliffs, NJ: Prentice-Hall.

Kochan, S. G. (1988). *Programming in ANSI C*, Indianapolis, Indiana: Hayden Books.

Kreyszig, E. (1988). *Advanced Engineering Mathematics, Sixth Edition*, New York: John Wiley.

Index